Spirituality and Religiousness and Alcohol/Other Drug Problems: Treatment and Recovery Perspectives

Spirituality and Religiousness and Alcohol/Other Drug Problems: Treatment and Recovery Perspectives has been co-published simultaneously as *Alcoholism Treatment Quarterly*, Volume 24, Numbers 1/2 2006.

Monographic Separates from *Alcoholism Treatment Quarterly*™

For additional information on these and other Haworth Press titles, including descriptions, tables of contents, reviews, and prices, use the QuickSearch catalog at http://www.HaworthPress.com.

Spirituality and Religiousness and Alcohol/Other Drug Problems: Treatment and Recovery Perspectives, edited by Brent B. Benda, PhD, and Thomas F. McGovern, EdD (Vol. 24, No. 1/2, 2006). *"Convincing evidence that spirituality and religiousness are not only relevant, but integral to our understanding the disease of addiction and the process of recovery." (Dr. Jeffry D. Roth, Editor, Journal of Groups in Addiction and Recovery; Author, Group Psychotherapy and Recovery from Addiction: Carrying the Message)*

Latinos and Alcohol Use/Abuse Revisited: Advances and Challenges for Prevention and Treatment Programs, edited by Melvin Delgado, PhD (Vol. 23, No. 2/3, 2005). *"For anyone interested in building a culturally competent system of care for Latinos, This book will provide invaluable guidance. . . . Fills a substantial gap in our knowledge about alcohol use and abuse among subgroups of Latinos. . . . Brings together research and practice knowledge on a broad range of topics, including the most recent trends in alcohol use and dependence among Latinos, service use and effectiveness, help-seeking behavior and barriers to treatment, the unmet needs of incarcerated Latinos, and ethnically sensitive interventions." (Carol Coohey, PhD, Associate Professor, University of Iowa School of Social Work)*

Responding to Physical and Sexual Abuse in Women with Alcohol and Other Drug and Mental Disorders: Program Building, edited by Bonita M. Veysey, PhD, and Colleen Clark, PhD (Vol. 22, No. 3/4, 2004). *"Highly recommended. Any clinician working with women (and their families) will appreciate the breadth and depth of this book and its use of clinical examples, treatment direction, and sobering statistics." (John Brick, PhD, MA, FAPA, Executive Director, Intoxikon International; Author of Drugs, the Brain, and Behavior and the Handbook of the Medical Consequences of Alcohol and Drug Abuse)*

Alcohol Problems in the United States: Twenty Years of Treatment Perspective, edited by Thomas F. McGovern, EdD, and William L. White, MA (Vol. 20, No. 3/4, 2002). *An overview of trends in the treatment of alcohol problems over a 20-year period.*

Homelessness Prevention in Treatment of Substance Abuse and Mental Illness: Logic Models and Implementation of Eight American Projects, edited by Kendon J. Conrad, PhD, Michael D. Matters, PhD, Patricia Hanrahan, PhD, and Daniel J. Luchins, MD (Vol. 17, No. 1/2, 1999). *Provides you with new insights into how you can help your clients overcome political, economic, and environmental barriers to treatment that can lead to homelessness.*

Alcohol Use/Abuse Among Latinos: Issues and Examples of Culturally Competent Services, edited by Melvin Delgado, PhD (Vol. 16, No. 1/2, 1998). *"This book will have widespread appeal for practitioners and educators involved in direct service delivery, organizational planning, research, or policy development." (Steven Lozano Applewhite, PhD, Associate Professor, Graduate School of Social Work, University of Houston, Texas)*

Treatment of the Addictions: Applications of Outcome Research for Clinical Management, edited by Norman S. Miller, MD (Vol. 12, No. 2, 1994). *"Ambitious and informative . . . Recommended to anybody involved in the practice of substance abuse treatment and research in treatment outcome." (The American Journal of Addictions)*

Self-Recovery: Treating Addictions Using Transcendental Meditation and Maharishi Ayur-Veda, edited by David F. O'Connell, PhD, and Charles N. Alexander, PhD (Vol. 11, No. 1/2/3/4, 1994). *"A scholarly trailblazer, a scientific first. . . . Those who work daily in the fight against substance abuse, violence, and illness will surely profit from reading this important volume. A valuable new tool in what may be America's most difficult battle." (Joseph Drew, PhD, Chair for Evaluation, Mayor's Advisory Committee on Drug Abuse, Washington, DC; Professor of Political Science, University of the District of Columbia)*

Treatment of the Chemically Dependent Homeless: Theory and Implementation in Fourteen American Projects, edited by Kendon J. Conrad, PhD, Cheryl I. Hultman, PhD, and John S. Lyons, PhD (Vol. 10,

Brent B. Benda, PhD
Thomas F. McGovern, EdD
Editors

Spirituality and Religiousness and Alcohol/Other Drug Problems: Treatment and Recovery Perspectives

Spirituality and Religiousness and Alcohol/Other Drug Problems: Treatment and Recovery Perspectives has been co-published simultaneously as *Alcoholism Treatment Quarterly*, Volume 24, Numbers 1/2 2006.

Pre-publication
REVIEWS,
COMMENTARIES,
EVALUATIONS . . .

"**B**enda and McGovern provide CONVINCING EVIDENCE THAT SPIRITUALITY AND RELIGIOUS-NESS ARE NOT ONLY RELEVANT, BUT INTEGRAL to our understanding the disease of addiction and the process of recovery."

Dr. Jeffry D. Roth
Editor, Journal of Groups in Addiction and Recovery
Author, Group Psychotherapy and Recovery from Addiction: Carrying the Message

More pre-publication
REVIEWS, COMMENTARIES, EVALUATIONS . . .

"In addiction treatment there has been a longstanding distinction between abstinence and sobriety, with an understanding that the difference has something to do with spirituality. This volume reflects the recent surge of research and scholarly interest in this relationship between spirituality and recovery. Who would have imagined, just two decades ago, that we would be reading scientific articles on love, forgiveness, and spiritual well-being? A RICH ARRAY OF POPULATIONS IS ADDRESSED IN THESE CHAPTERS, across cultures, ages, drugs, and life situations, offering more pieces of the puzzle of recovery."

William R. Miller, PhD
Distinguished Professor of Psychology and Psychiatry
University of New Mexico

"The connection of spirituality and/or religion to alcohol and other drug problems has been recognized since the beginning of the field of addiction studies; yet, research literature on this topic is rare. . . . This book attempts to fill the gap in the current state of knowledge and address this critical connection. In addition to providing an overview of the topic, the book addresses such issues as religiousness and substance abuse prevention among adolescents, the connection of spirituality and/or religion to the treatment of women and of homeless veterans, and examines the critical concept of forgiveness in the recovery processes. Each chapter PROVIDES AN EXCELLENT LITERATURE REVIEW, A THOROUGH DESCRIPTION OF THE METHODOLOGY USED IN THE RESEARCH AND AN EXCELLENT DISCUSSION OF THE APPLICATION OF FINDINGS TO TREATMENT. This is a book that will be of great interest to faculty and students in addiction training programs and to researchers as well as clinicians interested in better understanding this important topic and its critical role in the recovery process of so many individuals."

Dr. S. Lala Ashenberg Straussner, DSW
Professor and Director
Post-Master Certificate Program in The Clinical Approaches to Addictions
Editor, Journal of Social Work Practice in the Addictions
New York University
School of Social Work

No. 3/4, 1993). *"A wealth of information and experience. . . . A very useful reference book for everyone seeking to develop their own treatment strategies with this patient group or the homeless mentally ill." (British Journal of Psychiatry)*

Treating Alcoholism and Drug Abuse Among Homeless Men and Women: Nine Community Demonstration Grants, edited by Milton Argeriou, PhD, and Dennis McCarty, PhD (Vol. 7, No. 1, 1990). *"Recommended to those in the process of trying to better serve chemically dependent homeless persons." (Journal of Psychoactive Drugs)*

Co-Dependency: Issues in Treatment and Recovery, edited by Bruce Carruth, PhD, and Warner Mendenhall, PhD (Vol. 6, No. 1, 1989). *"At last a book for clinicians that clearly defines co-dependency and gives helpful treatment approaches. Essential." (Margot Escott, MSW, Social Worker in Private Practice, Naples, Florida)*

The Treatment of Shame and Guilt in Alcoholism Counseling, edited by Ronald T. Potter-Efron, MSW, PhD, and Patricia S. Potter-Efron, MS, CACD III (Vol. 4, No. 2, 1989). *"Comprehensive in its coverage and provides important insights into the treatment of alcoholism, especially the importance to the recovery process of working through feelings of overwhelming shame and guilt. Recommended as required reading." (Australian Psychologist)*

Drunk Driving in America: Strategies and Approaches to Treatment, edited by Stephen K. Valle, ScD, CAC, FACATA (Vol. 3, No. 2, 1986). *Creative and thought-provoking methods related to research, policy, and treatment of the drunk driver.*

Alcohol Interventions: Historical and Sociocultural Approaches, edited by David L. Strug, PhD, S. Priyadarsini, PhD, and Merton M. Hyman (Supp. #1, 1986). *"A comprehensive and unique account of addictions treatment of centuries ago." (Federal Probation: A Journal of Correctional Philosophy)*

Treatment of Black Alcoholics, edited by Frances Larry Brisbane, PhD, MSW, and Maxine Womble, MA (Vol. 2, No. 3/4, 1985). *"Outstanding! In view of the paucity of research on the topic, this text presents some of the outstanding work done in this area." (Dr. Edward R. Smith, Department of Educational Psychology, University of Wisconsin-Milwaukee)*

Psychosocial Issues in the Treatment of Alcoholism, edited by David Cook, CSW, Christine Fewell, ACSW, and Shulamith Lala Ashenberg Straussner, DSW, CEAP (Vol. 2, No. 1, 1985). *"Well-written and informative; the topic areas are relevant to today's social issues and offer some new approaches to the treatment of alcoholics." (The American Journal of Occupational Therapy)*

Alcoholism and Sexual Dysfunction: Issues in Clinical Management, edited by David J. Powell, PhD (Vol. 1, No. 3, 1984). *"It does a good job of explicating the linkage between two of the most common health problems in the U.S. today." (Journal of Sex & Marital Therapy)*

Spirituality and Religiousness and Alcohol/Other Drug Problems: Treatment and Recovery Perspectives

Brent B. Benda, PhD
Thomas F. McGovern, EdD
Editors

Spirituality and Religiousness and Alcohol/Other Drug Problems: Treatment and Recovery Perspectives has been co-published simultaneously as *Alcoholism Treatment Quarterly*, Volume 24, Numbers 1/2 2006.

The Haworth Press, Inc.

New York • London • Victoria (AU)
www.HaworthPress.com

HV
5275
.S665
2006

Spirituality and Religiousness and Alcohol/Other Drug Problems: Treatment and Recovery Perspectives has been co-published simultaneously as *Alcoholism Treatment Quarterly*, Volume 24, Numbers 1/2 2006.

The development, preparation, and publication of this work has been undertaken with great care. However, the publisher, employees, editors, and agents of The Haworth Press and all imprints of The Haworth Press, Inc., including The Haworth Medical Press® and Pharmaceutical Products Press®, are not responsible for any errors contained herein or for consequences that may ensue from use of materials or information contained in this work. With regard to case studies, identities and circumstances of individuals discussed herein have been changed to protect confidentiality. Any resemblance to actual persons, living or dead, is entirely coincidental.

The Haworth Press is committed to the dissemination of ideas and information according to the highest standards of intellectual freedom and the free exchange of ideas. Statements made and opinions expressed in this publication do not necessarily reflect the views of the Publisher, Directors, management, or staff of The Haworth Press, Inc., or an endorsement by them.

The Haworth Press, Inc., 10 Alice Street, Binghamton, 13904-1580 USA

Cover design by Karen M. Lowe

Library of Congress Cataloging-in-Publication Data

Spirituality and religiousness and alcohol/other drug problems : treatment and recovery perspectives / Brent B. Benda, Thomas F. McGovern, editors.
   p. cm.
   "Co-published simultaneously as Alcoholism treatment quarterly, volume 24, numbers 1/2 2006."
   Includes bibliographical references and index.
   ISBN-13: 978-0-7890-3299-7 (hard cover : alk. paper)
   ISBN-10: 0-7890-3299-6 (hard cover : alk. paper)
   ISBN-13: 978-0-7890-3323-9 (soft cover : alk. paper)
   ISBN-10: 0-7890-3323-2 (soft cover : alk. paper)
   1. Alcoholics–Rehabilitation. 2. Recovering alcoholics–Religious life. 3. Recovering addicts–Religious life. 4. Twelve-step programs–Religious aspects. 5. Alcoholism–Religious aspects. 6. Drug abuse–Religious aspects. 7. Spirituality. I. Benda, Brent B. II. McGovern, Thomas F. III. Alcoholism treatment quarterly.
 HV5275.S665 2006
 201'.7629–dc22

                              2006002582

Indexing, Abstracting & Website/Internet Coverage

This section provides you with a list of major indexing & abstracting services and other tools for bibliographic access. That is to say, each service began covering this periodical during the year noted in the right column. Most Websites which are listed below have indicated that they will either post, disseminate, compile, archive, cite or alert their own Website users with research-based content from this work. (This list is as current as the copyright date of this publication.)

Abstracting, Website/Indexing Coverage . . . . Year When Coverage Began

- *Abstracts in Anthropology <http://www.baywood.com/Journals/PreviewJournals.asp?Id=0001-3455>* **1991**
- *Academic Abstracts/CD-ROM* **1995**
- *Academic Search Elite (EBSCO)* **1995**
- *Academic Search Premier (EBSCO) <http://www.epnet.com/academic/acasearchprem.asp>* **1995**
- *Addiction Abstracts is a quarterly journal published in simultaneous print & online editions. This unique resource & reference tool is published in collaboration with the National Addiction Ctr & Carfax, Taylor & Francis <http://www.tandf.co.uk/addiction-abs>* **1995**
- *ATForum.com <http://www.pain-topix.com>* **2006**
- *Business Source Corporate: coverage of nearly 3,350 quality magazines and journals; designed to meet the diverse information needs of corporations; EBSCO Publishing <http://www.epnet.com/corporate/bsourcecorp.asp>* **1995**
- *Criminal Justice Abstracts* **1984**
- *e-psyche, LLC <http://www.e-psyche.net>* **2001**
- *EAP Abstracts Plus <http://www.eaptechnology.com>* **1995**

(continued)

(continued)

- *MasterFILE Select: coverage of nearly 770 periodicals covering general reference, business, health, education, general science, multi-cultural issues and much more; EBSCO Publishing <http://www.epnet.com/government/mfselect.asp>* 1995
- *National Criminal Justice Reference Service <http://www.ncjrs.org>* 1998
- *NewJour (Electronic Journals & Newsletters) <http://gort.ucsd.edu/newjour/>* 2005
- *OCLC ArticleFirst <http://www.oclc.org/services/databases/>* 2003
- *OCLC ContentsFirst <http://www.oclc.org/services/databases/>* 2003
- *Ovid Linksolver (OpenURL link resolver via CrossRef targeted DOI links) <http://www.linksolver.com>* 2005
- *Pain Treatment Topix <http://www.pain-topix.com>* 2006
- *PARINT (Publishing Addiction Research Internationally) <http://www.parint.org>* 2005
- *Project MAINSTREAM <http://www.projectmainstream.net>* 2005
- *Psychological Abstracts (PsycINFO) <http://www.apa.org>* 1984
- *Referativnyi Zhurnal (Abstracts Journal of the All-Russian Institute of Scientific and Technical Information–in Russian) <http://www.viniti.ru>* 1984
- *Scopus (Elsevier) <http://www.info.scopus.com>* 2005
- *Social Services Abstracts <http://www.csa.com>* 1990
- *Social Work Abstracts <http://www.silverplatter.com/catalog/swab.htm>* 1991
- *SocioAbs <http://www.csa.com>* 2003
- *Sociological Abstracts (SA) <http://www.csa.com>* 1990
- *Spanish Technical Information System on Drug Abuse Prevention "Sistema de Informacion Tecnica Sobre Prevention del Abuso de Drogas" (in Spanish) <http://www.idea-prevencion.com>* 1998
- *Studies on Women and Gender Abstracts <http://www.tandf.co.uk/swa>* 1989
- *SwetsWise <http://www.swets.com>* 2001
- *Violence and Abuse Abstracts: A Review of Current Literature on Interpersonal Violence (VAA)* 1995
- *zetoc <http://zetoc.mimas.ac.uk/>* 2004

(continued)

Special Bibliographic Notes related to special journal issues
(separates) and indexing/abstracting:

- indexing/abstracting services in this list will also cover material in any "separate" that is co-published simultaneously with Haworth's special thematic journal issue or DocuSerial. Indexing/abstracting usually covers material at the article/chapter level.
- monographic co-editions are intended for either non-subscribers or libraries which intend to purchase a second copy for their circulating collections.
- monographic co-editions are reported to all jobbers/wholesalers/approval plans. The source journal is listed as the "series" to assist the prevention of duplicate purchasing in the same manner utilized for books-in-series.
- to facilitate user/access services all indexing/abstracting services are encouraged to utilize the co-indexing entry note indicated at the bottom of the first page of each article/chapter/contribution.
- this is intended to assist a library user of any reference tool (whether print, electronic, online, or CD-ROM) to locate the monographic version if the library has purchased this version but not a subscription to the source journal.
- individual articles/chapters in any Haworth publication are also available through the Haworth Document Delivery Service (HDDS).

Spirituality and Religiousness and Alcohol/Other Drug Problems: Treatment and Recovery Perspectives

CONTENTS

ABOUT THE EDITORS

Brent B. Benda, PhD, is Professor, School of Social Work, University of Arkansas at Little Rock. He has published numerous articles on alcohol and other drug problems among adolescents and among homeless people. Also, he has written several articles on religion and spiritual well being and on the effects of these factors on delinquency and crime. Most of his career he has taught courses in delinquency, research and statistics.

Thomas F. McGovern, EdD, is Professor in the Department of Neuropsychiatry, Texas Tech University Health Sciences Center, Lubbock, Texas. He also directs the program in Health Care Ethics and Humanities for the School of Medicine. He has been actively involved in the treatment of alcohol and other drug problems, as clinician, educator and researcher for 25 years. He has served on the committee which authored the Institute of Medicine Study, *Broadening the Base of Treatment for Alcohol Problems* (1990). He has served as the Editor of *Alcoholism Treatment Quarterly* for 17 years.

Themes and Patterns of Spirituality– Religiousness and Alcohol/Other Drug Problems: Treatment and Recovery Perspectives

Thomas F. McGovern, EdD
Brent B. Benda, PhD

SUMMARY. The themes and patterns of spirituality-religiousness are explored, in their relevance to the treatment and recovery from alcohol-other drug problems, in this volume. The findings of the various authors are summarized, including descriptions of the populations studied across the life cycle, as they experience treatment and recovery. *[Article copies available for a fee from The Haworth Document Delivery Service: 1-800-HAWORTH. E-mail address: <docdelivery@haworthpress.com> Website: <http://www. HaworthPress.com>* © 2006 by The Haworth Press, Inc. All rights reserved.]

KEYWORDS. Spirituality, religiousness, treatment, recovery, alcohol-other drug problems (AOD), overview

Thomas F. McGovern is affiliated with the Department of Neuropsychiatry, Texas Tech University Health Sciences Center, Lubbock, TX 79430.

Brent B. Benda is affiliated with the School of Social Work, University of Arkansas at Little Rock, Little Rock, AR 72204.

Address correspondence to: Dr. Thomas F. McGovern, Department of Neuropsychiatry, Texas Tech University Health Sciences Center, Lubbock, TX 79430.

[Haworth co-indexing entry note]: "Themes and Patterns of Spirituality–Religiousness and Alcohol/Other Drug Problems: Treatment and Recovery Perspectives." McGovern, Thomas F., and Brent B. Benda. Co-published simultaneously in *Alcoholism Treatment Quarterly* (The Haworth Press, Inc.) Vol. 24, No. 1/2, 2006, pp. 1-5; and: *Spirituality and Religiousness and Alcohol/Other Drug Problems: Treatment and Recovery Perspectives* (ed: Brent B. Benda, and Thomas F. McGovern) The Haworth Press, Inc., 2006, pp. 1-5. Single or multiple copies of this article are available for a fee from The Haworth Document Delivery Service [1-800-HAWORTH, 9:00 a.m. - 5:00 p.m. (EST). E-mail address: docdelivery@haworthpress.com].

1

The spiritual and religious dimensions of healthcare enjoy a prominent place in contemporary treatment initiatives and outcome evaluations. This emphasis is especially true in settings which espouse a holistic approach to health care. The importance of spirituality and religiousness in addressing alcohol-other drug problems (AOD) has long been recognized. From ancient times, as documented in religious text and concomitant teachings and precepts across the ages, humans have sought to develop guidelines which would determine the appropriate use and non use of mind and mood changing agents. The American experience, in the richness of its cultural, spiritual, and religious responses to the use of alcohol and other drug problems, is elegantly captured in William White's *Slaying the Dragon* (1998). White, in this outstanding work and elsewhere describes the religious and spiritual themes which characterize treatment and recovery initiatives prior to and consequent upon the founding of Alcoholics Anonymous in 1935.

This volume focuses on a recent segment of treatment and recovery as experienced by various populations across the life cycle. A special emphasis is placed on the treatment and recovery experiences of adolescents, women, men and women Vietnam Veterans, and of homeless persons, all of whom have struggled with AOD problems in their manifold dimensions. A story of hope emerges from the promise of recovery evidenced in the lives of the participants whose journeys are described in the studies comprising this volume.

Spirituality and religiousness are concepts which are difficult to define and to operationalize for study and research in the healthcare field, in general, and in the AOD field, in particular. Significant efforts, with corresponding measures of success, characterize the work of researchers and commentators who describe spirituality and religiousness as an essential component and holistic account of the origins, diagnoses, treatments of alcohol and other drug problems. McGovern and McMahon, in the opening chapter of the volume, trace the conceptual origins of spirituality and religiousness in their application to the AOD field. They put a particular emphasis on recovering communities, especially Alcoholics Anonymous in terms of their ongoing conversations about spirituality and religiousness in the process of recovery. They identify the pioneering work of Ernest Kurtz, Charles Whitfield, Howard Brown, William Miller, Oliver Morgan, William White and others.

Belcher continues a focus on religiousness as he examines, from a religious and theological perspective, the attitudes of various protestant denominations to the use of alcohol. He identifies a wide spectrum of denominational responses, ranging from one extreme which denounces any use of alcohol as sinful to another viewpoint which accepts the moderate use of alcohol, up to the point of drunkenness. The author sees the attitudes of various Protestant communities of faith as coloring their responses to the needs of members with alcohol problems. Traditional and fundamentalist congregations see some form of religious conversion, a turning away from sin as the answer to alcohol dependency. Less fundamental congregations like the Methodists and Presbyterians view alcohol dependency as an illness to be treated and membership in AA as an important vehicle of recovery. Religiousness, in Belcher's view, is an important treatment consideration for persons who are active in various Protestant faith communities.

Laudet and her co-authors make a significant contribution to a deeper understanding of the process of recovery, including its spiritual dimensions, in their study of quality of life among recovering persons. They discuss the better life (quality of life) to which drug dependent aspire in their illness and which they achieve, following a challenging and stressful path, in recovery. Spirituality, religiousness, life meaning, and 12-step affiliation buffer the stress in the journey towards enhance life situation. The recovery of inner-city ethnic minority persons, dealing with dependency on many drugs, is recounted in a humane narrative which gives hope to treaters and sufferers alike.

Benda, Pope, and Kelleher continue an exploration of the significance of religiousness as a buffering factor against alcohol-other drug problems and delinquency in the lives of adolescents. It has been an assumption of the treatment field that attendance at church is a primary component of the buffering factor. This study shows that overall religiousness, values and attitudes are more important as a positive influence than church attendance alone. Persisting and ongoing values may be a greater safeguard for adolescents.

The research of Connors and her colleagues addresses the significance of spirituality and religiousness in the treatment of low-income pregnant and/or parenting women in a residential treatment setting. These women experienced AOD problems, with associated depression and post-traumatic stress illnesses. From the perspective of an established treatment community, characterized by a high degree of trust, the authors capture an intimate insight into the religious and spiritual struggles of the residents, using broader indices, derived from the Fetzer Study (1998). This study identifies positive and negative religious coping strategies, with special references to expression of mental health. Of particular significance is the identification of the negative effects of certain types of religiousness on the mental well-being of women. It reminds one of the need to realize that religion can have negative as well as positive effects on people because of differing frames of reference.

Benda, DiBlasio, and Pope continue a description of the struggles of homeless Vietnam Veterans to overcome their problems associated with alcohol and other drugs. Their illnesses, often co-existing with other chronic mental illness, are difficult to treat; the many admissions to treatment settings which characterize the care of these patients often engenders an attitude of hopelessness in treaters and treated alike. The authors identify and describe factors which promote recovery and hope: spiritual well-being, sustaining relationships, and work satisfaction. The importance of spiritual well-being as a component of recovery is particularly relevant to this volume.

An understanding of forgiveness is an important religious and spiritual element in the recovery process of persons and families experiencing alcohol problems. Worthington, Scherer, and Cooke apply the first author's long experience with a concept of forgiveness to the dynamics and treatment and recovery in the alcohol dependency field. Forgiveness and unforgiveness, in their association with many transgressions, individual and familial, associated with alcohol problems, are articulated in their cognitive, emotional, and spiritual dimensions. The brokenness and the healing involved in the treatment of AOD problems, in their personal and familial expressions, are tied in with the dynamics of forgiveness. The model of forgiveness, described in a five-step psycho-educational process, is connected in a most effective way with the broader reality of spiritual transformation espoused by the AA fellowship.

The insights of the Worthington et al. perspective provide an excellent context for the following study by Benda and Belcher. That study examines forgiveness in its application to the recovery process of a population of men and women associated with a Veterans Administration Treatment Program. The authors combine background in social work and pastoral care to highlight the importance of forgiveness in the restoration of the lives of veterans, women and men, which have been disrupted by AOD problems and other mental illness. Many veterans suffered traumatic events in their earlier lives and the authors show, in keeping with life-course theory, that earlier adversities can be reversed by healing events later in life. Forgiveness is seen as an important element in this process of healing.

This volume concludes with two studies which address broader aspects of the recovery process. Ripley and her co-authors investigate the importance of family involvement in the treatment of individual family members experiencing alcohol and other drug problems. White examines the dynamics of recovery across the lifecycle.

Ripley and her colleagues discuss pathways to recovery involving the entire family unit, with a special emphasis on the mediating effects of gender, investment in the relationship and perceived spousal support. The relevance of couples behavioral therapy and family systems approaches are examined in their effects on treatment outcome. Special attention is paid to the importance of Al-Anon in its ability to restore the overall well-being of families involved in the disease process of loved ones. The spiritual dimensions of Al-Anon are particularly relevant to the overall theme of this work.

White's insightful analysis of the dynamics of recovery across the lifecycle espouses a holistic approach of body-mind-spirit. This concluding piece frames, in a larger context, the other articles included in this volume. Recovery pathways, styles of recovery, developmental stages and recovery stability are discussed in a most informative fashion by one of the foremost commentators on the art and science of the treatment of alcohol and other drug problems in our day.

Spirituality and Religiousness and Alcohol/Other Drug Problems: Conceptual Framework

Thomas F. McGovern, EdD
Terry McMahon, MD

SUMMARY. Spirituality and religiousness are multidimensional concepts in their philosophical, theological and healthcare connotations. Both concepts have been discussed extensively in the literature describing the origins, diagnosis and treatment of alcohol and other drug problems. Recovery communities, especially Alcoholics Anonymous, have been studied in terms of their ongoing conversations about spirituality and religiousness in the process of recovery. The contributions of authors, such as James, Tiebout, Kurtz, Whitfield, Brown, Miller, Morgan and White to an understanding of those concepts are highlighted. *[Article copies available for a fee from The Haworth Document Delivery Service: 1-800-HAWORTH. E-mail address: <docdelivery@ haworthpress.com> Website: <http://www.HaworthPress.com> © 2006 by The Haworth Press, Inc. All rights reserved.]*

Thomas F. McGovern and Terry McMahon are affiliated with the Department of Neuropsychiatry, Texas Tech University Health Sciences Center, Lubbock, TX 79430.

Address correspondence to: Dr. Thomas F. McGovern, Department of Neuropsychiatry, Texas Tech University Health Sciences Center, 3601 4th Street, Lubbock, TX 79430-0001.

[Haworth co-indexing entry note]: "Spirituality and Religiousness and Alcohol/Other Drug Problems: Conceptual Framework." McGovern, Thomas F., and Terry McMahon. Co-published simultaneously in *Alcoholism Treatment Quarterly* (The Haworth Press, Inc.) Vol. 24, No. 1/2, 2006, pp. 7-19; and: *Spirituality and Religiousness and Alcohol/Other Drug Problems: Treatment and Recovery Perspectives* (ed: Brent B. Benda, and Thomas F. McGovern) The Haworth Press, Inc., 2006, pp. 7-19. Single or multiple copies of this article are available for a fee from The Haworth Document Delivery Service [1-800-HAWORTH, 9:00 a.m. - 5:00 p.m. (EST). E-mail address: docdelivery@haworthpress.com].

Available online at http://www.haworthpress.com/web/ATQ
© 2006 by The Haworth Press, Inc. All rights reserved.
doi:10.1300/J020v24n01_02

KEYWORDS. Spirituality, religiousness, multidimensional, treatment, recovery, alcohol/other drug problems

Spirituality and religiousness are essential components of the human experience. Around these concepts humankind has organized its deepest hopes and aspirations and it has appealed to either or both in its search for meaning, especially so when confronted by pain and suffering. Problems associated with alcohol and other drugs (AOD) have been framed over the ages by spiritual and religious considerations. Spirituality and religiousness are variously viewed as different, as the same and as overlapping in their interaction with human existence in general and in their interaction with health and illness issues, in particular. This article seeks to conceptualize and operationalize definitions of both concepts as they are found in the diagnosis of, treatment of and recovery from the suffering and brokenness associated with AOD problems.

A recent issue of *Newsweek,* September 5, 2005, has a special feature on Spirituality in America (Adler, 2005). It identifies the vast majority–88%–of Americans as either spiritual or religious. While describing the importance of both concepts in American life it also distinguishes, in the sample studied, between those who describe themselves as both religious and spiritual, those who see themselves as either/or, and those who view themselves as neither. This media report underscores the difficulty people experience in distinguishing between spirituality and religiousness in the general population; it can be assumed that the same holds true in particular populations, such as those experiencing AOD problems. Conceptualizing and operationalizing definitions of spirituality and religiousness in the addiction field is challenging but not impossible. A significant literature, drawn primarily from narrative and descriptive studies from early intervention and treatment studies, guides our journey.

DEFINITIONS OF SPIRITUALITY AND RELIGIOUSNESS

Descriptions of spirituality and religiousness have been formulated by theologians, philosophers, social scientists, and, of late, by healthcare professionals. Each definition is colored by the emphasis of the particular discipline from which it emanates. It is clearly beyond the scope of this article to summarize the contributions of the various disciplines to an understanding of the two concepts. Our focus of necessity is on the understanding attached to both realities in healthcare, with particular attention devoted to psychiatry and the behavioral sciences. Philosophers, theologians, and historians are, however, referenced in tracing the place of spirituality and religiousness in addressing AOD problems.

Miller (1998) distinguishes between spirituality and religiousness, with particular reference to alcohol and other drug problems, in the following terms. He describes the spiritual as that which is "transcendent and transpersonal," as an attribute of humanity which can be investigated scientifically, in keeping with the thought of philosopher William James (James, 1902). Spirituality in Miller's conceptual frame work, "defies customary conceptual boundaries." Miller cites Kurtz and Ketcham (1992) in describing religion as "being defined by its boundaries–by particular beliefs, practices, forms of government and rituals." Spirituality is a quality common to all human kind while religion tends to run along denominational lines, "making religions by nature exclusionary" (Smith and Seymour, 1999). Smith and Seymour (1999) further comment: no matter how broad based their frame of reference (religious) some are left out. Religiousness, in its own right, and as a variable in the study of AOD treatment and recovery, is easier to conceptualize, define and operationalize as a subject of scientific investigation. Spirituality, however, can also be conceptualized and is accessible to description and research as a multi-dimensional construct with identifiable demands such as other behaviors, beliefs, and experiences (Miller, 1998; Fetzer, 1999; Morgan, 1999).

Kurtz, an acknowledged authority on spirituality in the context of Alcoholics Anonymous (AA), differentiates between religiousness and spirituality in the AA experience in a very insightful and revealing fashion. In the context of AA, he writes of "A universal spirituality that can cohere with any religion or with none" (Kurtz 1989, 1999). He acknowledges the influence of William James and Carl Jung in influencing AA consciousness, as "two thinkers who reflected unconventional spirituality by their example of taking religious insights seriously without adhering to any special theology" (Kurtz 1989, 1999). Kurtz also identifies themes–release, gratitude, humility and tolerance–which can be described and studied in the context of the spiritual experience of AA fellowship (Kurtz 1989, 1999; Kurtz and Ketcham, 1992). The relevance of these themes, as part of a research agenda around spirituality and religiousness in the AOD field, will be discussed further in the research section of this paper.

SPIRITUALITY AND RELIGIOUSNESS:
ALCOHOL AND OTHER DRUG CONTEXT

Humankind has struggled with problems associated with the misuse and abuse of alcohol and other intoxicating and mind-altering substance since the dawn of human history. In the Jewish and Christian traditions the use of wine has both social and ritualistic significance. Scriptures, both Jewish and Christian, have injunctions against the misuse of alcohol, especially when it results in drunkenness; such behaviors are indeed seen as sinful (Miller 1995, 1998). The age old religious and spiritual struggles associated with the use/misuse of alcohol is captured in a modern citation of an ancient saying *spiritus contra spiritum* (spirit again spirit), as quoted by Carl Jung in his correspondence with Bill Wilson, the cofounder of Alcoholics Anonymous (Jung 1961, 1975).

In the American experience, the birth of Alcoholics Anonymous in 1935 brings an increased emphasis on the spiritual as one of three components of alcoholism as a three-fold malady involving body, mind and spirit. In this respect, it is wise to note Kurtz's (2002) caveat that AA "neither originated nor promulgated the disease concept of alcoholism." While the concept of "illness" did help many of the earlier and later members of AA, Kurtz (1999) insists that the emphasis on the spiritual, as an essential component of recovery, has always been AA's primary contribution to the well-being of its members. He sees the story telling in AA "as revealing the connection between thinking, acting, willing and feeling, in the purity that is at the core of the experience of sobriety" (Kurtz 1989, 1999). Spirituality, as reflected in AA story-telling, involves "not talking about it but as the actual living of certain qualities" (Kurtz 1989, 1999).

PRE-AA EXPERIENCES OF SPIRITUALITY
AND RELIGIOUSNESS

Before embarking on any further exploration of AA spirituality, as an attribute of illness and recovery, it may be enlightening to explore this spiritual legacy of pre-AA alcoholic mutual aid societies (White, 2001). In the late 18th and 19th century, a variety of Native American Temperance Societies, through the use of local "circles," addressed the issues associated with alcohol in Native American communities. White (2001) notes these initiatives as the first geographically centralized alcohol recovery efforts in America, in that they address spiritual concerns in addition to political, economic and social concerns.

The needs of Euro-American alcoholics are variously addressed also, in the pre-AA era, by Mutual Aids Societies like the Washingtonians and Fraternal Temperance Societies, the Emmanuel Movement and Jacoby Club. All espoused a self help ethos, with particular emphasis on transformation and formation in a new way of life. Their rise and decline often depends on the vagaries of charismatic leadership. The foibles of leaders of these groups are often the determining factor in their success or failure. Some of these groups are distinctly non-religious and non-spiritual, as evidenced by the Washingtonians. Others, like the Emmanuel Club, espoused religious and spiritual orientations. A common process of experimentation and discovery is a shared characteristic of these mutual aids societies. In addition, to a distinctly secular approach to recovery, many of these 19th century mutual aid societies espoused a model of treatment and recovery which involved religious conversion, personal transformation, and often provided religious networks which promoted and maintained sobriety in terms of long-term recovery (White, 1998, pp. 71-78).

RELIGIOUS AND SPIRITUAL TRENDS IN THE 19TH CENTURY

Throughout the 19th century, one finds a consistent emphasis on religious conversion as a remedy for alcohol problems, including drunkenness (White, 1998, pp. 71-78). Conversion and recovery are themes stressed in the great religious revivals of the 1850s and 1860s. Efforts to provide ongoing support to recovering persons are evidenced in the Rescue Missions, an outstanding example of which is the Water Street Mission in New York, founded under the inspiration of a recovering alcoholic, Jerry McCauley, and grounded in an evangelical religious tradition. The Salvation Army, from 1880 onwards, likewise provides a haven for persons with alcohol problems, stressing confession and transformation and personal identity as components of recovery (White 1998).

The most profound 19th century influence on AA can be traced to William James and to his classic work The Varieties of Religious Experience (1902). James espouses the 19th century theme that religious conversion can be instrumental in profoundly transforming the lives and behaviors of alcohol dependent persons. He describes two aspects of conversion, one gradual and one sudden and dramatic. James incorporates psychological and religious insights into his descriptions of the stressors of alcoholics; these insights have a profound influence on Bill Wilson, when AA comes into existence in 1935.

The religious initiatives of the 19th century receive mixed reviews from the religious commentators at the end of that century. While acknowledging the contributions of religious inspired efforts to address the suffering of persons with alcohol problems, they note that recovery through religious conversion was limited (White, 1998). A religious focus, which addresses alcohol problems from a religious perspective, persists and passes into the 20th century. The Oxford Movement, with its focus on the need for spiritual change at the personal level, begins in the early 1900s. This movement, and especially as it was refined by Dr. Sam Shoemaker, emphasizes four absolutes—honesty, purity, unselfishness and love—as the foundation of sobriety. The Oxford Movement and Shoemaker in particular have intimate connections with the origins and early history of AA.

SPIRITUALITY AND RELIGIOUSNESS: THE AA EXPERIENCE

The origins of AA, with particular emphasis on the spirituality as an essential component of fellowship, are described in the writings of Tiebout, Kurtz, White and Morgan. Before undertaking a brief analysis of these writers' contributions to an understanding of AA spirituality, one must first recognize the admonition of Kurtz (1999) that we first "understand any phenomenon (AA) in and on its own terms." The most basic understanding of AA's spirituality is derived from AA's description of itself as enshrined in Alcoholics Anonymous (AA, 1976) and The Twelve Steps and Twelve Traditions (AA, 1981). As members of AA address alcohol and other drug problems and achieve sobriety and ongoing recovery they consistently reference these two foundational texts. A careful reading of these texts, supported by the testimony of AA members who incorporate their (texture) wisdom into daily living, provides an essential insight into the workings of AA, including an appropriate recognition of spirituality and religiousness involved in the process of recovery.

Morgan describes the core experience of the spirituality of AA and other recovery groups, "as a tale of degeneration, surrender and transformation" (Morgan, 2002b). The testimony of AA members over the past 70 years attests to the accuracy of this description. Tiebout, Bill Wilson's psychiatrist and a life-long student of the AA experience, was very impressed by the remarkable transformation his patients experienced as a result of their participation in AA. Tiebout (1944) writes: "I find myself facing the question what had happened? My answer is that the patients had a religious or spiritual experience." The dynamics of conversion are no longer "an event out of the blue" but as growing out of identifiable human experiences. Tiebout's writings (1944, 1961) capture the spiritual dimensions of alcoholism as an illness and he also describes a like spiritual dimension in the processes of treatment and recovery.

One cannot overestimate the importance of Kurtz as historian and analyst par excellence of the early history and subsequent development of AA. His classic work Not God: A History of Alcoholics Anonymous (1979), followed by his ground-breaking article on the intellectual significance of AA (Kurtz, 1982), introduce the general public and specialists–including researchers–to the conceptual, spiritual underpinnings of AA. In addition to identifying the essential spiritual nature of AA, he also captures with outstanding perception and description the nature of the surrender process, together with the qualities of spirit which grace the recovery experience. Kurtz (1992) writes that "history and imperfection are my specialties, not necessarily in that order." In identifying the spiritual dimensions of the recovery process, Kurtz consistently proposes a spirituality of imperfection (Kurtz and Ketcham, 1992). It is experienced, according to Kurtz, "as a willingness to learn, a gratitude that sees gifts in all reality, a humility that relieves the pain of comparisons, a tolerance that accepts differences, a forgiveness that invites healing and, (above all) a being-at-home-ness that is found in accepting ones story (McGovern, 1999).

Whitfield (1985) is also a significant contributor to understanding of spirituality and religion in the identification of and treatment of the recovery of AOD problems. He appeals to many religious and spiritual traditions, including eastern religions and philosophies, in describing the mystical dimensions of recovery; he also pioneers a measure of spirituality, which encompasses the assessment and measurement of the qualities associated with recovery.

Miller, Morgan and White, individually and collectively have advanced our appreciation of the conceptual and research dimensions of the spiritual and religious dimensions of AOD problems. Miller's analysis (1998) of the extant research and of future research possibilities and changes provides outstanding clarity and direction to the field. White, the consummate historian and faithful observer of the varieties of religious and spiritual experiences in all aspects of treatment and recovery, paints a back drop against which the story of addiction field can be presented in a most coherent fashion. Morgan delights in pulling together the interdisciplinary threads of religiousness and spirituality, weaving them into a coherent whole which incorporate insights from theology, philosophy and behavioral sciences. Morgan, commenting on efforts to capture the essence of spirituality and religiousness research over the past 70 years (since the founding of AA in 1935), writes: "taken together the classic literature of spirituality and addiction studies illustrate both the core experiences of addiction and recovery and spirituality and the effects of these experiences" (Morgan, 1999).

SPIRITUAL AND RELIGIOUS DIMENSIONS OF THE AOD RESEARCH

Morgan (1999) describes the research literature dealing with spirituality and religiousness in the AOD field "as reflective and speculative in nature, often rooted in the lived experiences of the addicts themselves and gathered by clinical, qualitative, and narrative research." Kurtz (1999) applauds the qualitative approach "as ingrained in the reality of personal experience, that attest to narrative and story as the only way the spiritual dynamics will fully reveal themselves." He distinguishes between qualitative and quantitative research, in terms of the former involving "distancing" and the later involving "immersion." He cautions against a quantitative approach that would demand that the spiritual be "somehow material," approaches which would deny the spiritual, especially in the context of AA, the respect and impartiality it deserves. Many of the domains of the spiritual–including the themes of release, gratitude, humility, and tolerance–can be successfully investigated (Kurtz, 1999; Morgan, 2002b). Paradox and metaphor, the "both-and-ness" of the human condition (Kurtz, 1999), are constant features of the language and practice of AA. It is important that the richness and complexity of the language of spirituality be captured in AOD research approaches, whether qualitative and quantitative or a combination of both. Howard Brown, before his untimely death, and his colleague, J. H. Peterson, likewise deceased, combine qualitative and quantitative aspects of spirituality research in a most insightful and creative fashion (Brown and Peterson 1999, 1991). Brown, in particular, coalesces the reality of the lived spirituality of the AA fellowship with insights drawn from psychology, transpersonal-psychology, psychiatry and various religious traditions. The Brown-Peterson Recovery Progress Inventory (Brown and Peterson 1991, Morgan 2000a) offers a conceptual framework of AA spirituality together with measures of spiritual domains, including behaviors, thought patterns and beliefs.

ASSESSMENT AND MEASUREMENT

Assessment and measurement of spirituality and religiousness, together with the various domains or attributes associated with both constructs, are indispensable elements of research in the AOD field. Gorsuch and Miller (1996) see assessment as addressing relevant domains within the broader constructs of spirituality and religiousness and, then, reliable ways (instrumentation) to address to assess (measure) them. Miller (1998) and Hill and Hood (1999) concur that adequate measures and reliable instrumentation exists to promote and support effective research. Morgan (2002a) lists and critiques a variety of measures, with particular relevance to spiritual research in the AOD field. Among the instruments which Morgan (2002a) rates as significant are: Brief Multidimensional Measures Religiousness/Spirituality (Fetzer, 1999); Brown-Peterson Recovery Progress Inventory (Brown and Peterson, 1991); Spiritual-Well-Being Scale (Ellison, 1993); Index of Core Spiritual Experiences (Standard, Sandhu and Painter, 2000); Spiritual Health Inventory (Veach and Chappel, 1992); Religious Background Behavior Questionnaire (Conners, Tonnigan and Miller 1996); and Spiritual Belief Scale (Schaler, 1996). Whitfield's (1985) pioneering work, in describing the spiritual dimensions of alcoholism and recovery, is previously noted in this article. The most comprehensive listing of instruments is found in Hill and Hood (1999); the Fetzer Study (1999) is also an excellent resource for concepts of spirituality and religiousness and also for measures of various domains encompassed by both disciplines.

RECOVERY:
A VARIETY OF RELIGIOUS AND SPIRITUAL EXPERIENCES

Recovery from alcohol and other drug problems is a constant theme in the addiction literature. White and Kurtz (2005) identify "three styles of recovery initiation: quantum change, incremental change and a less conscious process that sociologists refer to as 'drift.'" Bill Wilson, cofounder of AA, describes his personal and sudden transformation as one whose "special feature was the electric suddenness and the over-whelming and immediate conviction that it carried to me" (Wilson, 1962). Wilson cautions against over dramatizing this experience of quantum change (Miller and CdeBaca, 2001); he is also aware of incre-mental recovery, involving a slower process of transformation, with phases of change across time. These phases are cyclic in nature rather than lock step and fixed in a particular order. The third step to recovery, identified by White and Kurtz (2005) as "drift," speaks to "gradual ces-sation/reduction of AOD use and related problems as a matter of cir-cumstances rather than choice." It can be surmised that spiritual and/or religious factors are at work in all these three styles of recovery and es-pecially so, in styles one and two. White and Kurtz (2005), with typical thoroughness, also note styles of recovery which divorce themselves from religious and spiritual ideals. Secular recovery rests in "the belief of each individual to rationally direct his/her own self change process." Such an approach has features in common with the Washingtonian Movement in the late 19th century.

White (2002) and White and Kurtz (2005) have been encouraged by the emergence of the recovery concept as a "governing principle" of the AOD field. Enshrined in this principle is a shift in a preoccupation with treatment concerns to "anchoring recovery within the client's natural environment" (White, 2005). This natural environment incorporates the cultural, economic, social, spiritual and religious factors around which a recovering person's life is organized. Such a supportive and inclusive environment is conceivably one in which various spiritual frameworks of recovery (AA and other recovery groups) can overlap with religious pathways (White and Kurtz, 2005). Devising interconnectedness and networks of recovery along community lines, which includes spiritual-ity and religiousness as specific components, is an exciting prospect for ongoing study and implementation.

CONCLUSION

Kurtz (1996, 1999) advocates that close attention be paid to the real history of AA. He writes: "there is a link between memory and hope; both are fragile so each sustains the other, and each needs all the help it can get from the other." In applying Kurtz's wisdom to the broader world of AOD problems one might conjecture that the articles in this volume will generate hope for the present and the future, grounded as they are in the experiences and memories of the past. Spirituality and religiousness are essential ingredients of memory and hope. This volume as a whole, including this article in particular, honors this essential connection.

REFERENCES

Adler, J. (2005). Spirituality in America. *Newsweek*, Sept. 5, 2005, 48-65.

Alcoholics Anonymous World Services. (1937/1976). *Alcoholics Anonymous: The story of how many thousands of men and women have recovered from alcoholism, third edition.* New York: Author.

Alcoholics Anonymous World Services. (1953/1981). *Twelve Steps and twelve traditions.* New York: Author.

Brown, H.P. and Peterson, J.H. (1990). Rationale and procedural suggestions for defining and actualizing spiritual values in the treatment of dependency. *Alcoholism Treatment Quarterly, 7*(3), 17-46.

Brown, H.P. and Peterson, J.H. (1991). Assessing spirituality in addiction treatment and follow-up: Development of the Brown-Peterson Recovery Progress Inventory. *Alcoholism Treatment Quarterly, 8*(2). 21-50.

Connors, G.J., Tonigan, J.S. and Miller, W.R. (1996). A measure of religious background and behavior for use in behavior change research. *Psychology of Addictive Behaviors, 10*(2), 90-96.

Ellison, C.W. (1983). Spiritual well-being: Conceptualization and measurement. *Journal of Psychology and Theology, 11*, 330-340.

Gorsuch, R.L. and Miller, W.R. (1999). Assessing spirituality. In W.R. Miller (Ed.), *Integrating spirituality into treatment: Resources for practitioners* (pp. 47-64). Washington, DC: American Psychological Association.

Hill, P.C. and Hood, R.W., Jr. (Eds.). (1999). *Measures of religiosity.* Birmingham, AL: Religious Education Press.

James, W. (1902, 1982). *The varieties of religious experience.* New York: Penguin.

John E. Fetzer Institute. (1999b, October). *Multidimensional measurement of religiousness/spirituality for use in health research: A report of the Fetzer Institute/National Institute on Aging Working Group with additional psychometric data.* Kalamazoo, MI: Fetzer Institute.

Jung, C.J. (1961/1975). Letter to William G. Wilson, 30 January, 1961, in G. Adler (Ed.) *Letters of Carl J. Jung,* Vol. 2 (pp. 623-625), London; Routledge and Kegen Paul.

Kurtz, E. (1982). Why A.A. works–The intellectual significance of Alcoholics Anonymous. *Journal of Studies on Alcohol, 43*, 38-80.

Kurtz, E. (1979). *Not-god: A history of Alcoholics Anonymous.* Center City, MN. Hazelden Educational Materials.

Kurtz, E. (1989) "Spiritual Rather Than Turn Religious: The contributions of Alcoholics Anonymous" in R.B. Waahlberg (Ed.), Prevention and Control/Realities and

Aspirations: Volume II (pp. 678-86). Oslo, Norway: National Directive for the Prevention of Alcohol and Drug Problems.

Kurtz, E. (1996). Origins of A.A. spirituality. *Blue Book, 38*, 35-42.

Kurtz, E. (1999). The Collected Ernie Kurtz. Wheeling, WV: The Bishop of Books.

Kurtz, E. (2002). Alcoholics Anonymous and the disease concept of alcoholism. *Alcoholism Treatment Quarterly, 20*(3/4), 5-59.

Kurtz, E. and Ketcham, K. (1992). *The spirituality of imperfection: Modern wisdom from classic stories.* New York: Bantam Books.

McGovern, T.F. (1999). Foreword in E. Kurtz *The Collected Ernie Kurtz.* Wheeling, WV: The Bishop of Books.

Miller, W.R. (1995). Towards a biblical perspective on drug use. *Journal of Ministry in Addiction and Recovery, 2*(2), 77-86.

Miller, W.R. (1997). Spiritual aspects of addictions treatment and research. *Mind/Body Medicine, 2*(1), 37-43.

Miller, W.R. (1998). Researching the spiritual dimensions of alcohol and other drug problems. *Addiction, 93*(7), 971-982.

Miller, W.R. and CdeBaca (2001). Quantum change: When epiphanies and sudden insights transform ordinary lives. New York, NY: Guilford Press.

Miller, W. and Kurtz, E. (1994). Models of Alcoholism used in treatment: Contrasting AA and other perspectives with which it is often confused. *Journal of Studies on Alcohol, 55*(2), 159-166.

Morgan, O.J. (1999). Addiction and spirituality in context. In O.J. Morgan and M. Jordan (Eds.), *Addiction and spirituality: A multidisciplinary approach* (pp. 3-30). St. Louis, MO: Chalice.

Morgan, O.J. (2002a). Alcohol problems, alcohol and spirituality: An overview of measurement and scales. *Alcoholism Treatment Quarterly, 20*(1), 1-18.

Morgan, O.J. (2002b). Spirituality, alcohol and other drug problems: Where Have We Been? Where Are We Going? *Alcoholism Treatment Quarterly, 20*(3/4), 61-82.

Schaler, J.A. (1996). Spiritual thinking in addiction-treatment providers: The Spiritual Belief Scale (SBS). *Alcoholism Treatment Quarterly, 14*, 7-33.

Smith, D.E. and Seymour, R.B. (1999). Overcoming cultural points of resistance of spirituality. In O.J. Morgan and M. Jordan (Eds.), *Addiction and Spirituality: A Multidisciplinary Approach* (pp. 95-109). St. Louis, MO. Chalice Press.

Stanard, R.P., Sandhu, D.S., and Painter, L.C. (2000). Assessment of spirituality in counseling. *Journal of Counseling and Development, 78*, 204-210.

Tiebout, H.M. (1961). Alcoholics Anonymous–An experiment in nature. *Quarterly Journal of Studies on Alcohol, 22*, 52-68.

Tiebout, H.M. (1946). Psychology and treatment of alcoholism. *Quarterly Journal of Studies on Alcohol, 7*, 214-227.

Tiebout, H.M. (1944). Therapeutic mechanisms of Alcoholics Anonymous. *American Journal of Psychiatry, 100*, 468-473.

Veach, T.L. and Chappel, J.N. (1992). Measuring spiritual health: A preliminary study. *Substance Abuse, 13*, 139-147.

White, W. (2001). Pre-AA alcoholic mutual aid societies. *Alcoholism Treatment Quarterly 19*(1), 1-21.

White, W.L. (2005). Recovery: Its history and renaissance as an organizing construct concerning alcohol and other drug problems. *Alcoholism Treatment Quarterly*, 23(1), 3-15.

White, W.L. (1998). *Slaying the dragon: The history of addiction treatment and recovery in America*. Bloomington, IL: Chesnut Health Systems.

White, W.L. and Kurtz, E. (2005). The varieties of recovery experience. Chicago, IL: Great Lakes Addiction Technology Transfer Center.

Whitfield, C.L. (1985). *Alcoholism attachments and spirituality: A transpersonal approach*. East Rutherford, NJ: Thomas Perrin.

Wilson, B. (1962). Spiritual experiences. *A.A. Grapevine*, July 1962; 2-3.

Protestantism and Alcoholism:
Spiritual and Religious Considerations

John R. Belcher, MDiv, PhD, LCSW-C

SUMMARY. This article provides an overview of Protestant perspectives on alcohol use and abuse. It discusses the dissimilar views of alcohol consumption among Protestant denominations. While there is a consensus that abuse of alcohol is morally wrong and spiritually debilitating, some denominations have theological positions that any alcohol use is harmful spiritually and psychologically. Some treatment implications of these positions are discussed. *[Article copies available for a fee from The Haworth Document Delivery Service: 1-800-HAWORTH. E-mail address: <docdelivery@haworthpress.com> Website: <http://www.HaworthPress. com> © 2006 by The Haworth Press, Inc. All rights reserved.]*

KEYWORDS. Alcohol, religion, spirituality, Protestantism

John R. Belcher is Professor, School of Social Work, University of Maryland, and Adjunct Faculty Member, The Ecumenical Institute of Theology, St. Mary's Seminary and University, Baltimore, MD.

Address correspondence to: Dr. John R. Belcher, School of Social Work, University of Maryland, 525 West Redwood Street, Baltimore, MD 21201 (E-mail: Jbelcher@ssw.umaryland.edu).

[Haworth co-indexing entry note]: "Protestantism and Alcoholism: Spiritual and Religious Considerations." Belcher, John R. Co-published simultaneously in *Alcoholism Treatment Quarterly* (The Haworth Press, Inc.) Vol. 24, No. 1/2, 2006, pp. 21-32; and: *Spirituality and Religiousness and Alcohol/Other Drug Problems: Treatment and Recovery Perspectives* (ed: Brent B. Benda, and Thomas F. McGovern) The Haworth Press, Inc., 2006, pp. 21-32. Single or multiple copies of this article are available for a fee from The Haworth Document Delivery Service [1-800-HAWORTH, 9:00 a.m. - 5:00 p.m. (EST). E-mail address: docdelivery@haworthpress.com].

Available online at http://www.haworthpress.com/web/ATQ
© 2006 by The Haworth Press, Inc. All rights reserved.
doi:10.1300/J020v24n01_03

The use of alcohol and religious views about its use are mixed. For instance, wine is used in many Protestant and Jewish rituals (Koenig, McCullough, & Larson, 2001; Miller, 1998). Many religions forbid the use of alcohol (Akabaliev & Dimitrov, 1997) and other religious groups suggest not using it (Phillips, Kuzma et al., 1980). For purposes of study, religion and alcohol is a very broad subject area. Therefore, this paper will focus on Protestantism and alcohol.

Protestant religious doctrine varies in its stance towards alcoholism. Thus, many alcohol treatment specialists are often in a quandary because of the various denominational stances and conflicting and varying views on alcohol use. The varying views stem in part from the various ways in which certain scriptures of the Bible have been interpreted–it is the interpretation rather than the message that is inconsistent. Partial revelation invites contradictory perspectives (1 Corinthians 13).

Isaiah 25:6 points out that banquets (feasts) are marked by rich food and aged wine. At the Last Supper, Jesus talks about the coming eschatological banquet when he says, "I will never again drink of the fruit of the vine until that day when I drink it new with you in my father's kingdom" (Matthew 26:29). The Bible also lists as villains, drunkards (Ryken, Wilhoit, & Longman, 1998). Moreover, Isaiah 5:22 notes, "Woe to those who are heroes at drinking . . . "

Interestingly, but not surprisingly, a denomination's view of alcohol usually determines their view of how alcoholism should be treated. There is far from a unified stance towards alcohol and alcohol treatment among the denominations.

Some denominations, for example, make it a point of preaching about the "evils" of alcohol, whereas other denominations do not sermonize that alcohol per se is evil, but the decision to abuse it means that the person is both ill and separated from God. Some denominations do not accept the framework of addictions being an illness and instead argue that recovery from alcoholism predominantly requires rededication to Christ. This paper will explore these various beliefs and attempt to make some sense of how denominations integrate their view of alcohol into a framework for recovery.

PROTESTANTISM AND ALCOHOL: HISTORICAL CONTEXT

First of all it needs to be noted that Protestantism is a complex phenomenon in which there are many different beliefs and views of such basic principles as the existence of Christ. Some denominations, for example, the Church of God (Cleveland, Tennessee), hold that Christ is divine and omnipresent whereas other denominations, for example, the Episcopal Church, are less dogmatic about Christ's omnipresence.

Up until the Protestant Reformation much of the Christian community was not particularly concerned about alcohol. Certainly, the Catholic Church, which was the predominant Christian church, did not condone alcoholism, but it did not single out the use of alcohol as a sin. The Protestant Reformation changed views towards alcohol and other practices that were considered to be contrary to God's purpose (Cherry, 1971; Tuveson, 1968). Puritans practiced a theology of sin, repentance and strict discipline to ordained Godly principles, which included abstinence from alcohol (Hall, 1997). Repentance in which a person admitted their past and current "sins" such as alcohol use, was necessary for sanctification and/or holiness (Hall, 1962). Seventeenth century America quickly became a Protestant melting pot with variations of Presbyterianism, Congregationalism, and later Methodism dominating the religious landscape (Lucas, 1976; Pope, 1969).

What emerged from Puritanism was a tension between society and religion in which no state religion would emerge; instead, a variety of Protestant beliefs would live in tension with an emerging secular society (Chu, 1985; McLoughlin, 1971; Peterson, 1997). Despite their best efforts, clergy in Colonial American were not able to "discipline" the people into accepting codes that would prohibit practices such as the use of alcohol. Protestant views would vary as to alcohol use and abuse and would often come in conflict with society.

The Great Awakening swept through the eastern seaboard between 1739-1742. Most historians note that it was a time when America broke with the Middle Ages and Catholicism. Discussions of soteriology (the ways in which people draw closer to God) and ecclesiology (how Christians should be organized into congregations and who should rule them) dominated the era. A colorful figure that emerged during the Great Awakening was Johnathan Edwards (Kerr, 1966). Edwards preached a mix of "Hell fire and repentance" in which the evils of practices such as the use of alcohol, were condemned.

Following the Great Awakening, movements emerged that specifically sought to convince society of the need for total abstinence. The American Society for the Promotion of Temperance formed in 1826; later in 1836 the American Temperance Union would emerge (Ahlstrom, 1972). During the Second Great Awakening, practices associated with alcohol, such as dancing, theatergoing, and lotteries also became suspect. Religious movements, such as American Pentecostalism, an off-spring of the Wesleyan Holiness Movement, emerged and "Christian Perfection" was urged (Dayton, 1975).

For instance, the Methodist Church condemned the use of alcohol and in revivals of the 18th century the issue of alcohol as sin was often a cornerstone of the revival (Ahlstrom, 1972). Other revivalists from this era also condemned alcohol. The Southern United States developed a unique relationship between alcohol and religion. Scholars point out that the South and Christianity created an environment where revivalism flourished, conservative and fundamental Christianity took root, and Christianity itself took on a unique Southern flavor (Matthews, 1977; Wyatt-Brown, 1982). The South's view of alcohol use was to often tolerate its use and sometimes encourage its use, yet also subscribe to religious doctrine that condemned its use (Ayers, 1992). What was created was a kind of paradoxical environment in which people used alcohol during the week and attended church on Sunday to seek forgiveness for its use. This kind of behavior continues today.

Since the 19th century there has been a major denominational shift with the mainline denominations (United Methodist, Presbyterian USA, United Church of Christ, Disciples of Christ, Episcopalian, American Baptist, and Lutheran) losing membership to conservative Christian movements, such as the Evangelical, Charismatic, Pentecostal (Church of God, Cleveland, Tennessee), Assembly of God, Presbyterian Church of America, Vineyard and other conservative non-denominational movements (Miller, 1997). Conservative Christians particularly hold the view that the use of alcohol is a sin and treatment for alcohol problems should involve an "altar" experience in which the alcoholic approach the "altar" for forgiveness and redemption. These groups are less likely in general to openly support the use of traditional treatments such as Alcoholics Anonymous.

In mainline-Protestant circles, for example, in the United Methodist Church, there is growing interest in the use of spirituality in the treatment of substance abuse (Borman & Dixon, 1998). Alcoholics Anonymous (AA), which is one of the most widely used methods to treat alcoholism, although spiritual, may not be associated with a formal religion (Goldsmith, 1992). It is the fact that AA is not connected to a formal religion that causes some denominations, usually conservative Christian groups, to reject its use. Not surprisingly, AA chapters can be found in many churches, usually Catholic or mainline Protestant, but not in conservative Christian groups.

Rooted in conservative Christianity is a deep concern about the use of alcohol. There is often a belief that use leads to abuse, which means that alcohol use is often viewed as a sin. Treatment relies on the use of repentance as opposed to the medical model, which often combines treatment (counseling), medication and some form of a 12-step program. For instance, the goal of spirituality (for Wesleyans, Pentecostals and Charismatics spirituality has an element of the forensic) is to "bring the converted believer (once converted the believer does not drink) into the experience of the sanctifying grace whereby inner sin is cleansed" (Tracy, 2002, p. 324).

The division in the Protestant community over the use of alcohol and when its use constitutes abuse has created a kind of schism in terms of views towards alcohol use and treatment. There are those denominations that approach alcohol use in the same way as does the scientific community, i.e., the Presbyterian church USA; other denominations hold little regard for the views of the scientific community, i.e., the Church of God, Cleveland, Tennessee. The scholarly and treatment communities are often unaware of these distinctions.

RESEARCH ON THE RELATIONSHIP
BETWEEN RELIGION AND ALCOHOL

The scholarly community is often deeply divided over the relationship between religion and social deviance (alcohol use/abuse is considered a social deviance) (Richard, Bell, & Carlson, 2000). In fact, religion is frequently studied as to its effect on alcohol use because religion is considered a form of social control (McIntosh et al., 1981). For example, in a study done in 1969, non-religious respondents were just as likely as religious respondents to commit delinquent acts, such as abusing alcohol (Hirschi & Stark, 1969). Some recent research, including research done by Stark (1996), has found that religion deters alcohol use (Peek, Curry, & Chalfant, 1985; Benda, 1994; Cochran, Wood, & Amklev, 1994). Moreover, religious beliefs and practices–or religiousness–provide moral proscriptions against unlawful behavior, and reinforce a sense of responsibility toward others, individually and corporately.

The relationship between religion and alcohol, while showing that it can reduce substance abuse also shows that it has minimal influence. Stark and Bainbridge (1998) note that regional differences are important to consider when evaluating the influence of religion on alcohol.

For example, many studies have been conducted in the Pacific coast area where church attendance is low. Evans and colleagues (1995) found that church attendance, because it affects moral community, is a much more powerful predictor of alcohol use than is individual religiousness. Other areas of the U.S., such as the South, generally have higher levels of religious attendance, which hypothetically reduce alcohol abuse. However, the South's unusual relationship with religion needs to be also considered.

Religious communities, or what Stark (1987) refereed to as "moral communities," exert direct influence over people who "belong" to that community as well as indirect influence on people who do not regularly attend, but either attend occasionally or their relatives attend. Unfortunately, Stark and his colleagues looked at religious/moral communities as equal in terms of the kind of influence they exerted. There is a vast difference between these communities that most likely determines the kinds of influence that an attendee experiences. Those denominations that single out alcohol as a sin, and argue that its use leads a person away from God, most likely exert a different kind of influence than does a denomination that holds the view that alcohol abuse is wrong, but responsible consumption does not draw someone away from God. For example, some conservative Christians believe that divine healing (God's direct intervention) is guaranteed, and when a person is not healed, they have generally failed to be healed because they do not meet a certain condition such as continued alcohol use (Nathan & Wilson, 1995). Moreover, these groups tend to blame alcohol use for a myriad of problems ranging from employment to marital conflict.

Research shows that many people continue to support and hold resentment towards these beliefs as adults (Greene, Ball, Belcher, & McAlpine, 2003). Denominations such as the Presbyterian Church (USA) generally take a stance in which alcohol use is not wrong, but abuse of alcohol is viewed as both wrong and is an illness. A person attending one of these congregations may not see the Church as presenting a moral argument against alcohol use, which can be both positive and negative. For the person who is prone to abuse alcohol, lack of moral sanction may actually contribute towards abuse. On the other hand, the presentation of non-negative arguments against its use may be beneficial for the person who is not likely to abuse it. In fact, some studies have found that individual religiousness (which is directly related to church experience) has little influence on drug and alcohol use (Amey, Albrecht, & Miller, 1996).

Larson and Wilson (1980) found that some spiritual practices reduce alcohol and other drug abuse. Interestingly, the specific spiritual practices or the kind of spiritual environment that affects substance abuse is not clear. What about attending church or belonging to a religious community seems to be most beneficial in protecting against alcohol abuse? One possible answer is that belonging to church for many people increases their levels of self-esteem (Belcher & Vining, 2000; Ellison & Smith, 1991; Koenig, McCullough, & Larson, 2000). It may not be that the religious/moral community provides negative sanction against addictions, but the person who attends feels more positive about themselves, has greater self-esteem and is less likely to engage in alcohol or other drug abuse. The disease model of addictions suggests that one of the "triggers" for substance abuse is poor self-esteem/self-worth (Kaplan & Sadock, 1998). Moreover, a faith based community can decrease stress and depression (Koenig, George, & Peterson, 1998; Larson et al., 1992), which can also act as triggers for chemical abuse. Prayer, for example, may "facilitate or augment various psychotherapeutic efforts" (Belcher & Benda, 2005; Magaletta & Brawer, 1998), which can help to create a supportive environment that further acts to reduce potential triggers for alcohol abuse.

Many religious institutions create environments that foster the kinds of support that reduce the "triggers" so often associated with alcohol problems. Certainly, many religious denominations continue their primary focus on the "evils" of alcohol use. However, other denominations focus more on creating positive environments that support addictions' treatment. There are two major studies that support the role of faith based treatment in addictions.

The first, conducted in 1975 and funded in part by the U.S. Department of Health, Education and Welfare, found that 67% of people who completed a religion-oriented drug abuse treatment program remained abstinent for five years after completion (Hess, 1975). One of the findings often not reported in the literature is the fact that Teen Challenge created an environment where the participants increased their sense of belonging. It provided teens' with an opportunity to be part of something they had previously not experienced. In the case of Teen Challenge, the missing ingredient in the teens' lives was faith. Another major study in 1981 reported that heroin addicts who participated in faith based treatment were more likely to remain abstinent than were those not in faith based treatment (Desmond & Maddux, 1981). Interestingly, both of these studies evaluated the effect of faith-based addiction's programs, but specific programs differ in many respects from the effect of churches on addictions. In addition, one study focused on teenagers. More recent research shows that spirituality can reduce the problem of substance abuse among women (Greene et al., 2003).

Embedded within the Protestant community is a growing culture known as pastoral counseling. Much of the secular scientific world is unfamiliar with how pastoral counseling addresses the problem of alcohol abuse. Pastoral counseling is used to varying degrees by all Protestant denominations, although some denominations remain cautious towards the theory and practice of it.

PASTORAL COUNSELING

Browning (1985, p. 9) notes that "psychiatry, psychology, and social work . . . promoted their own conceptual tools and specialized frameworks for the interpretation of human behavior." These tools, while useful to conceptualize illness, do not provide a useful framework to understand the tension that often occurs between man/woman and God. For example, many people suffer from clinical depression; psychology, psychiatry and social work are often able to only conceptualize the problem from the viewpoint of the Diagnostic and Statistical Manual of Mental Disorders (DSM-IV-TR). However, these groups are often not able to also understand that depression means separation from God.

Much like depression, alcohol and other drug abuse also contributes to separation from God and the goal of pastoral counseling with substance abusers is to reconnect them to God. Ideally, this reconnection will decrease their substance abuse. Most mainline Protestant denominations use pastoral counseling, which means they use pastoral counselors, to treat those mental health and addictions problems. Pastoral counseling is taught in most mainline seminaries and many pastoral counselors have a Masters of Divinity as well as a clinical degree in psychology, social work or marriage and family therapy. Moreover, most pastoral counselors work with psychiatrists, psychologists and social workers to create a therapeutic environment for the client. This often means, for example, encouraging the client to also see a psychiatrist for psychotropic medication.

There have been no large controlled studies that have examined the efficacy of pastoral counseling with mental health and/or addiction problems. The field has not progressed to the point that the field is willing to be critically examined. Instead, there are many anecdotal and small studies, which suggest that pastoral counseling is effective in the treatment of addictions (Royce, 1985). It is difficult to say at this time that it is more or less effective than other forms of treatment.

Some Protestant denominations do not "buy" into the pastoral counseling movement. Instead, denominations such as the Church of God, which is a conservative Christian group, prefer to encourage people with problems to approach the altar for healing (Belcher & Hall, 2001). Conservative Christian groups often distrust pastoral counseling because it "dabbles" in the scientific world. It borrows from other disciplines, such as psychiatry, psychology, and/or social work. Conservative Christian groups often argue–"Why borrow from these disciplines when God heals?"

CONCLUDING REMARKS

In many respects a person's decision to use alcohol will be tolerated or not tolerated by different Protestant denominations. Some denominations condemn the use of alcohol as a sin, while other denominations tolerate its use. For someone who does abuse alcohol, the kind of Protestant denomination they attend will certainly determine the treatment they receive. For example, if a person attends the Presbyterian Church, USA, they will most likely be offered pastoral counseling and the pastoral counselor most likely will suggest AA and possible involvement with a psychiatrist. The abuse will be viewed as an illness and the person as separated from God.

If a person attends a conservative Christian church, they will most likely be viewed as a sinner because they chose to drink in the first place. They will most likely be encouraged to approach the altar for healing. If they do receive counseling it will be provided as an adjunct to support healing and repentance. The abuse will not be viewed as an illness.

Such contrasting approaches to the use and abuse of alcohol suggest that both the clinical and the scholarly community should use caution when either treating and/or studying Protestants who undergo "treatment" for addictions. It should be clear that views of use and abuse vary among the Protestant community and one should also assume that "treatment" will vary widely. It is important to note that conservative Christians tend to view the "world" with suspicion, whereas other Protestant groups do not. One's view of the world will certainly affect treatment.

REFERENCES

Ahlstrom, S.E. (1972). *A religious history of the American People*. New Haven and London: Yale University Press.

Akabaliev, & Dimitrov, I. (1997). Attitudes towards alcohol use among Bulgarian-Christians and Turks-Muslims. *Folia Med (Plovdiv)*, 39, 7-12.

Amey, C.H., S.L. Albrecht, & M.K. Miller (1996). Racial differences in adolescent drug use: The Impact of religion. *Substance Use & Misuse*, 31, 1311-1332.

Ayers, E.L. (1982). *The promise of the New South: Life after reconstruction*. New York: Oxford University Press.

Belcher, J.R., & Benda, B.B. (2005). Issues of divine healing in psychotherapy: Opening a dialog. *Journal of Religion & Spirituality in Social Work*, 24, 21-38.

Belcher, J.R., & Hall, S.M. (2001). Healing and psychotherapy: The Pentecostal tradition. *Pastoral Psychology*, 50, 63-75.

Belcher, J.R., & Vining, J.K. (2000). Counseling Pentecostals: The process of change. *Marriage and Family: A Christian Journal*, 3, 383-392.

Benda, B. (1994). Testing competing theoretical concepts: Adolescent alcohol consumption. *Deviant Behavior*, 15, 375-395.

Borman, P.D., & Dixon, D.N. (1998). Spirituality and the 12 steps of substance abuse recovery. *Journal of Psychology and Theology*, 26, 287-291.

Cherry, C. (1971). *God's New Israel: Religious interpretations of American destiny*. Englewood Cliffs, NJ: Prentice-Hall.

Chu, J. (1985). *Neighbors, Friends, or madmen: The Puritan adjustment to Quakerism in Seventeenth-Century Massachusetts Bay*. Westport, CT: Greewood.

Cochran, J.K., P.K. Wood, & B.J. Arneklev (1994). Is the religiosity-delinquency relationship spurious? A test of arousal and social control theories. *Journal of Research on Crime and Delinquency*, 31, 92-123.

Dayton, D.W. (1975). From "Christian Perfectionism" to the Baptism of the Holy Ghost. In V. Synan (Ed.), *Aspects of Pentecostal-Charismatic Origins*. Plainfield, NJ: Logos International.

Desmond, D.P., & J.F. Maddux (1981). Religious programs and careers of chronic heroin users. *American Journal of Drug & Alcohol Abuse*, 8, 71-83.

Ellison, C.G., & Smith, J. (1991). Toward an integrative model of health and well-being. *Journal of Psychology & Theology*, 19, 35-48.

Evans, D.T., Cullen, F.T., Burton, V.S., Dunaway, R.G., Payne, G.L., & Kethineni, S.R. (1995). Religion, Social bonds and Delinquency. *Deviant Behavior*, 17, 43-70.

Goldsmith, R.J. (1992). The essential features of alcohol and drug treatment. *Psychiatric Annuals*, 22, 419-424.

Greene, J., Ball, K., Belcher, J.R., & McAlpine, C. (2003). Addictions, homelessness, spirituality: A women's health issue. *Journal of Social Work Practice in the Addictions*, 3, 39-56.

Hall, B. (1962). Calvin against the Calvinists. Proceedings of the Huguenot Society of London, 20, 284-301.

Hall, D.D. (1997). Narrating Puritanism. In H.S. Stout & D.G. Hart (Eds.), *New Directions in American Religious History* (pp. 51-83). New York: Oxford University Press.

Hess, C. (1975). Research summation: HEW Study on Teen Challenge Training Center. Rehersburg, PA. Springfield, MO: National Teen Challenge.

Hirschi, T., & Stark, R. (1969). Hellfire and delinquency. *Social Problems*, 17, 202-213.

Kaplan, H.I., & Sadock, B.J. (1998). *Synopsis of psychiatry: Behavioral sciences and clinical psychiatry.* 8th ed. Baltimore, MD: Williams and Williams.

Kerr, H.T. (Ed.) (1966). *Readings in Christian thought.* Nashville: Abingdon.

Koenig, H.G., George, L.K., & Peterson, B.L. (1998). Religiosity and remission from depression in medically ill older patients. *American Journal of Psychiatry*, 155, 536-542.

Koenig, H.G., McCullough, M.E., & Larson, D.B. (2001). *Handbook of religion and health.* New York: Oxford University Press.

Larson, D.B., Sherrill, S., & Lyons et al. (1992). Associations between dimensions of religious commitment and mental health reported in the American Journal of Psychiatry and Archives of General Psychiatry, 1978-1989. *American Journal of Psychiatry*, 19, 557-559.

Larson, D.B., & Wilson, W.P. (1980). Religious life of alcoholics. *Southern Medical Journal*, 73, 723-727.

Lucas, P.R. (1976). *Valley of discord: Church and Society along the Connecticut River, 1625-1725.* Hanover, NH: University Press of New England.

Magaletta, P.R., & Brawer, P.A. (1998). Prayer in psychotherapy: A model for its use, ethical considerations, and guidelines for practice. *Journal of Psychology and Theology*, 26, 322-330.

Matthews, D.G. (1977). *Religion in the Old South.* Chicago, Chicago University Press.

McIntosh, W.A., Fitch, S.D., Wilson, J.B., & Nyberg, K.L. (1981). The effects of mainstream religious social controls on adolescent drug use in rural areas. *Review of Religious Research*, 23, 54-75.

McLoughlin, W. (1971). *New England Dissent, 1630-1833: The Baptists and the separation of Church and state, 2 vols.* Cambridge, MA: Harvard University Press.

Miller, D.E. (1997). *Reinventing American Protestantism: Christianity in the new millennium.* Berkeley, CA: University of California Press.

Miller, W.R. (1998). Researching the spiritual dimensions of alcohol and other drug problems. *Addictions*, 93, 979-990.

Nathan, R., & Wilson, K. (1995). *Empowered evangelicals: Bringing together the best of evangelical and charismatic worlds.* Ann Arbor, MI: Vine Books.

Peek, C.W., Evans, C.W., & P.H. Chalfant (1985). Religiosity,and delinquency over time-deviance deterrence and deviance amplification. *Social Science Quarterly*, 66, 120-131.

Peterson, M.A. (1997). *The price of redemption: The spiritual economy of Puritan New England.* Stanford, CA: Stanford University Press.

Phillips, R.L., Kuzma, J.W., Beeson, W.L., & Lotz, T. (1980). Influence of selection versus lifestyle on risk of fatal cancer and cardiovascular disease among Seventh-Day Adventists. *American Journal of Epidemiology*, 112, 296-314.

Pope, R.G. (1969). *The Half Way Covenant: Church Membership in Puritan New England.* New Haven, CT: Yale University Press.

Richard, A.J., Bell, D.C., & Carlson, J.W. (2000). Individual religiosity, moral community and drug user treatment. *Journal for the Scientific Study of Religion*, 39, 218-294.

Royce, J.E. (1985). Alcohol and other drug dependencies. In Wicks, R.J., Parsons, R.D., & Capps, D. (Eds.), *Clinical handbook of pastoral counseling volume I (expanded edition)* (pp. 502-519). New York: Integration Books.

Ryken, L., Wilhoit, J.C., & Longman, III, T. (Eds.) (2000). Character Types. In *Dictionary of Biblical Imagery* (pp. 137-138). Downers Grove, IL: Inter-Varsity Press.

Stark, R. (1996). Religion as context: Hellfire and delinquency one more time. *Sociology of Religion*, 57, 163-173.

Stark, R. (1987). Religion and deviance: A new look. In W. S. Laufer (Ed.), *Crimes, values, and religion*. Norwood, NJ: Ablex.

Stark, R., & Bainbridge, W.S. (1998). *Religion, Deviance, and Social Control*. New York and London: Routledge.

Tracy, W.D. (2002). Spiritual direction in the Wesleyan-Holiness movement. *Journal of Psychology and Theology*, 30, 323-335.

Tuveson, E.L. (1968). *Redeemer Nation: The idea of America's millennial role*. Chicago: University of Chicago Press.

Wyatt-Brown, B. (1982). *Southern Honor: Ethics and Behavior in the Old South*. New York: Oxford University Press.

The Role of Social Supports, Spirituality, Religiousness, Life Meaning and Affiliation with 12-Step Fellowships in Quality of Life Satisfaction Among Individuals in Recovery from Alcohol and Drug Problems

Alexandre B. Laudet, PhD
Keith Morgen, PhD
William L. White, MA

Alexandre B. Laudet is Director, Center for the Study of Addictions and Recovery (C-STAR), National Development and Research Institutes, Inc. (NDRI), 71 West 23rd Street, 8th floor, NY, NY 10010 (E-mail: laudet@ndri.org).

Keith Morgen is Senior Research Associate, C-STAR at NDRI (E-mail: morgen@ndri.org).

William L. White is Senior Research Consultant, Chestnut Health Systems/Lighthouse Institute, 720 West Chestnut Street, Bloomington, IL 61701 (E-mail: bwhite@ chestnut.org).

Address correspondence to: Alexandre B. Laudet at the above address.

The authors gratefully acknowledge the contribution of the members of the recovering community who shared their experiences, strength and hope with our staff for this project.

This work was supported by NIDA Grant R01 DA14409 and by a grant from the Peter McManus Charitable Trust to the first author.

[Haworth co-indexing entry note]: "The Role of Social Supports, Spirituality, Religiousness, Life Meaning and Affiliation with 12-Step Fellowships in Quality of Life Satisfaction Among Individuals in Recovery from Alcohol and Drug Problems." Laudet, Alexandre B., Keith Morgen, and William L. White. Co-published simultaneously in *Alcoholism Treatment Quarterly* (The Haworth Press, Inc.) Vol. 24, No. 1/2, 2006, pp. 33-73; and: *Spirituality and Religiousness and Alcohol/Other Drug Problems: Treatment and Recovery Perspectives* (ed: Brent B. Benda, and Thomas F. McGovern) The Haworth Press, Inc., 2006, pp. 33-73. Single or multiple copies of this article are available for a fee from The Haworth Document Delivery Service [1-800-HAWORTH, 9:00 a.m. - 5:00 p.m. (EST). E-mail address: docdelivery@haworthpress.com].

SUMMARY. Many recovering substance users report quitting drugs because they wanted a better life. The road of recovery is the path to a better life but a challenging and stressful path for most. There has been little research among recovering persons in spite of the numbers involved, and most research has focused on substance use outcomes. This study examines stress and quality of life as a function of time in recovery, and uses structural equation modeling to test the hypothesis that social supports, spirituality, religiousness, life meaning, and 12-step affiliation buffer stress toward enhanced life satisfaction. Recovering persons ($N = 353$) recruited in New York City were mostly inner-city ethnic minority members whose primary substance had been crack or heroin. Longer recovery time was significantly associated with lower stress and with higher quality of life. Findings supported the study hypothesis; the 'buffer' constructs accounted for 22% of the variance in life satisfaction. Implications for research and clinical practice are discussed. *[Article copies available for a fee from The Haworth Document Delivery Service: 1-800-HAWORTH. E-mail address: <docdelivery@haworthpress.com> Website: <http://www.HaworthPress.com> © 2006 by The Haworth Press, Inc. All rights reserved.]*

KEYWORDS. Recovery, addiction, 12-step, spirituality, social support, quality of life, meaning

Two of the reasons frequently cited by alcohol and other drug users for seeking recovery are negative consequences of drug use (past consequences and fear of future consequences) and "wanting a better life" (e.g., Laudet, Savage, & Mahmood, 2002; also see Burman, 1997). Several researchers have noted that the process of recovery is often precipitated by a combination of avoidance-oriented and approach-oriented goals (Walters, 2000; also see Granfield & Cloud, 2001). Although there has been little research in this area, what empirical evidence there is suggests that quality of life among active drug users is very poor and that stress levels are high. The road of recovery is both the path to and the promise of a better life. Recovery is a continuous, lifelong process and a difficult path for most (Flynn, Joe, Broome, Simpson, & Brown, 2003; Margolis, Kilpatrick, & Mooney, 2000). So, does recovery lead to a better life? As recently noted by White (2004), the problems created by excessive alcohol and drug use are well documented, but there is no comparable body of research on the recovery benefits that accrue to individuals, families and communities. Little research has been conducted in the recovering community; most of what is known of the recovery process emanates from treatment evaluations using short follow-up periods. The few empirical investigations conducted on recovery are typically exploratory, qualitative and methodologically limited (e.g., small sample size and/or restricted sample characteristics). There is a critical need for knowledge about the process of addiction recovery, about the challenges, about useful resources as well as about the positive outcomes of recovery. Such knowledge can provide recovering persons, their families and service professionals with realistic expectations for recovery outcomes, knowledge about the timeframes within which such outcomes are likely to be achieved, and the strategies and processes through which they are facilitated. To maximize its usefulness, research on recovery must use state of the art methodology including large representative samples, quantitative methods and sophisticated statistical techniques that help elucidate the critical processes at work (White, 2004). The present study is a first step in that direction. We examine stress and life satisfaction among recovering persons, and investigate the role of social supports, spirituality, religiousness, life meaning, and 12-step affiliation as recovery capital–buffering stress and enhancing life satisfaction.

STRESS

Stress is closely linked to substance abuse; alcohol and drug use are regarded by some as self-treatment for existential pain (Ventegodt, Merrick, & Andersen, 2003). A recent teen survey found that high stress teens are twice as likely as low stress teens to smoke, drink, get drunk and use illegal drugs (The National Center on Addiction and Substance Abuse at Columbia University, 2003). The multiple negative consequences of substance use, that may include poor physical and mental health, financial difficulties, homelessness, criminal justice involvement, and estrangement from family and friends, suggest that stress levels are very high among active users. Stress is also cited often as a relapse trigger (e.g., Laudet, Magura, Vogel, & Knight, 2004; Titus, Dennis, White, Godley, Tims, & Diamond., 2002). Virtually nothing is known about stress levels among recovering persons. A cross-sectional study of 102 women in recovery reported that perceived stress in 16 life domains significantly decreased from pre-recovery to recovery (Weaver, Turner, & O'Dell, 2000). An informative, albeit small-scale, exploratory study of drug-dependent persons abstinent for an average of 9 years speaks to the demands recovery places on the individual (Margolis, Kilpatrick, & Mooney, 2000): the majority of subjects reported passing through an initial phase (lasting one to three years) almost solely focused on remaining abstinent, particularly the first year (early recovery). Only once a solid recovery foundation was established could subjects concentrate on "living a normal life," where abstinence was no longer the main focus. That middle recovery phase was a transitional period involving a conscious decision to change life focus: after years of addiction centered on drug use and a period focused on remaining abstinent, the addict is left with "well, what do I do now?" (Chapman, 1991, p. 11). Following that transitional period, the addict enters late recovery, a time of individual growth and search for meaning (Freyer-Rose, 1991). Each of these phases presents new challenges, responsibilities, and potential sources of stress.

QUALITY OF LIFE

Quality of life (QOL) has become an important endpoint in clinical trials and studies for many chronic disorders, but has not been widely studied in the substance abuse field (Smith & Larson, 2003). The QOL construct is an important diagnostic and outcome criterion because it incorporates the individual's subjective view and informs on the living situation of a given population (Rudolf & Watts, 2002). In the addiction field, the few studies available have been conducted mostly on restricted populations–e.g., heroin users, clients in substance abuse treatment and HIV-positive individuals. In particular, individuals abusing crack cocaine have rarely been studied (Rudolf & Watts, 2002). Findings from existing studies suggest that QOL among substance users is poor (e.g., Te Vaarwerk & Gaal, 2001). This is especially true of drug injectors and of users of 'hard' drugs such as cocaine, heroin and amphetamines (Brogly, Mercier, Bruneau, Palepu, & Franco, 2003; Havassy & Arns, 1998; Ventegodt & Merrick, 2003). A recent study reported that QOL among substance abuse treatment patients receiving public assistance was significantly lower than for the general population, and as low or lower as that of patients with other serious chronic disorders and health conditions such as lung disease and diabetes; addiction treatment clients' QOL was significantly lower than that of individuals interviewed one week prior to cardiac surgery (Smith & Larson, 2003). Quality of life among active substance users is negatively associated with frequency of use and with the drug composite score of Addiction Severity Index (ASI–McLellan, Cacciola, Kushner, Peters, Smith, & Pettinati, 1992; e.g., Falk, Wang, Carson, & Siegal, 2000). Very little is known about the association between recovery and QOL; one study reported that QOL increased among recovering alcohol users whereas it decreased among those who relapsed (Foster, Marshall, & Peters, 2000). To date, the relationship between length of abstinence and life satisfaction remains unclear (Rudolf & Watts, 2002).

Overall, available evidence suggests that alcohol and other drug users are under high levels of stress and that QOL is poor. Little is currently known of QOL as a function of recovery. In the next section, we review briefly a number of factors that have been found to buffer stress and to enhance quality of life and/or recovery from addictions; they are: social supports, spirituality, life meaning, religiousness, and affiliation with 12-step fellowships.

SOCIAL SUPPORTS

Granfield and Cloud (2001) recently noted that "though we live in a society that glorifies a meritocratic ideology of 'pulling oneself up by the bootstrap,' it is largely a cultural myth" (p. 1566). The importance of social support in influencing behavior has been shown in a large number of different contexts. Social relationships are hypothesized to be helpful in two ways: indirectly by buffering stress in difficult times, and directly, by providing assistance, emotional support and a sense of belonging that can alleviate or buffer stress as well as improve satisfaction with life, whether or not stress is present (Caplan & Caplan, 2000; Dalgard & Tambs, 1997). A large body of literature has elucidated the mechanisms through which social support promotes physical and mental health and buffers psychological stresses (Greenblatt, Becerra, & Serafetinides, 1982; Taylor & Aspinwall, 1996; for a review, see Taylor, 1995). Empirical evidence has linked social support to increased health, happiness and longevity (Berkman, 1985; Lin, 1986). Among substance users, lower levels of social support prospectively predict relapse (Havassy, Hall, & Wasserman, 1991) while higher levels predict decreased substance use (Humphreys & Noke 1997; Noone, Dua, & Markham, 1999; Rumpf, Bischof, Hapke, Meyer, & John, 2002; for review, see El-Bassel, Duan-Rung, & Cooper, 1998). Moreover, social support has been linked to better quality of life both among substance users and individuals with a mental disorder (e.g., Brennan & Moos,

1990; Nelson, 1992) and is a significant correlate of subjective well-being among recovering substance users who are dually-diagnosed with comorbid psychiatric disorder (Laudet et al., 2000).

While general friendship is important for overall well-being, specific domains are predicted more strongly by the behavior and orientation of one's social network (e.g., Beattie & Longabaugh, 1997). Alemi and colleagues demonstrated empirically the importance of the orientation of social support networks and noted "that people are likely to adopt roles supported by the individuals who they see most often and whose opinions are important to them" (Alemi, Stephens, Llorens, Schaefer, Nemes, & Arendt, 2003, p. 1294). In the addiction field, recovery-oriented support may foster greater self-efficacy toward ongoing abstinence because recovering persons can acquire effective coping strategies from their peers (e.g., Finney, Noyes, Coutts, & Moos, 1998). Support, and in particular, recovery-oriented support, is likely to be critical to alcohol and other drug users, especially early on, as there is evidence that friendships erode with the cessation of substance use–in all likelihood because the individual is moving away from substance using associates but may not have yet developed a healthier network (e.g., Ribisl, 1997). Friends' support for substance use is a negative predictor of abstinence (e.g., Havassy, Wasserman, & Hall, 1993; Longabaugh et al., 1998; Project MATCH Research Group, 1997). Conversely, having a recovery-oriented network predicts subsequent decreased alcohol use (e.g., Humphreys, Moos, & Cohen, 1997; Humphreys, Mankowski, Moos, & Finney, 1999; Weisner, Delucchi, & Matzger, 2003). Many former recovering persons report that being in the company of other recovering individuals is helpful (e.g., Granfield & Cloud, 2001; Margolis et al., 2000; Nealon-Woods, Ferrari, & Jason, 1995; Richter, Brown, & Mott, 1991; Trumbetta Mueser, Quimby, Bebout, & Teague 1999). At least one study has reported that the effect of support for abstinence on reduced substance use was stronger than that for general friendship quality (Humphreys et al., 1999).

SPIRITUALITY, RELIGIOUSNESS AND LIFE MEANING

Human beings have long looked to faith for strength and support, particularly in difficult times. Scientific research and clinical practice were slow to acknowledge and to investigate the role of this dimension of the human experience, in large part because it is not easily defined or captured using traditional quantitative measures. In the last twenty years and especially in the last ten years, several groups of researchers have developed and tested instruments to assess the constructs of religiosity and spirituality, contributing to refined definitions of the terms and to a growing understanding of their critical importance in clinical research and practice. A large body of empirical research has investigated the role religion and spirituality play in people's lives, particularly but not only, in the lives of individuals struggling with chronic and terminal illness.

Before proceeding with a brief overview of the literature, working definitions of key terms are in order. Cook (2004) recently surveyed 265 published works on spirituality and addiction and concluded that "spirituality as understood within the addiction field is currently poorly defined" (p. 539). In this paper, we adopt the definitions put forth by the Fetzer Institute in preparation for developing a multidimensional measure of religiousness/spirituality(1999):

> *Religiousness* has specific behavioral, social, doctrinal, and denominational characteristics because it involves a system of worship and doctrine that is shared within a group. *Spirituality* is concerned with the transcendent, addressing ultimate questions about life's meaning, with the assumption that there is more to life than what we see or fully understand. (. . .) While religions aim to foster and nourish the spiritual life–and spirituality is often a salient aspect of religious participation–it is possible to adopt the outward forms of religious worship and doctrine without having a strong relationship to the transcendent. (p. 2)

Although other definitions have been proposed, they generally preserve the essential distinction between the two concepts (e.g., Elkins, Hedstrom, Hughes, Leaf, & Saunders, 1988; Corrigan, McCorkle, Schell, & Kidder, 2003; The National Center on Addiction and Substance Abuse, 2001; for review, see Cook, 2004). As the above definitions suggest, spirituality is generally thought of as more basic, more inclusive and more universal than is religiousness; spirituality is a subjective experience that exists both within and outside of traditional religious systems (Vaughan, 1998). Spirituality and religiousness are both latent (multidimensional) constructs that can include behavioral, cognitive, existential, spiritual, ritualistic and social components (Connors, Tonigan, & Miller, 1996; Miller & Thoresen, 2003). Religiousness and spirituality are generally conceptualized as overlapping but distinguishable constructs that share some characteristics but retain non-shared featured (e.g., Miller &

Thoresen, 2003; Zinbauer, Pargament, Cole, Rye, Butter, Belavich et al., 1997). For instance, while some religious behaviors (e.g., frequent religious practice, prayer, and church attendance) are correlated with some dimensions of spirituality, many aspects of spirituality are independent of self-reported religious behaviors (Heintz & Baruss, 2001).

The "will to meaning"–constructing meaning from life's events–is an essential human characteristic, a critical element of psychological well-being (Fetzer Institute, 1999; Ryff 1989), and one that can lead to physical and mental discomfort if blocked or unfulfilled (Frankl, 1963). Antonovsky (1979) has noted the importance of meaning or purpose in life as part of a sense of coherence; meaning provides context that is essential to understand and successfully cope with life's difficulties (Fife, 1994; Park & Folkman, 1997). Life meaning is an inherent part of the spiritual pursuit (e.g., Speck, 2004); it has received virtually no attention in the addiction field to date.

Scientific literature strongly supports the notion that spirituality and religiousness can enhance health and QOL. In a review of 200 + studies, positive relationships were documented with physical and functional status, reduced psychopathology, greater emotional well-being and improved coping (Matthews, Larson, & Barry, 1993; Matthews & Larson 1995). These studies show that religious/spiritual beliefs typically play a positive role in adjustment and in better health (Brady, Peterman, Fitchett, Mo, & Cella, 1999; for review, Koenig, MuCullough, & Larson, 2001). Spirituality was included in the World Health Organization's Quality of Life instrument (WHOQOL) after focus group participants worldwide reported that spirituality was an important component of their QOL (The WHOQOL Group, 1995). Persons with strong religious faith report higher levels of life satisfaction, greater happiness, and fewer negative psychosocial consequences of traumatic life events (Ellison, 1991).

A large body of research has investigated the role of religiousness and spirituality in dealing with stressful situations. In that context, religious and spiritual beliefs and practices appear to function as protective factors or buffers that mediate or moderate the relationship between life stressors and quality of life (e.g., Culliford, 2002; Miller & Thoresen, 2003; for review, see Fetzer Institute, 1999). For example, Landis (1996) has reported findings suggesting that spirituality buffers uncertainty in the face of chronic illness. Reliance on spiritual beliefs and engaging in spiritual activities can give hope, strength, and provide meaning during stressful periods (e.g., Galanter, 1997); Underwood and Teresi (2002) use the expression 'social support from the divine' (p. 31). The extant literature has documented a strong and consistent inverse relationship between spiritual well-being (SWB–a multidimensional construct that incorporates both existential well-being or life meaning, and spiritual beliefs–Ellison, 1983) and negative affect among persons in stressful situations (e.g., Fehring, Brennan, & Keller, 1987). In one study among persons with chronic illnesses, the 'non-spiritual' group reported lower levels of QOL and life satisfaction than did the 'existential' and the 'religious' groups (Riley, Perna, Tate, Forchheimer, Anderson, & Luera, 1998); SWB has also been shown to contribute to QOL even after controlling for the influence of mood, emotional well-being and social desirability (Brady et al., 1999). Studies of persons with chronic and/or terminal illness (e.g., cancer, HIV disease) have reported positive associations between spiritual well-being and QOL (e.g., Cohen, Hassan, Lapointe, & Mount, 1996; Coleman, 2004; Cotton, Levine, Fitzpatrick, Dold, & Targ, 1999; Fry, 2001; Laudet et al., 2000; Levine & Targ, 2002; Nelson, Rosenfeld, Breitbart, & Galietta, 2002; Volcan, Sousa, Mari Jde, & Horta, 2003). One study demonstrated significant associations between spiritual well-being and hardiness, as well as between existential well-being and hardiness among persons who were HIV positive or who had diagnoses of acquired immunodeficiency syndrome (AIDS)-related complex (ARC) or AIDS, supporting the notion that spirituality may confer resiliency in stressful situations (Carson & Green, 1992); hardiness is a personality trait that buffers stress toward positive outcomes in a variety of contexts (Kobassa, 1979). The few studies that sought to assess independently the role of religiousness and spiritual beliefs in moderating stress have reported findings suggesting that the beneficial aspects of religion on QOL may be primarily related to spiritual well-being and to life meaning rather than to religious practices per se (e.g., Cotton et al., 1999; Mickley, Soeken, & Belcher, 1992; Nelson Rosenfeld, Breitbart, & Galietta, 2002; Tsuang, Williams, Simpson, & Lyons, 2002).

In addition to enhancing QOL and to offering resiliency in stressful situations, spirituality and religiousness have also been studied in association with substance use behavior. A fairly large body of evidence shows an inverse relationship between involvement in religion (e.g., attending services, considering religious beliefs important) and likelihood of substance use across life stages (Benson, 1992; Johnson, 2001; Koenig et al., 2001; The National Center on Addiction and Substance Abuse (CASA) at Columbia University, 1998, 1999; Stewart, 2001); most results from a large scale study using latent growth analysis showed that religiosity reduced the impact of (buffered) life stress on initial level of substance use and on rate of growth in substance use over time among adolescents (Wills, Yaeger, & Sandy, 2003). Possible protective mechanisms conferred by religious involvement may include avoidance of drugs, social support advocating abstinence or moderation, time-occupying activities that are incompatible with drug use, and the promotion of pro-social values by the religious affiliation that includes leading a drug-free life (Morjaria & Orford, 2002). The association between religiosity/spirituality and lower substance use, together with the growing interest in the role of spirituality and religious faith in QOL and in clinical care, have resulted in renewed interest in this topic in the addiction field: "if religious and spiritual involvement can act as a protective factor, it should come as no surprise that it could act as a means of ridding oneself of an addiction" (Morjaria & Orford, 2002, p. 226). Evidence for the growing interest in spirituality and religion among addiction professionals include the recent publication of white papers (e.g., The National Center on Addiction and Substance Abuse (CASA) at Columbia University, 2001) as well as by a request for applications (RFA) entitled "Studying Spirituality and Alcohol," sponsored jointly by the National Institute on Alcohol Abuse and Alcoholism of the National Institutes of Health and the John E. Fetzer Institute (RFA: AA-00-002, 2000). This is historically significant. Nearly seventy years ago, when the recovery program of Alcoholic Anonymous was first put forth in the Big Book, Bill W. wrote "for we have not only been mentally and physically ill, we have been spiritually sick. When the spiritual malady is overcome, we straighten out mentally and physically" (Alcoholics Anonymous World Services, 3rd edition, 1939/1976, p. 64). The suggested strategies to overcome the "spiritual malady" of alcoholism as put forth in the 12-steps that provide the spiritual foundation of the AA recovery program can be summarized thus: "The alcoholic at certain times has no effective defense against the first drink. (. . .) His defense must come from a Higher Power" (p. 43–see next section for discussion). Subsequently, as the professionalization and the medicalization of addiction treatment grew, the spiritual emphasis of the 12-step program came to be–and often remains–one of its more controversial and criticized aspects (e.g., Connors & Dermen, 1996; Davis & Jansen, 1998; Klaw & Humphreys, 2000).

Nonetheless, a growing body of empirical research supports the notion that religiousness and spirituality may enhance the likelihood of attaining and maintaining recovery from addictions, and recovering persons often report that religion and/or spirituality are critical factors in the recovery process (e.g., Christo & Franey, 1995; Green et al., 1998; Kus, 1995; Matthew & Saunders, 1997; Margolis et al., 2000; McDowell, Galanter, Goldfarb, & Lifshutz, 1996; Morjaria & Orford, 2002; Richard et al., 2000). Most studies in this area have been somewhat limited by methodological shortcomings (e.g., small sample). Recently, a growing number of large-scale, well-designed studies using quantitative methods have also documented the importance of spirituality to maintaining recovery (e.g., Flynn, Joe, Broome, Simpson, & Brown, 2003; Laudet et al., 2000) and a handful of long-term studies documented the association between increased involvement in religion and remission among alcoholic individuals (Vaillant & Milofsky, 1982; also see Moos & Finney, 1990). Moreover, there is evidence that spirituality increases from pre- to post-recovery (Mathew, Georgi, Wilson, & Mathew, 1996; Miller, 1998) and that among recovering individuals, higher levels of religious faith and spirituality are associated with cognitive processes previously linked to more positive health outcomes including more optimistic life orientation, higher resilience to stress, lower levels of anxiety, and positive effective coping skills (Pardini, Plante, Sherman, & Stump, 2000; Kondo, Iimuro, Iwai, Kurata, Kouda, Tachikawa, Nakashima, & Munakata, 2000). In sum, there is support for the positive role that spirituality and religiosity can play in minimizing substance use behavior, and preliminary evidence that this dimension may also facilitate the process of recovery from addictions.

AFFILIATION WITH 12-STEP FELLOWSHIPS

Twelve-step fellowships (e.g., Narcotics and Alcoholics Anonymous) are the most widely available addiction recovery resource in the US. Affiliation with 12-step fellowships, both during and after treatment, is a cost-effective and useful approach to promoting recovery from alcohol–and other drug-related problems (e.g., Christo & Franey, 1995; Fiorentine & Hillhouse, 2000, Humphreys & Moos, 2001; McKay, Merikle, Mulvaney, Weiss, & Kopenhaver, 2001; Miller, Ninonuevo, Klamen, & Hoffmann., 1997; Montgomery, Miller, & Tonigan, 1995; Morgenstern, Labouvie, McCray, Kahler, & Frey, 1997; Project MATCH Research Group, 1997; Timko, Moos, Finney, & Lesar, 2000; for reviews: Tonigan, Toscova, & Miller, 1996; Humphreys, Wing, McCarty, Chappel, Gallant, Haberle et al., 2004). Although the bulk of 12-step studies have focused on substance use as the primary outcome, there is also some evidence that the benefits of 12-step affiliation extend to other areas of psychosocial functioning including less severe distress and psychiatric symptoms, higher likelihood of being employed, and enhanced quality of life (e.g., Gossop, Harris, Best, Man, Manning, Marshall, & Strang, 2003; Moos, Finney, Ouimette, & Suchinsky, 1999).

The 12-step program of recovery as formulated by its founders (AA, 1939/1976) uses a 3-pronged approach: unity (fellowship, traditions and principles of the program), service (chairing meetings, qualifying, setting up the meeting space), and recovery ("working" the 12-step program). The recovery program is a set of suggested strategies that are based on a spiritual foundation whereby the individual is encouraged to rely on an external power greater than him/herself (Higher Power that many choose to call God), although no religious affiliation or belief is a requirement for 12-step membership. In fact, the AA founders specifically address this issue in one of the early chapters of the Big Book[1] ("We agnostics," AA World services, 1939/1976) and the few empirical investigations of the association between religiosity and 12-step participation have found that extent of religious beliefs does not appear to affect the benefits derived from 12-step participation (Tonigan, Miller, & Schermer, 2002; Winzelberg & Humphreys, 1999).

Meeting attendance is the most popular and the most researched form of 12-step participation. Members attend meetings to share "their experiences, strength and hope" in an accepting environment; new members gain hope and coping strategies from more experienced "old-timers" and more experienced members come to "keep it green" (i.e., to remember their past experiences with drug use by listening to new members). Fellowship with other recovering persons is one of the cornerstones of 12-step recovery and is credited by recovering individuals as a critical source of support (e.g., Laudet et al., 2002; Margolis et al., 2000; Nealon-Woods, Ferrari, & Jason, 1995). Twelve-step affiliation requires more than attending meetings, however. The benefits of meeting attendance can be enhanced through other suggested affiliative practices (e.g., Montgomery et al., 1995) and associated with more stable abstinence (Caldwell & Cutter, 1998). These practices include having a sponsor, working the 12-steps, having a home group, reading recovery literature, being active before and after meetings (e.g., setting up chairs and making coffee), and having between-meeting contact with other 12-step members (Caldwell & Cutter, 1998). In the absence of engaging in these activities, meeting attendance is associated with high attrition and with the consequent loss of the potential benefits of affiliation

(Walsh, Hingson, & Merrigan, 1991). There is also evidence that embracing 12-step ideology (e.g., commitment to abstinence, reliance on a Higher Power, needing to work the 12-step program) predicts subsequent abstinence independently of meeting attendance (e.g., Fiorentine & Hillhouse, 2000). The benefits of working the 12-step program are likely to be at least partially independent of meeting attendance, and available in the absence of attendance, especially when recovery has stabilized and a program of recovery has been largely internalized. This does not imply that meeting attendance is not critical to the recovery process, especially early on; rather, it may be that over time, recovery becomes less dependent upon meeting attendance among persons who have come to embrace the program and strive to incorporate its principles in their life. One of a handful of long-term studies found that the most stable abstinence from alcohol over 10 years came from being a sponsor (Cross, Morgan, Moony, Martin, & Rafter, 1990) and working the steps has been shown to stabilize abstinence (Chappel, 1993; Vaillant, 1995). Large-scale prospective studies using long-term follow-ups are critically needed. Overall, 12-step affiliation is a multifaceted process, combining cognitive, behavioral, social and spiritual components. It provides exposure to similar status persons (peers) as well as to the organization's ideology about these persons and their problems (Katz, 1993). This exposure is believed to lead to certain social and cognitive changes among members that, in time affect their behavior and well-being (Kingree & Thompson, 2000a and 2000b).

STUDY OBJECTIVES

The main objectives of this study are to examine stress and life satisfaction as a function of length of recovery, and to assess the role of a number of protective factors as "recovery capital" that may buffer stress and enhance life satisfaction among recovering persons. Specifically, we address two research questions: (1) Does quality of life improve over time?; and (2) Do factors previously identified as buffering stress and promoting stable recovery contribute to enhancing QOL among recovering persons? Using structural equation modeling (SEM), we test a model where social supports, spirituality, life meaning, religious practices, and affiliation with 12-step fellowships are hypothesized to buffer stress and to enhance quality of life satisfaction.

MATERIALS AND METHOD

This study was conducted in the context of a NIDA-funded prospective investigation of factors associated with stable abstinence from illicit drugs over time.

Sample

Recruiting was conducted in New York City through media advertisements placed in free newspapers (e.g., the *Village Voice*) and flyers posted throughout the community (e.g., libraries, coffee shops, and YMCAs). Recruiting was conducted over a one-year period starting in March 2003. The study maintained a toll-free telephone number that interested persons were directed to call. Callers were screened briefly (10-12 minutes). Information was collected on basic demographics, past and current drug use, lifetime dependence severity (using the Drug Abuse Screening Test–DAST 10–Skinner, 1982), current utilization of treatment services and contact information. Eligibility criteria for the study were: (1) fulfilling for a year or longer the DSM-IVR criteria for substance abuse or dependence of any illicit drug, (2) self-reported abstinence for at least one month, and (3) not being enrolled in residential treatment.[2] Eligible callers were contacted within a week to schedule an in-person interview. Seven hundred and two unduplicated screeners were conducted; of those, 440 were eligible; 353 were interviewed (82% of eligibles). [Reasons why 87 eligibles were not interviewed: unable to contact with information given at screener–e.g., disconnected telephone (39), did not come to appointment and unable to contact to reschedule (22), refused (10), relapsed between screening and scheduling call (6), data collection ended (10).]

The interview session started by explaining the voluntary nature of the study, what participation in the study entails; the signed informed consent procedure was then administered and the interview was conducted, lasting two and a half hours on average. Participants were paid $30 for their time. The study was reviewed and approved by the NDRI Institutional Review Board (IRB) and we obtained a certificate of confidentiality from our funding agency. The analyses presented here were conducted on the baseline cohort of 353 participants.

Measures

The study used a semi-structured instrument; in addition to sociodemographics and background, we used the measures described below.

Unless otherwise stated, higher scores represent a higher level of the construct under study; Chronbach Alpha reliability scores reported are those obtained for this dataset.

Dependence severity: We used the Lifetime Non-alcohol Psychoactive Substance Use Disorders subscale of the The Mini International Neuropsychiatric Interview (M.I.N.I.), a short structured diagnostic interview developed in the United States and Europe for DSM-IV and ICD-10 psychiatric disorders (Sheehan, Lecrubier, Harnett-Sheehan, Amorim, Janavs, Weiller et al., 1998). The MINI has become the structured psychiatric interview of choice for psychiatric evaluation and outcome tracking in clinical psychopharmacology trials and epidemiological studies. The M.I.N.I. has been validated against the much longer Structured Clinical Interview for DSM diagnoses (SCID-P) in English and French and against the Composite International Diagnostic Interview for ICD-10 (CIDI) in English, French and Arabic. The 14 items answered in a yes/no format yield a single score ranging from 0 to 14. Sample item: "When you were using [primary substance], did you ever find that you needed to use more [primary substance] to get the same effect that you did when you first started taking it?" Cronbach's Alpha = .81.

Clean time: Drug and alcohol use history was collected using a list of 13 substances based on the ASI (McLellan, Kushner, Metzger et al., 1992). For each substance 'ever' used once or more, participants provided the last date of use; a variable was computed for clean time from each substance ever used; the clean time variable used in the analyses represents time since *most recent use of any of the illicit drug* ever used, in months (i.e., if participant last used heroin 4 years ago and crack 5 months ago, clean time for the present analyses is 5 months).

Stress: "Overall, how stressed have you been in the past year?" Answer scale: 0 = not at all to 10 = extremely.

Stressful life events: We used an 11-item inventory developed by the first author; participants indicate whether they have experienced each event in the past year; sample items: "personal injury or illness," "Increased responsibility (e.g., financial, home, work)" and "death of a loved one." The analyses use a sum score so that a higher score reflects a greater number of stressful events in the past year.

Recovery support: The Social Support for Recovery Scale (SSRS) consists of 11 items rated on a Likert-type scale (1 = strongly disagree to 4 = strongly agree); sample item: "The people in my life understand that I am working on myself" (Laudet et al., 2000). Negatively phrased items are reversed and the score used here is the sum of the 11 items. Cronbach's Alpha = .88.

Social support: The 23-item Social Support Appraisal Scale (SSA; Vaux & Harrison, 1985; Vaux, 1988) measures the degree to which a person feels cared for, respected, and involved with friends, family and other people. Items are rated on a Likert-type scale (1 = strongly disagree to 4 = strongly agree). Sample item: "My friends respect me," "I don't feel close to members of my family." Cronbach's Alpha = .92.

Spirituality, life meaning and religious practices: (1) The *Spirituality* subscale of the Spiritual Well-Being Scale (SWBS–Paloutzian & Ellison, 1982) consists of 6 items rated on a Likert-type scale (1 = strongly disagree to 4 = strongly agree) and yields one score representing "the affirmation of life in relationship with God, self, community and environment" (Ellison, 1983, p. 331). We adapted the wording of the items to a broader dimension of spirituality (from "God" to "God/Higher Power"). Sample items: "I don't get much personal strength and support from God/my Higher Power" and "I have a personally meaningful relationship with God/my Higher Power." Cronbach Alpha = . 82. (2) *Life meaning* was assessed using the *Existential* Subscale of the Spiritual Well-Being Scale (Paloutzian & Ellison, 1982), consisting of 6 items rated as described above; it yields a score (after reversing the three that are negatively phrased) representing one's perception of life's purpose, apart from any religious reference. Sample items: "Life doesn't have much meaning," and "I believe there is some real purpose for my life." Alpha = .87. (3) We used the *Religious Background and Behavior* (RBB) questionnaire to assess religious activities in the past year (Connors, Tonigan, & Miller, 1996). The instrument measures frequency of (a) thinking about God; (b) prayer or meditation; (c) attending worship services; (d) reading/studying scriptures or holy writings; and (e) having a direct experience with God; answer categories range from never to once a day. Cronbach's Alpha = .81.

Twelve-step affiliation: Affiliation consists of two dimensions: meeting attendance and involvement in 12-step suggested activities. (a) *Meeting attendance* is the number of 12-step addiction recovery meetings attended in the past year (AA, NA or CA); (b) *12-step involvement* is the sum of nine 12-step activities in the past year: having a sponsor; sponsoring someone; considering oneself a member of AA, NA or CA; having a home group; working the steps; doing service; having contact with 12-step fellowship members outside of meetings; reading 12-step or recovery literature outside of meetings; and socializing with 12-step members outside of meetings.

Quality of life satisfaction: The main dependent variable in the analyses was measured with the following item: "Overall, how satisfied are you with your life right now?" answered on a visual scale where 1 = "not at all," and 10 "completely." We used this measure because we were interested in assessing participants' overall evaluation of their life satisfaction, taking into account the balance between positive and negative as it was relevant to their individual experience.

Analytic Plan

The analyses were conducted in several stages. First, descriptive statistics examine the key variables under study, and bivariate associations among these variables are examined. Next, we used structural equation modeling (SEM) to test a model assessing the collective effect of length of time in recovery time, social support, recovery support, spirituality, life meaning, religious practices, and 12-step affiliation as hypothesized mediators of stress on quality of life. A simple graphic representation of our hypothesized model, developed from the literature reviewed above, is presented in Figure 1. Finally, a simple linear regression was conducted to assess the magnitude of the influence of *each individual* observed variable hypothesized to influence quality of life satisfaction, since SEM results bear on the *simultaneous* influence of all variables in the latent variable but not on the strength of their individual influence.

FIGURE 1. Hypothesized model: Supports, spirituality/religiousness and 12-step affiliation that buffer quality of life satisfaction from stress.

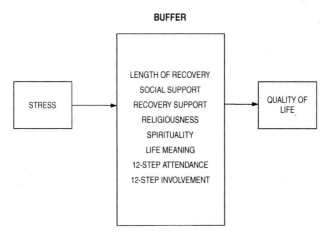

The structural equation modeling (SEM) analyses tested the appropriateness of the model in Figure 1 using maximum-likelihood estimation within AMOS 4.0 (Arbuckle, 1999). SEM analyses examine observed and unobserved (or latent) constructs to ascertain a relationship among all variables. Observed variables, represented as boxes in the SEM figures discussed in the Results section (Figures 2 and 3), are measurable (e.g., a scale score). Unobserved or latent variables are represented by an oval in the SEM figures.

FIGURE 2. Original hypothesized SEM with all error terms covarying.

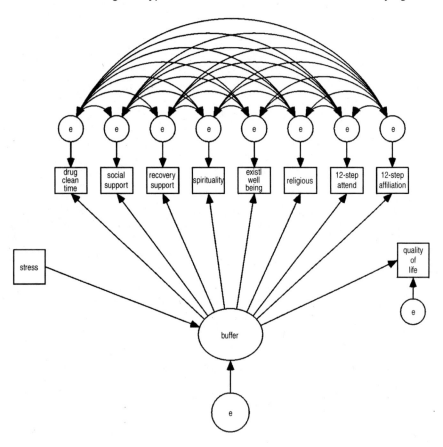

e = measurement error for that specific item

FIGURE 3. Final structural equation model.

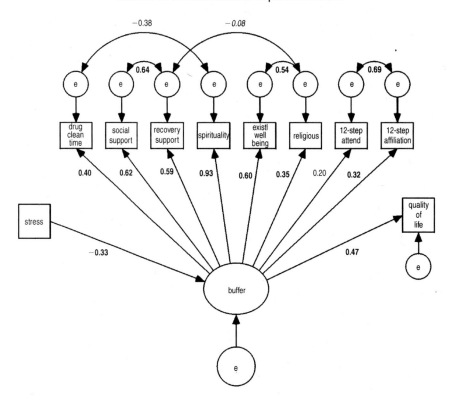

e = measurement error for that specific item; error terms not reported in figure for clarity
all reported findings in the figure are standardized and significant
BOLD type indicates *p* < .001; REGULAR type indicates *p* < .01; *ITALICS* type indicates *p* < .05

In this study, we tested the hypothesized model whereby recovery time, general social support, recovery support, spirituality, life meaning, religious practices, and 12-step affiliation constitute a buffer that mediates the relationship between life stress and overall quality of life satisfaction. Figure 2 reflects the tested model and shows paths that were modeled from the observed general measure of perceived stress in the past year to the latent variable *buffer*. Another path was then modeled from the latent variable to the observed quality of life measurement. This represents a full Structural Equation Model as it reflects both a path analysis (stress → buffer → quality of life) and a confirmatory factor analysis (the eight observed measurements that explain the latent variable). Adequacy of model fit was assessed with standardized coefficients obtained from the maximum likelihood method of estimation. To determine model fit, we used the comparative fit index (CFI), the Tucker-Lewis index, the chi-square/degrees of freedom ratio, and the root mean square of approximation (RMSEA). Once modeled, the significance of path coefficients, variances, and covariances is determined by examining the critical ratio (CR). Any $CR > 1.96$ is significant at the .05 level and indicates that path coefficient or covariance has a significant effect on the model. In addition, the R-squared (or squared multiple correlation) shows the percent of variance explained by the model for that particular endogenous (dependent) variable (Byrne, 2001). Although model fit indices and significance of path coefficients and covariances assist in model evaluation, the final determination of the "best" model tends to be a subjective and theoretical judgment.

RESULTS

Descriptives

Sample. The sample was 56% male; 62% African-American, 16% non-Hispanic white, and 22% of other or mixed ethnic/racial background; 19% were of Hispanic origin. Participants ranged in age from 19 to 65 years (mean = 43, Std. Dev. = 8). Educational attainment ranged from 5 to 19 years of schooling (mean = 12 year, Std. Dev. = 2). Nineteen percent were employed part-time, 21% full time; 60% cited government or other benefits (e.g., Veteran's pension) as primary source of income. Over half (56%) were single, 16% were married and 28% were widowed, separated or divorced. Nearly one quarter (22%) reported being seropositive for HIV antibodies. The majority (82%) had no current involvement with the criminal justice system; 18% were on probation or parole. The majority of participants were polysubstance users; lifetime dependence severity was high. Most frequent primary problem substance was crack followed by heroin (18.5%). Clean time ranged from one months to ten years. Means and standard deviations for key variables under study are displayed in Table 1.

On average, stress level and number of stressful life events in the past year were moderate; life satisfaction was high, as were levels of both recovery-specific support and general social support, as well as life meaning (existential well-being) and spirituality. Religious activities were

TABLE 1. Key Variables Descriptives (N = 353)

	Possible Range	Mean	Standard Deviation
Clean time from drugs (in months)	1-120	26.5	31.5
Dependence severity	0-14	11.7	2.4
Stress	0-10	6.3	2.6
Stressful Life events	0-11	3.9	2.1
Recovery Support	1-4	3.0	.30
Social Support	1-4	3.0	.35
Spirituality	0-4	3.0	.39
Religious activities	0-8	5.1	1.7
Life Meaning	1-4	3.2	5.1
Twelve-step affiliation:			
Ever Narcotics Anonymous (NA)	----	87%	
Ever Alcoholics Anonymous (AA)	----	72%	
Past year Narcotics Anonymous	----	69%	
Past year Alcoholics Anonymous	----	47%	
Any 12-step attendance past year (NA or AA)	----	73%	
Total (NA+AA) meetings past year*	----	141	135
12-step involvement (activities in NA+AA)*	0-9	4.2	3.5
Quality of life satisfaction	0-10	7.5	1.9

* among past year attenders

more moderate.[3] Nearly three-quarter of participants had attended a 12-step meeting in the past year; involvement in 12-step activities was more moderate.

Bivariate associations among key variables. First we examined whether there were significant differences in either stress level or in quality of life between men and women, between individuals who reported being HIV seropositive and seronegative, and as a function of age. No differences emerged for quality of life. Stress was significantly and negatively correlated with age (older age, less stress. $r = -.14, p = .01$) but the association lost statistical significance when recovery time was held constant (partial correlation, $r = -.07, p = .20$). This is not unexpected as older individuals are more likely to have been in recovery longer.

Next we examined the bivariate associations among key variables. Zero-order two-tailed Pearson R coefficients are reported in Table 2.

TABLE 2. Bivariate Associations Among Key Variables

	1	2	3	4	5	6	7	8	9	10	11	12
1. Clean time from drugs (in months)	1	.01	−.27**	−.20**	.08	.14**	.14*	.13*	.11*	.09	.06	.21**
2. Dependence severity		1	.09	.10	−.03	−.11*	−.03	.16**	.13*	.13	.27**	−.04
3. Stress			1	.30	−.18**	−.22**	−.27**	−.11*	−.10	−.14*	−.12*	−.29**
4. Stressful Life events				1	−.07	−.08	−.04	.04	.09	.15*	.00	−.09
5. Recovery Support					1	.77**	.56**	.11*	.31**	.23**	.26**	.31**
6. Social Support						1	.58**	.18**	.38**	.19**	.19**	.33**
7. Spirituality							1	.35**	.58**	.20**	.26**	.44**
8. Religious activities								1	.67**	.13	.32**	.33**
9. Life Meaning									1	.19**	.26**	.28**
10. Total (NA+AA) meetings past year										1	.54**	.07
11. 12-step involvement											1	.22**
12. Quality of life satisfaction												1

* $p < .05$. ** $p < .01$; all correlations are two-tailed

Longer duration of clean time was significantly associated with lower levels of stress (overall stress rating and fewer stressful events in the past year), greater levels of social (but not recovery) support, greater spirituality, more religious activities, greater meaning in life and greater quality of life. Dependence severity was not significantly associated with either stress levels or quality of life. Higher stress levels were significantly associated with lower recovery and social supports, with lower spirituality levels, fewer religious activities, less 12-step meeting attendance and involvement, and lower quality of life satisfaction. Finally, in addition to longer recovery time and lower stress, significant correlates of quality of life were: greater levels of recovery an social support, higher spirituality ratings, greater involvement in religious activities, grater level of life meaning and, greater 12-step involvement (but not attendance).

Structural Equation Modeling[4]

Data were examined for normality prior to testing the model. With exception of the 12-step involvement and recovery support, all study variables were significantly skewed. Transformations were performed to bring the values closer to a normal distribution. Logarithmic transformations were performed on positively skewed variables and the quadratic transformation was performed on negatively skewed variables, using the In SPSS 11.5 software.[5]

Initial model. The first model (Figure 2) estimated all error terms as co-varying with one another and produced a good fit to the data. The $\chi^2/df = 1.49$, CFI = 1.000, Tucker-Lewis = .997, RMSEA = .037 (95% CI: 0 to .081). All the observed loadings on the latent variable were significant ($p < .001$), thus the latent variable appears adequately measured by the indicators. The two paths leading into and out of the latent variable were also significant. However, less than one-third of the co-variances were significant. Although a discrepancy between the good fit indices and many insignificant co-variances appears, the good fit of the model may have been due to this model being overly fitted with 58 parameters and only 7 degrees of freedom (see Kline, 1998). Therefore, we tested a revised model with only the significant co-variances remaining.

Final model. Though not fitting as well as the original model, the revised (final) model adequately fit the data (Figure 3). The $\chi^2/df = 3.58$, CFI = .99, Tucker-Lewis = .985, RMSEA = .086 (95% CI: .068 to .103).

Again, all latent variable and path loadings were significant. In addition, the remaining error co-variances were significant. The error co-variances refer to situations in which knowing the residual of one indicator helps in knowing the residual associated with another indicator. Knowing that a respondent gave a certain response to one item increases the probability that a similar response will be given to another item. Such an example exhibits correlated error terms. Uncorrelated error terms are an assumption of regression, whereas the correlation of error terms may and should be explicitly modeled in SEM. That is, in regression the researcher models variables, whereas in SEM the researcher must model error as well as the variables.

We found significant positive relationships between the error terms of recovery support and social support ($p < .001$), the number of 12-step meetings attended in the past year and the degree of active involvement in the 12-step program ($p < .001$), religious involvement and existential well-being ($p < .001$), while finding significant negative relationships between time abstinent from drug use and spiritual well-being ($p < .01$), and between religious involvement and recovery support ($p < .05$).

The squared multiple correlation (SMC) is independent of measurement units and represents the proportion of variable variance explained by the predictors of that variable. The analyzed model was designed to explain the influence of variables under study on quality of life, and results from the final model showed that 22.2% of the variance associated with quality of life is accounted for by its predictors in the model.

We also tested the significance of the indirect effect of stress on quality of life, as mediated through the latent variable buffer. Using the Sobel Test (see Baron & Kenny, 1986; Shrout & Bolger, 2002; Sobel, 1982), we found a significant indirect effect of stress of quality of life (critical ratio = -3.20, $p < .001$), indicating that as stress is reduced via interaction with the latent variable buffer, quality of life increases.

Findings from the linear regression analysis examining the *individual* contribution of each of the eight variables assessed in combination as 'buffer' in the SEM analyses reported above were significant ($p < .001$) for all variables except 12-step attendance: length of clean time for length of clean time (0.302), social support (0.310), recovery support (0.270), spirituality (0.412), existential well-being (.237), religiousness (0.292), and 12-step affiliation (0.186). The percentage of variance explained by each individual variable ranged from 0 to 17%; taken together, the individual contribution of these eight variables accounted for 60.6% of the variance in quality of life satisfaction.

DISCUSSION

Our findings suggest that the hope for "a better life" that motivates alcohol and drug users to initiate the recovery process may become a reality for many; moreover, findings supported our hypothesis that social supports, spirituality, life meaning, religiousness and 12-step affiliation buffer stress significantly and enhance quality of life among recovering persons. First, overall stress levels were moderate and QOL was relatively high in this sample of inner-city former polysubstance users, most of whom were members of ethnic/racial minority groups. Moreover, findings suggest that stress levels decrease significantly as time in recovery increases, and that life satisfaction increases over time. This study is among the first to address this important research questions and to do using a relatively large, diverse sample of polysubstance drug users; our findings are consistent with previous study and extend their generalizability (e.g., Weaver et al., 2000; Foster et al., 2000).

Second, levels of factors previously identified as enhancing QOL and recovery were also generally high. This was particularly true of general social support and recovery support, spirituality, life meaning, and 12-step attendance. In addition, a number of these protective factors were significantly and positively correlated with recovery time, suggesting that levels increases over time: in particular, social support, spirituality, religious activities and life meaning. Recovery-specific support did not increase; this may be because over time, recovering persons become less focused on abstinence and concentrate more on "living a normal life" where recovery-specific support may be less critical than is general social support; that transition occurs after a more intense abstinence-focused period lasting from one to two-years (Margolis et al., 2000); we note that over one half (56%) of our sample was in recovery for longer than one year; further, examination of recovery support over the course of length of recovery traced an inverted U-shaped curve, starting relatively low, increasing to a peak at between one and two years of recovery, and slopping down gradually to more moderate levels.

Twelve-step attendance and involvement did not increase over time; few studies have examined 12-step affiliation over the course of recovery so that little is known about this important topic. Here, the finding was unexpected because we have reported elsewhere that in this sample, among those who reported lifetime 12-step participation ('ever'), NA attendance increased over the course of recovery while AA participation decreased (Laudet & White, 2004). Thus, we believe that the finding that 12-step affiliation did not correlate significantly with length of recovery may be due to a measurement artifact in the present study where attendance and involvement in Alcoholics and Narcotics Anonymous were combined, a decision we made based on the study aims to examine the role of 12-step affiliation overall, on QOL. Zemore and Kaskutas (2004) recently reported that among recovering alcoholics, levels of AA involvement (attendance and activities–e.g., reading recovery literature) were *not* associated with length of sobriety, but that what the authors termed "AA achievement" ("the degree to which respondents had worked the program," p. 385) was significantly and positively associated with length of sobriety. Future research is needed that examines separately NA and AA affiliation among recovering polysubstance users; we plan such analyses using longitudinal data in the future.

Present findings also suggest that spirituality, religious practices and life meaning increase moderately as recovery progresses. A handful of previous reports have indicated that spirituality increases from pre- to post-recovery (e.g., Mathew et al., 1996; Miller, 1998). Substance users often come into recovery feeling abandoned by God or alienated from God or from the religious community, as expressed by a research participant cited by The National Center on Addiction and Substance Abuse (2001):

> Being in recovery has changed the way I see God. I came into recovery with a God, but it was a punishing, vengeful and unforgiving God. I had done so many things . . . I knew were ungodly, that I thought for sure I was going to Hell. . . . When I came into recovery I found a new God. I found a God that was loving, forgiving, understanding and responsive to the need that I have. In retrospect, I can see that God has been with me all the time. Craig, Age 44, African American Male (p. 41)

Spirituality, religiousness and life meaning enhance coping, confer hope for the future, provide a heightened sense of control, security and stability; they confer support and strength to resist the opportunity to use substances, all of which are very much needed to initiate and maintain recovery (for reviews, see Cook, 2004; The National Center on Addiction and Substance Abuse, 2001; The Fetzer Institute, 1999). While not all recovering persons embrace spirituality/religiousness, many report that a spiritual or religious connection to the transcendent is part of their recovery. Recovering participants in one study expressed a sense of needing something to depend on that could be trusted and that was there always (Morjaria & Orford, 2002). Recovering person also express often that lack of a spiritual or religious connection contributed to the escalation of their problem (National Center on Addiction and Substance Abuse, 2001). Of note, previous religiousness or spirituality is not a prerequisite to gaining the benefit of spirituality in recovery (e.g., Christo & Franey, 1995; Jones, 1994), suggesting that this critical recovery resource may be available to all who seek it (see later discussion).

Third, findings supported the hypothesized role of social supports, spirituality/religiousness, life meaning and 12-step affiliation in buffering stress and in enhancing quality of life in this recovering sample. Granfield and Cloud's (1999) concept of *recovery capital* may help interpret this finding. Recovery capital is the amount and quality of internal and external resources that one can bring to bear to initiate and sustain recovery from addiction. Social supports and 12-step affiliation are among key external resources previously associated with stable recovery; spirituality and faith, as well as the benefits they confer–hope, a sense of control and security, and emotional support–constitute internal resources that have been linked to positive health outcomes. This study extends current knowledge about the benefits of these resources to QOL in the recovering community. This is important for several reasons. First, little is known about the recovery experience beyond the short post-treatment period that is typical of most addiction research designs. Recovery is a lifelong, dynamic process and it is therefore critical to learn more about relevant challenges and helpful resources (recovery capital) over the course of the process in order to enhance the likelihood that stable recovery be maintained. Second, most studies in the addiction field focus on substance use as the primary outcome. Recovery goes well beyond substance use; in particular, quality of life is a critical domain in behavioral health research that has been neglected thus far by addiction researchers. As Stanton Peele wrote, addicts improve when their relationships to work, family, and other aspects of their environment improve (1985); that is to say, quality of life is critical to the recovery process and it is critical that we identify factors that influence (enhance and/or threaten) QOL among recovering persons. Third, substance use begins and continues in the broader psychosocial context of the user (including one's social network, beliefs, and social environment–see Moos, 2003). Therefore, recovery must be studied in that context as well, lest we obtain only a fragmented picture of a complex and dynamic process. In the same way as an individual's existential beliefs, community participation, socioeconomic factors and peer network (to name only a few) influence substance use behavior, these factors play a key role in the initiation and maintenance of personal change (recovery). The concept of recovery capital opens up the possibility of broadening an understanding of recovery through a greater appreciation of a person and his/her embeddedness within social and cultural life (Granfield & Cloud, 2001).

This study has a number of limitations that must be considered when interpreting findings, chief of which are the non-random sample and the cross-sectional design. As a result of the latter, our findings cannot speak to causation or to the mechanisms underlying the stress buffering effect of the domains under study. Fieldwork on the first of three yearly waves of follow-up data collection began in the spring of 2004; the questions addressed here will be re-examined using a longitudinal design. With respect to sample representativeness, the scarcity of information on the recovering community makes it extremely difficult to determine how representative the present sample is from the recovering population as a whole. This study was conducted in New York City and recruited primarily inner-city, ethnic/racial minority members whose primary substances were crack and heroin. The associations investigated here should be examined again among diverse samples of participants to determine whether present findings are generalizable. Finally, using single items to assess stress and quality of life may be viewed as a limitation; we selected these measurements because we were interested in participants' overall subjective assessment of stress and life satisfaction. Present findings are consistent with prior reports on both stress and QOL that used a variety of measures ranging from single items to sophisticated scales, suggesting that this measurement limitation may not significantly compromise the interpretation of results presented here.

This study also has a number of strengths and implications for both researchers and for clinicians. We used a relatively large sample of mostly inner-city members of minority groups who are under-represented in behavioral health research. The quantitative approach and the use of sophisticated statistical techniques applied to the study of recovery, spirituality/religion, and QOL contribute to current knowledge that, for the most part, has been obtained from small-scale qualitative studies. Further, empirical studies to date have generally not recognized the distinctions between spirituality and religions but instead have treated them as the same general concept, often using a single item (Connors, Tonigan, & Miller, 1996; Cook, 2004; Miller & Thoresen 2003; Speck, 2004); we assessed separately spirituality, religiosity and life meaning.

Although the history of alcohol and other drug use is intertwined with spirituality and religion, there has been relatively little attention among researchers on the incorporation of spirituality in the treatment of addictions (Miller, 1998, 1999) or in studying their role in the process of recovery (Morjaria & Osford, 2002).

This study represents but a first step in a much-needed investigative effort that would focus on the role of spirituality and faith as recovery capital. As recently noted in the white paper *So Help me God: Substance Abuse, Religion and Spirituality*, by the National Center on Addiction and Substance Abuse, more research is needed to document pathways through which religion and spirituality work to prevent substance abuse and aid in recovery (2001). Previously, Finney (1995) has argued for the need to identify the mechanisms underlying the beneficial effects of factors associated with positive health outcomes. We plan on examining the research questions addressed here and to investigate the underpinning of the association between spirituality/religion and quality of life using longitudinal data. We also hope that the present study will stimulate research interest in this critical yet under-investigated area.

Additional implications for research include: (1) The importance of extending the investigative scope of studies on addiction and particularly, on recovery, beyond substance use; QOL is a critical yet under-investigated domain in the addiction field thus far. Here, the hypothesized buffers accounted for only 22% of the explained variance in QOL, suggesting that other factors are at play that were not measured in this study. (2) The need to incorporate spirituality and religiousness measures in the study of addiction and recovery, and to assess these constructs separately. (3) The importance of using statistical models that assess simultaneously, multiple domains of participants' experience or recovery capital when seeking to identify factors contributing to the recovery experience. Here, each hypothesized protective domain accounts for a relatively small amount of the variance in QOL (regression results). Examining these factors simultaneously as *recovery capital* has greater explanatory power; it also lends greater external validity to the analyses by modeling statistically the real-life recovery experience as a dynamic process where a multiplicity of influences come to bear simultaneously on the individual.

Clinical Implications

Findings also have a number of implications for clinicians and for the recovering community. First, the finding that quality of life increases and that stress decreases as recovery progresses can give hope for a better future to individuals in early recovery who are struggling to stay drug-free and to move forward, often doing so "one day at a time." Second, findings emphasize the importance of the recovery capital ingredients examined here (social supports, spirituality, religiousness, life meaning and 12-step affiliation) in minimizing the stress attendant to the recovery process, and in enhancing life satisfaction. While necessarily focusing on substance use, clinicians should also take into account individual clients' life situation, satisfaction levels and goals for the future, as well as clients' social context and available recovery capital; this includes identify deficits in available recovery resources, and working with the individual to suggests supportive recovery resources that fit the person's situation, needs, and beliefs (for discussion, see Granfield & Cloud, 2001; Moos, 2003; White & Sanders, 2004).

As discussed earlier, there is already overwhelming empirical evidence that 12-step affiliation is beneficial to the recovery process; present findings suggest that these benefits extend to the critical and most general domain of life satisfaction. The importance of general social support and domain-specific support (recovery support) in buffering stress and enhancing QOL emphasizes the need for recovering persons to establish a social network of persons who can provide encouragement, acceptance, and a sense of belonging. In that regard, affiliation with 12-step fellowships has been shown to minimize or eliminate the erosion of friendship networks that often attends the cessation of substance use (e.g., Ribisl, 1997; Humphreys, Mankowski, Moos, & Finney, 1999). However, many recovering persons drop out of 12-step fellowships relatively early on, and some never attend (e.g., Caldwell & Cutter, 1998; Fiorentine, 1999; Klaw & Humphreys, 2000; McCrady, Epstein, & Hirsch, 1996; McIntire, 2000; Morgenstern et al., 1996), so clinicians should not stop at encouraging 12-step affiliation as a source of recovery support. Rather, clinicians should work in partnership with clients on a case-by-case basis to develop strategies that maximize recovery capital (and its utilization) tailored to the individual's situation; these strategies should be revisited periodically since needs and available resources make change as recovery progresses (for more substantial discussion of *recovery management*, we refer readers to McLellan, Lewis, O'Brien, & Kleber, 2000; White, Boyle, & Loveland, 2002, 2003; Dennis, Scott, & Funk, 2003). Participation in religious/spiritual congregations can also provide a supportive network (Berkman & Syme, 1979; House et al., 1988; for review, see Fetzer Institute, 1999). Again, as with 12-step fellowships, however, religious/spiritual group membership, while potentially beneficial for some, may not appeal to others. Thus, one of the most promising and potentially useful implication of our findings for clinicians centers on the beneficial role of spirituality and life meaning as a critical ingredient of recovery capital; these resources tend to be underutilized by clinical service providers (e.g., Miller, 1998). There is overwhelming evidence that persons receiving mental health services, including addiction services, view spirituality as essential to recovery, and a number of researchers have emphasized the need for clinicians to give more attention to clients' spiritual needs (e.g., Arnold, Avants, Margolin, & Marcotte, 2002; McDowell, Galanter, Goldfarb, & Lifshutz, 1996; National Center on Addiction and Substance Abuse, 2001). As noted by Arnold and colleagues (2002), interventions that attempt to address spiritual needs must be flexible enough to allow for several interpretations of spirituality, including conceptualizations of spirituality that do not include belief in a "higher power"; that is, the individual should be able to define spirituality for him/herself; this recommendation is consistent with the initial suggestion of Bill W. as set forth in the Big Book and discussed briefly earlier. Perhaps most promising and vastly neglected up to now is the importance of life meaning in the recovery process. Life meaning helps transcend the here and now, re-establish hope and the ability to cope (Speck 2004); this is particularly important for recovering individuals who may face painful and difficult realizations about the destructive consequences of their past use on their life and that of their loved ones, in addition to the difficulties they are encountering in the present. Life meaning does not need to be tied to specific sets of religious or spiritual beliefs, so that the pursuit of meaning as defined by the individual should be encouraged and fostered as part of rehabilitative and recovery services.

Overall, present findings suggest that the hope for a better life that sets many substance users on the path to recovery can be a reality; there is light at the end of the dark tunnel of active addiction for those who choose to change course and 'to go to any length' to seek recovery. That pursuit is stressful, challenging, lengthy, and requires a capital of recovery resources. With the ultimate goal of enhancing overall life satisfaction, present findings indicate that social supports, 12-step affiliation, spirituality, religiousness and life meaning have the potential of contributing to the overall recovery experience and thus, should be made an integral part of the menu of resources offered to the recovering community.

NOTES

1. "Much to our relief, we discovered that we did not need to consider another's conception of God. Our own conception, however inadequate, was sufficient to make the approach and to effect a contact with Him. (. . .) To us, the Realm of Spirit is broad, roomy, all-inclusive; never exclusive or forbidding to those who honestly seek. It is open, we believe, to all men" (3rd edition, p. 46).

2. This is because the study is a naturalistic investigation of the role of psychosocial factors on long-term recovery, and we wanted to be able to assess the role of baseline community-related factors on subsequent outcome.

3. With respect to individual religious activities, 85% of participants reported thinking about God 'daily' or 'almost daily,' 78% prayed or mediated 'daily' or 'almost daily,' 33% attended worship services weekly or more often, 37% read or studied scriptures or holy writings at least weekly and 43% had a direct experience with God 'daily' or 'almost daily' whereas 29% never did and 20% rarely did.

4. Readers interested in more detailed statistical information pertaining to the analyses summarized here should contact the second author, Keith Morgen, at *morgen@ ndri.org*

5. In the case of the stressful events variables, there were 24 individuals in the dataset who had reported no stressful event in the past year; these cases were considered statistical outliers from the remaining sample and were dropped from the analysis.

REFERENCES

Alcoholics Anonymous World Services (1939/1976). *Alcoholics Anonymous: The story of how many thousands of men and women have recovered from alcoholism.* 3rd Ed. NY: Alcoholics Anonymous World Services Inc.

Alemi, F., Stephens, R., Llorens, S., Schaefer, D., Nemes, S., & Arendt, R. (2003). The Orientation of Social Support measure. *Addictive Behaviors, 28,* 1285-1298.

Antonovsky, A. (1979). *Health, stress, and coping.* San Francisco, CA: Jossey-Bass.

Arbuckle, J. (1999). AMOS 4.0 [computer software]. Chicago: SmallWaters.

Arnold, R., Avants, S., Margolin, A., & Marcotte, D. (2002). Patient attitudes concerning the inclusion of spirituality in addiction treatment. *Journal of Substance Abuse Treatment, 23,* 319-326.

Baron, R., & Kenny, D. (1986). The moderator-mediator distinction in social psychological research: Conceptual, strategic, and statistical considerations. *Journal of Personality and Social Psychology, 51,* 1173-1182.

Beattie, M., & Longabaugh, R. (1997). Interpersonal factors and post-treatment drinking and subject well-being. *Addiction, 92,* 1507-1521.

Benson, P. L. (1992). Religion and substance use. In J. F. Schumaker (Ed.), *Religion and mental health* (pp. 211-221). New York: Oxford University Press.

Berkman, L., & Syme, S. (1979). Social networks, host resistance, and mortality: A nine-year follow-up study of Alameda County residents. *American Journal of Epidemiology, 109,* 186-204.

Berkman, L. (1985). The relationship of social networks and social support to morbidity and mortality. In S. Cohen and S. Syme (Eds.), *Social support and health*. Orlando, FL: Academic Press, pp. 241-262.

Bollen, K. (1989). *Structural equations with latent variables*. New York: John Wiley & Sons.

Brady, M., Peterman, A., Fitchett, G., Mo, M., & Cella, D. (1999). A case for including spirituality in quality of life measurement in oncology. *Psycho-Oncology, 8*, 417-428.

Brennan, P., & Moos, R. (1990). Life stressors, social resources, and late-life problem drinking. *Psychology and Aging, 5*, 491-501.

Brogly, S., Mercier, C., Bruneau, J., Palepu, A., & Franco, E. (2003). Towards more effective public health programming for injection drug users: Development and evaluation of the injection drug user quality of life scale. *Substance Use and Misuse, 38*, 965-992.

Burman, S. (1997). The challenge of sobriety: Natural recovery without treatment and self-help programs. *Journal of Substance Abuse, 9*, 41-61.

Byrne, B. (2001). *Structural equation modeling with AMOS: Basic concepts, applications, and programming*. Mahwah, NJ: Lawrence Erlbaum Associates, Publishers.

Caldwell, P., & Cutter, H. (1998). Alcoholics anonymous affliction during early recovery. *Journal of Substance Abuse Treatment, 15*, 221-28.

Caplan, G., & Caplan, R. (2000). Principles of community psychiatry. *Community Mental Health J., 36*, 7-24.

Carson, V., & Green, H. (1992). Spiritual well-being: A predictor of hardiness in patients with acquired immunodeficiency syndrome. *Journal of Professional Nursing, 8*, 209-20.

Chapman, R. (1991). Middle recovery: An introspective journey. *Addiction and Recovery*, Sept-October, 8-12.

Chappel, J. (1993). Long term recovery from alcoholism. *Psychiatric Clin. N. Amer., 169*, 17-187.

Christo, G., & Franey, C. (1995). Drug users' spiritual beliefs, locus of control and the disease concept in relation to Narcotics Anonymous attendance and six-month outcomes. *Drug and Alcohol Dependence, 38*, 51-56.

Cohen, S., Hassan, S., Lapointe, B., & Mount, B. (1996). Quality of life in HIV disease as measured by the McGill quality of life questionnaire. *AIDS, 10*, 1421-7.

Coleman, C. (2004). The contribution of religious and existential well-being to depression among African American heterosexuals with HIV infection. *Mental Health Nursing, 25*, 103-10.

Connors, G., & Dermen, K. (1996). Characteristics of participants in Secular Organization for Sobriety (SOS). *American Journal Drug Alcohol Abuse, 22*, 281-295.

Connors, G., Tonigan, S., & Miller, W. (1996). A measure of Religious Background and Behavior for use in behavior change research. *Psychology of Addictive Behaviors, 10*, 90-96.

Cook, C. (2004). Addiction and spirituality. *Addiction, 99*, 539-551.

Corrigan, P., McCorkle, B., Schell, B., & Kidder, K. (2003). Religion and spirituality in the lives of people with serious mental illness. *Community Mental Health Journal, 3*, 487-99.

Cotton, S., Levine, E., Fitzpatrick, C., Dold, K., & Targ, E. (1999). Exploring the relationship among spiritual well-being, quality of life and psychological adjustment in women with breast cancer. *Psycho-Oncology, 8,* 429-438.

Cross, G., Morgan, C., Moony, A., Martin, C., & Rafter, J. (1990). Alcoholism treatment: A ten-year follow-up study. *Alcoholism Clinical and Experimental Research, 14,* 169-173.

Culliford, L. (2002). Spirituality and clinical care: Spiritual values and skills are increasingly recognised as necessary aspects of clinical care. *British Medical Journal (bmj.com), 325,* 1434-1435.

Dalgard, O., & Tambs, K. (1997). Urban environment and mental health: A longitudinal study. *British Journal of Psychiatry, 171,* 530-536.

Dennis, M.L., Scott, C.K., & Funk, R. (2003). An experimental evaluation of recovery management checkups (RMC) for people with chronic substance use disorders. *Evaluation and Program Planning, 26,* 339-352.

El-Bassel, N., Duan-Rung, C., & Cooper, D. (1998). Social support and social network profiles among women in methadone. *Social Service Review,* 379-401.

Elkins, D., Hedstrom, L., Hughes, L., Leaf, J., & Saunders, C. (1988). Toward a humanistic phenomenological spirituality. *Journal of Humanistic Psychology, 28,* 5-18.

Ellison, C. (1991). Religious involvement and subjective well-being. *J Health Soc Behav., 32,* 80-99.

Ellison, C. (1983). Spiritual Well-Being: Conceptualization and measurement. *Journal of Psychology and Theology, 11,* 330-340.

Falck, R., Wang, J., Carlson, R., & Siegal, H. (2000). Crack-cocaine use and health status as defined by the SF-36. *Addictive Behaviors, 25,* 579-584.

Fehring, R., Brennan, P., & Keller M. (1987). Psychological and spiritual well-being in college students. *Res Nurs Health, 10,* 391-8.

Fetzer Institute, National Institute on Aging Working Group (1999). Multidimensional measurement of religiousness/spirituality for use in health research. *A report of a national working group supported by the Fetzer institute in collaboration with the national institute on aging.* Kalamazoo, MI: Fetzer Institute.

Fife, B. (1994). The conceptualization of meaning in illness. *Social Science and Medicine, 38,* 309-316.

Finney, J. (1995). Enhancing substance abuse treatment evaluations: Examining mediators and moderators of treatment effects. *Journal of Substance Abuse, 7,* 135-50.

Finney, J., Noyes, C., Coutts, A., & Moos, R. (1998). Evaluating substance abuse treatment process models: Changes on proximal outcome variables during 12-step and cognitive-behavioral treatment. *Journal of Studies on Alcohol, 59,* 371-380.

Fiorentine R, & Hillhouse, M. (2000). Drug treatment and 12-step program participation: The additive effects of integrated recovery activities. *Journal of Substance Abuse Treatment, 18,* 65-74.

Fiorentine, R. (1999). After drug treatment: Are 12-step programs effective in maintaining abstinence? *American Journal of Drug Alcohol Abuse, 25,* 93-116.

Flynn, P., Joe, G., Broome, K., Simpson, D., & Brown, B. (2003). Looking back on cocaine dependence: Reasons for recovery. *American Journal on Addictions, 12,* 398-411.

Foster, J., Marshall, E., & Peters, T. (2000). Application of a quality of life measure, the life situation survey, to alcohol-dependent subjects in relapse and remission. *Alcohol: Clinical & Experimental Research, 24,* 1687-92.

Frankl, V. (1963). *Man's search for meaning.* New York, NY: Washington Square Press.

Freyer-Rose, K. (1991). Late recovery: A process of integration. *Addiction and Recovery,* Nov-Dec., 20-23.

Fry, P. (2001). The unique contribution of key existential factors to the prediction of psychological well-being of older adults following spousal loss. *Gerontologist, 41,* 69-81.

Galanter, M. (1997). Spiritual recovery movements and contemporary medical care. *Psychiatry, 60,* 211-23.

Gossop, M., Harris, J., Best, D., Man, L., Manning, V., Marshall, J., & Strang J. (2003). Is attendance at alcoholics anonymous meetings after inpatient treatment related to improved outcomes? A 6-month follow-up study. *Alcohol and Alcoholism, 38,* 421-426.

Granfield, R., & Cloud, W. (2001). Social context and "natural recovery": The role of social capital in the resolution of drug-associated problems. *Substance Use and Misuse, 36,* 1543-1570.

Granfield, R., & Cloud, W. (1999). *Coming clean: Overcoming addiction without treatment.* New York: New York University Press.

Green, L., Fullilove, M., & Fullilove, R. (1998). Stories of spiritual awakenings: The nature of spirituality in recovery. *Journal of Substance Abuse Treatment, 15,* 325-331.

Greenblatt, M., Becerra, R., & Serafetinides, E. (1982). Social networks and mental health: An overview. *American Journal of Psychiatry, 139,* 977-984.

Havassy, B., Wasserman, D., & Hall, S. (1993). Relapse to cocaine use: Conceptual issues. *In cocaine treatment: Research & clinical perspectives.* Research Monograph # 135. Rockville, MD: National Institute on Drug Abuse.

Havassy, B., & Arns, P. (1998). Relationship of cocaine and other substance dependence to well-being of high-risk psychiatric patients. *Psychiatric Services, 49,* 935-940.

Heintz, L. & Baruss, I. (2001). Spirituality in late adulthood. *Psychological Reports, 88,* 651-4.

House, J., Landis, K., & Umberson, D. (1988). Social relationships and health. *Science, 241,* 540-545.

Humphreys, K., Wing, S., McCarty, B., Chappel, J., Gallant, L., Haberle, B., Horvath, T., Kaskutas, L., Kirk, T., Kivlahan, D., Laudet, A., McCrady, B., McLellan, T., Morgenstern, J., Townsend, M., & Weiss, R. (2004). Self-help organizations for alcohol and drug problems: Toward evidence-based practice and policy. *Journal of Substance Abuse Treatment, 26,* 151-158.

Humphreys, K., & Moos, R. (2001). Can encouraging substance abuse patients to participate in self-help groups reduce demand for health care: A quasi-experimental study. *Alcoholism: Clinical and Experimental Research, 25,* 711-716.

Humphreys, K., Mankowski, E., Moos, R., & Finney, J. (1999). Do enhanced friendships networks and active coping mediate the effect of self-help groups on substance use? *Annals of Behavioral Medicine, 21,* 54-60.

Humphreys, K., Moos, R., & Cohen, C. (1997). Social and community resources and long-term recovery from treated and untreated alcoholism. *Journal of Studies on Alcohol, 58,* 231-238.

Humphreys, K., & Noke, J.M. (1997). The influence of post-treatment mutual help group participation on the friendship networks of substance abuse patients. *American Journal of Community Psychology, 25,* 1-16.

Johnson, B. (2001). *A better kind of high: How religious commitment reduces drug use among poor urban teens.* Report #2001-2. University of Pennsylvania: Center for Research and Urban Civil Society.

Jones, G. S. (1994). The surrender experience in recovery from substance dependence: A multiple case study. Ann Arbor, MI: UMI Dissertation Services.

Katz, A. (1993). *Self-help in America: A social movement perspective.* New York, NY: Twayne.

Kingree, J., & Thompson, M. (2000a). Mutual aid groups, perceived status benefits and well-being: A test with adult children of alcoholics with personal substance abuse problems. *American Journal of Community Psychology, 28,* 325-342.

Kingree, J.B., & Thompson, M. (2000b). 12-step groups, attributions of blame for personal sadness, psychological well-being, and the moderating role of gender. *Journal of Applied Social Psychology, 30,* 499-517.

Klaw, E., & Humphreys, K. (2000). Life stories of Moderation Management mutual help group members. *Contemporary Drug Problems, 27,* 779-803.

Kline, R. B. (1998). *Principles and practice of structural equation modeling.* New York: Guilford.

Kobasa, S. (1979). Stressful life events, personality, and health: An inquiry into hardiness. *Journal of Personality and Social Psychology, 37,* 1-11.

Koenig, H., McCullough, M., & Larson, D. (2001). *Handbook of religion & health.* New York: Oxford University Press.

Kondo, C., Iimuro, T., Iwai, K., Kurata, K., Kouda, M., Tachikawa, H., Nakashima, K., & Munakata, T. (2000). [A study of recovery factor about drug addiction recovery center "DARC"] *Nihon Arukoru Yakubutsu Igakkai Zasshi, 35,* 258-70.

Kus, R. (Ed.). (1995). *Spirituality and chemical dependency.* New York: The Haworth Press, Inc.

Laudet, A., Magura, S., Vogel, H., & Knight, E. (2004). Perceived reasons for substance use among persons with a psychiatric disorder. *American Journal of Orthopsychiatry, 74,* 365-375.

Laudet, A., & White, W. (2004). Correlates of 12-step affiliation in a community-based sample of former substance users. Poster Presented at the 66th Annual Scientific Meeting of the College on Problems of Drug Dependence, San Juan, Puerto Rico, June 2004.

Laudet, A., Savage, R., & Mahmood, D. (2002). Pathways to long-term recovery: A preliminary investigation. *Journal of Psychoactive Drugs, 34,* 305-311.

Laudet, A., Magura, S., Vogel, H., & Knight, E. (2000). Support, mutual aid and recovery from dual diagnosis. *Community Mental Health Journal, 36,* 457-476.

Levine, E., & Targ, E. (2002). Spiritual correlates of functional well-being in women with breast cancer. *Integrated Cancer Therapies, 1,* 166-74.

Lin, N. (1986). Conceptualizing social support. In N. Lin, A. Dean and W. Ensel (Eds.), *Social support, life events and depression.* New York: Academic Press, pp. 17-30.

Longbaugh, R., & Lewis, D. (1988). Key issues in treatment outcome studies. *Alcohol Health Research World, 12,* 168-175.

Margolis, R., Kilpatrick, A., & Mooney, B. (2000). A retrospective look at long-term adolescent recover: Clinicians talk to researchers. *Journal of Psychoactive Drugs, 32, 117-125.*

Mathew, R., Georgi, J., Wilson, W., & Mathew, V. (1996). Retrospective study of the concept of spirituality as understood by recovering individuals. *Journal of Substance Abuse Treatment, 13,* 67-73.

Matthews, D.A., & Larson, D.B. (1995) *The Faith factor: An annotated bibliography of clinical research on spiritual subject,* Vol. 3. National Institute for Healthcare Research, Rockville, MD.

McCrady, B., Epstein, E., & Hirsch, L. (1996). Issues in the implementation of a randomized clinical trial that includes Alcoholics Anonymous: Studying AA-related behaviors during treatment. *Journal of Studies on Alcohol, 57,* 604-12.

McDowell, D., Galanter, M., Goldfarb, L., & Lifshutz, H. (1996). Spirituality and the treatment of the dually diagnosed: An investigation of patient and staff attitudes. *Journal of Addictive Disorders, 15,* 55-68.

McIntire, D. (2000). How well does AA work? An analysis of published AA surveys (1968-1996) and related analyses/comments. *Alcoholism Treatment Quarterly, 18,* 1-18.

McKay, J., Merikle, E., Mulvaney, F., Weiss, R., & Kopenhaver, J. (2001). Factors accounting for cocaine use two years following initiation of continuing care. *Addiction, 96,* 213-225.

McLellan, A.T., Lewis, D., O'Brien, C., & Kleber, H. (2000). Drug dependence, a chronic medical illness: Implications for treatment, insurance and outcomes evaluation. *Journal of the American Medical Association, 284,* 1689-1695.

McLellan, A., Kushner, H., Metzger, D. et al. (1992). The fifth edition of the Addiction Severity Index. *Journal of Substance Abuse Treatment, 9,* 199-213.

Mickley, J., Soeken, K., & Belcher, A. (1992). Spiritual well-being, religiousness and hope among women with breast cancer. Image. *J. Nurs. Scholarsh., 2,* 267-272.

Miller, N., Ninonuevo, F., Klamen, D., & Hoffmann, N. (1997). Integration of treatment and posttreatment variables in predicting results of abstinence-based outpatient treatment after one year. *Journal of Psychoactive Drugs, 29,* 239-248.

Miller, W. (1999). *Integrating spirituality into treatment.* Washington, DC: American Psychological Association.

Miller, W. (1998). Researching the spiritual dimensions of alcohol and other drug problems. *Addiction, 93,* 979-990.

Miller, W., & Thoresen, C. (2003). Spirituality, religion and health: An emerging research field. *American Psychologist, 58,* 24-35.

Montgomery, H., Miller W., & Tonigan J. (1995). Does Alcoholics Anonymous involvement predict treatment outcome? *Journal of Substance Abuse Treatment, 12,* 241-246.

Moos, R. (2003). Addictive disorders in context: Principles and puzzles of effective treatment and recovery *Psychology of Addictive Behaviors, 17,* 3-12.

Moos, R, Finney, J, Ouimette, P., & Suchinsky, R. (1999). A comparative evaluation of substance abuse treatment: I. Treatment orientation, amount of care, and 1-year outcomes. *Alcoholism Clinical and Experimental Research, 23,* 529-536.

Morgenstern, J., Kahler, C., Frey, R., & Labouvie, E. (1996). Modeling therapeutic responses to 12-step treatment: Optimal responders, non-responders, and partial responders. *Journal of Substance Abuse, 8,* 45-59.

Morgenstern, J., Labouvie, E., McCray, B., Kahler, C., & Frey, R. (1997). Affiliation with Alcoholics Anonymous after treatment: A study of its therapeutic effects and mechanisms of action. *Journal of Consulting and Clinical Psychology, 65,* 768-777.

Morjaria, A., & Orford, J. (2002) The role of religion and spirituality in recovery from drink problems: A qualitative study of Alcoholics Anonymous members and South Asian men. *Addiction Research & Theory, 10,* 225-256.

National Institute on Alcohol Abuse and Alcoholism [NIAAA] (2000, February 7). *Studying spirituality and alcohol.* RFA: AA-00-002. Washington, DC: Author. Co-sponsored with the Fetzer Institute.

Nealon-Woods, M., Ferrari, J., & Jason. L. (1995). Twelve-step program use among Oxford House residents: Spirituality or social support in sobriety? *Journal of Substance Abuse, 7,* 311-318.

Nelson, C., Rosenfeld, B., Breitbart, W., & Galietta, M. (2002). Spirituality, religion, and depression in the terminally ill. *Psychosomatics, 43,* 213-20.

Nelson, G., Hall, G.B., Squire, D., & Walsh-Bowers, R. (1992). Social network transactions of psychiatric patients. *Social Science and Medicine, 34,* 433-445.

Noone, M., Dua, J., & Markham, R. (1999). Stress, cognitive factors, and coping resources as predictors of relapse in alcoholics. *Addictive Behaviors, 24,* 687-693.

Paloutzian, R., & Ellison, C. (1982). Loneliness, spiritual well-being and qualify of life. In: L. Peplau and D. Perlman (Eds.), *Loneliness: A sourcebook of current theory research and therapy.* New York: Wiley.

Pardini, D.A., Plante, T.G., Sherman, A., & Stump, J.E. (2000). Religious faith and spirituality in substance abuse recovery: Determining the mental health benefits. *Journal of Substance Abuse Treatment, 19,* 347-54.

Park, C., & Folkman, S. (1997). Meaning in the context of stress and coping. *General Review of Psychology, 1,* 115-144.

Peele, S. (1985). *The meaning of addiction: Compulsive experience and its interpretation.* Lexington, MA: D.C. Heath.

Project MATCH Research Group (1997). Matching alcoholism treatment to client heterogeneity: Project MATCH post-treatment drinking outcomes. *Journal of Studies on Alcohol, 58,* 7-29.

Ribisl, K. (1997). The role of social networks in predicting substance abuse treatment outcome in a dual diagnosis sample. Paper presented at the annual meeting of the Society for Behavioral Medicine, San Francisco.

Richter, S., Brown, S., & Mott, M. (1991). The impact of social support and self-esteem on adolescent substance abuse treatment outcome. *Journal of Substance Abuse, 3*, 317-85.

Riley, B., Perna, R., Tate, D., Forchheimer, M., Anderson, C., & Luera, G. (1998). Types of spiritual well-being among persons with chronic illness: their relation to various forms of quality of life. *Archives of Physical and Medical Rehabilitation, 79*, 258-64.

Rudolf, H., & Watts, J. (2002). Quality of life in substance abuse and dependency. *International Review of Psychiatry, 14*, 190-197.

Rumpf, H., Bischof, G., Hapke, U., Meyer, C., & John, U. (2002). The role of family and partnership in recovery from alcohol dependence: Comparison of individuals remitting with and without formal help. *European Addiction Research, 8*, 122-127.

Ryff, C. (1989). Happiness is everything, or is it? Explorations on the meaning of psychological well-being. *Journal of Personality and Social Psychology, 57*, 1069-1081.

Schumaker, J. (1992). *Religion and mental health.* New York: Oxford University Press.

Sheehan, D., Lecrubier, Y., Harnett-Sheehan, K., Amorim, P., Janavs, J., & Weiller, E. et al. (1998) The Mini International Neuropsychiatric Interview (M.I.N.I.): The Development and Validation of a Structured Diagnostic Psychiatric Interview. *Journal of Clinical Psychiatry, 59*, 22-33.

Shrout, P., & Bolger, N. (2002). Mediation in experimental and nonexperimental studies: New procedures and recommendations. *Psychological Methods, 7*, 422-445.

Skinner, H. (1982). The Drug Abuse Screening Test (DAST). *Addictive Behaviors, 7*, 363-371.

Smith, K., & Larson, M. (2003). Quality of life assessments by adult substance abusers receiving publicly funded treatment in Massachusetts. *American Journal of Drug and Alcohol Abuse, 29*, 323-335.

Sobel, M. (1982). Asymptotic confidence intervals for indirect effects in structural equation models. In S. Leinhardt (Ed.), *Sociological methodology*, (pp. 290-312). Washington, DC: American Sociological Association.

Speck, P. (2004). Spiritual needs in health care may be distinct from religious ones and are integral to palliative care. *BMJ (17 JULY 2004 bmj.com), 329*, 124-126.

Stewart, C. (2001). The influence of spirituality on substance use of college students. *Journal of Drug Education, 31(4)*, 343-51.

Taylor, S.E., & Aspinwall, L.G. (1996). Mediating and moderating processes in psychosocial stress. In: Kaplan, H.B. (Ed.), *Psychosocial stress.* New York: Academic Press, pp. 71-110.

Taylor, S.E. (1995). *Health psychology,* New York: McGraw.

Te Vaarwerk, M., & Gaal, E.A. (2001). Psychological distress and quality of life in drug-using and non drug-using HIV-infected women. *European Journal of Public Health, 11*, 109-115.

The National Center on Addiction and Substance Abuse (CASA) at Columbia University (2003, Unpublished). *The National Center on Addiction and Substance Abuse (CASA) at Columbia University's analysis of 1999 CASA teen survey data.* New York: The National Center on Addiction and Substance Abuse (CASA) at Columbia University.

The National Center on Addiction and Substance Abuse (CASA) at Columbia University (2001). So help me God: Substance abuse, religion and spirituality. New York: The National Center on Addiction and Substance Abuse (CASA) at Columbia University.

The National Center on Addiction and Substance Abuse (CASA) at Columbia University (1998). *Under the rug: Substance abuse and the mature woman*. New York: The National Center on Addiction and Substance Abuse (CASA) at Columbia University.

The WHOQOL Group (1995) The World Health Organization quality of life assessment (WHOQOL): Position paper from the World Health Organization. *Social Science and Medicine, 41*, 1403-1409.

Timko, C., Moos, R., Finney, J., & Lesar, M. (2000). Long-term outcomes of alcohol use disorders: Comparing untreated individuals with those in alcoholics anonymous and formal treatment. *Journal of Studies on Alcohol, 61*, 529-540.

Titus, J., Dennis, M., White, M., Godley, S., Tims, F., & Diamond, G. (2002). An examination of adolescents' reasons for starting, quitting, and continuing to use drugs and alcohol following treatment. Poster presented at the 64th Annual Scientific Meeting of the College on Problems of Drug Dependence, Quebec City, June 8-13.

Tonigan J., Miller, W., & Schermer, C. (2002). Atheists, agnostics and Alcoholics Anonymous. *Journal of Studies on Alcohol, 63*, 534-41.

Tonigan, J., Toscova, R., & Miller, W. (1996). Meta-analysis of the literature on Alcoholics Anonymous: Sample and study characteristics moderate findings. *Journal of Studies on Alcohol, 57*, 65-72.

Trumbetta, S., Mueser, K., Quimby, E., Bebout, R., & Teague, G. (1999). Social networks and clinical outcomes of dually diagnosed homeless persons. *Behavior Therapy, 30*, 407-430.

Tsuang M., Williams, W., Simpson, J., & Lyons, M.J. (2002). Pilot study of spirituality and mental health in twins. *American Journal of Psychiatry, 159*, 486-8.

Underwood, L., & Teresi, J. (2002). The Daily spiritual experience scale: Development, theoretical description, reliability, exploratory factor analysis, and preliminary construct validity using health-related data. *Annals of Behavioral Medicine, 24*, 22-33.

Vaillant G. (1983/1995). *The Natural history of alcoholism revisited*. Cambridge, MA: Harvard University Press.

Vaillant, G., & Milofsky, E. (1992). Natural history of male alcoholism: IV. Paths to recovery. *Archives of General Psychiatry, 39*, 127-133.

Vaughan, F., Wittine, B., & Walsh, R. (1998). Transpersonal psychology and the religious person, in *Religion and the clinical practice of psychology* (E.P. Shafranske Ed.). Washington, DC: American Psychological Association, pp. 483-509.

Vaux, A. (1988). *Social support: Theory, research, and intervention*. NY: Praeger.

Vaux, A., & Harrison, D. (1985). Support network characteristics associated with support satisfaction and perceived support. *American Journal of Community Psychology, 13*, 245-268.

Ventegodt, S., Merrick, J., & Andersen, N. (2003). Quality of life theory I. The IQOL theory: An integrative theory of the global quality of life concept. *Scientific World Journal, 13*, 1030-40.

Ventegodt, S., & Merrick, J. (2003). Psychoactive drugs and quality of life. *Scientific World Journal, 18*, 694-706.

Volcan, S., Sousa, P., Mari, Jde J., & Horta, B. (2003). Relationship between spiritual well-being and minor psychiatric disorders: A cross-sectional study. *Revista Saude Publica, 37*, 440-445.

Walsh, D., Hingson, R., & Merrigan, D. (1991). A randomized trial of treatment options for alcohol-abusing workers. *The New England Journal of Medicine, 325*, 775-782.

Walters, G. (2000). Spontaneous Remission From Alcohol, Tobacco, and Other Drug Abuse: Seeking Quantitative Answers to Qualitative Questions. *American Journal Drug Alcohol Abuse, 26*, 443-460.

Weaver, G., Turner, N., & O'Dell, K. (2000). Depressive symptoms, stress, and coping among women recovering from addiction. *Journal of Substance Abuse Treatment, 18*, 161-167.

Weisner, C., Delucchi, K., Matzger, H., & Schmidt, L. (2003). The role of community services and informal support on five-year drinking trajectories of alcohol dependent and problem drinkers. *Journal of Alcohol Studies, 64*, 862-873.

White, W. (2004). Recovery: The next frontier. *Counselor, 5*, 18-21.

White, W., & Sanders, M. (2004). Recovery management and people of color: Redesigning addiction treatment for historically disempowered communities. Posted at *http://www.bhrm.org*.

White, W., Boyle, M., & Loveland, D. (2003). Recovery management: transcending the limitations of addiction treatment. *Behavioral Health Management, 23*, 38-44.

White, W., Boyle, M., & Loveland, D. (2002). Alcoholism/Addiction as chronic disease: From rhetoric to clinical reality. *Alcoholism Treatment Quarterly, 20*, 107-130.

Wills, T. Yaeger, A., & Sandy, J. (2003). Buffering Effect of Religiosity for Adolescent Substance Use. *Psychology of Addictive Behaviors, 17*, 24-31.

Winzelberg, A., & Humphreys, K. (1999). Should patients' religiosity influence clinicians' referral to 12-step self-help groups? Evidence from a study of 3,018 male substance abuse patients. *Journal of Clinical and Consulting Psychology, 67*, 790-794.

Zemore, S., & Kaskutas, L. (2004). Helping, spirituality and alcoholics anonymous in recovery. *Journal of Studies on Alcohol, 65*, 383-391.

Zinnbauer, B., Pargament, K., Cole, B., Rye, M., Butter, E., Belavich, T., Hipp, K., Scott, A., & Kadar, J. (1997). Religion and spirituality; Unfuzzying the fuzzy. *Journal of Scientific Study of Religion, 36*, 549-564.

Church Attendance or Religiousness: Their Relationship to Adolescents' Use of Alcohol, Other Drugs, and Delinquency

Brent B. Benda, PhD
Sandra K. Pope, PhD
Kelly J. Kelleher, MD, MPH

SUMMARY. The purpose of the study was to determine if religiousness, instead of church attendance, was related to alcohol consumption, other drug use, and delinquency after considering socio-demographic, familial and peer factors. Many researchers argue that religion only inhibits relative minor, or ascetic, offenses, such as underage consumption of alcohol. They also argue that religion ceases to be related to offenses when more important influences like peer associations are considered.

This study consisted of a stratified random sample of 3,551 adolescents, grades seven through nine, from 66 public high schools in a south-

Brent B. Benda is Professor, School of Social Work, University of Arkansas at Little Rock, Little Rock, AR.

Sandra K. Pope is Assistant Professor, Department of Geriatrics, College of Medicine and Department of Epidemiology, College of Public Health, University of Arkansas for Medical Sciences, Little Rock, AR.

Kelly J. Kelleher is Director, Office of Clinical Sciences, Columbus Children's Research Institute and Professor of Pediatrics and Public Health, The Ohio State University, Columbus, OH.

Address correspondence to: Dr. Brent Benda, School of Social Work, University of Arkansas at Little Rock, Little Rock, AR 72204.

[Haworth co-indexing entry note]: "Church Attendance or Religiousness: Their Relationship to Adolescents' Use of Alcohol, Other Drugs, and Delinquency." Benda, Brent B., Sandra K. Pope, and Kelly J. Kelleher. Co-published simultaneously in *Alcoholism Treatment Quarterly* (The Haworth Press, Inc.) Vol. 24, No. 1/2, 2006, pp. 75-87; and: *Spirituality and Religiousness and Alcohol/Other Drug Problems: Treatment and Recovery Perspectives* (ed: Brent B. Benda, and Thomas F. McGovern) The Haworth Press, Inc., 2006, pp. 75-87. Single or multiple copies of this article are available for a fee from The Haworth Document Delivery Service [1-800-HAWORTH, 9:00 a.m. - 5:00 p.m. (EST). E-mail address: docdelivery@ haworthpress.com].

ern state. The findings indicate that religiousness is significantly related to all three offenses studied when other study factors are simultaneously considered, whereas church attendance has a modest relationship to drug use. The treatment implications of these findings are discussed. *[Article copies available for a fee from The Haworth Document Delivery Service: 1-800-HAWORTH. E-mail address: <docdelivery@haworthpress. com> Website: <http://www.HaworthPress.com> © 2006 by The Haworth Press, Inc. All rights reserved.]*

KEYWORDS. Religiousness, church attendance, adolescent alcohol and drug use, delinquency

BACKGROUND

There are cogent reasons for thinking that religion promotes a healthy lifestyle and the avoidance of alcohol consumption, use of other drugs, and delinquency (Baier & Wright, 2001; George, Larsons, Koeing, & McCullough, 2000). Religion offers divine principles concerning the sanctity of one's physical, mental, and spiritual being (Worthington, 1993). Religion also consists of moral imperatives of self-control and personal virtue, grounded in the authority of a Creator (Regnerus, 2003). The focus of the present study is on Judeo-Christian religions, which have specific proscriptions against breaking societal laws, such as underage alcohol consumption.

Several studies have emerged showing that religious measures are inversely related to unlawful behaviors among adolescents (e.g., Benda, 1995; Cochran, Wood, & Arneklev, 1994; Mason & Windle, 2002; Regnerus, 2003). A meta-analysis finds a moderate effect of $-.12$ across 60 recent studies–the majority of which observed a statistically significant inverse relationship between a measure of religion and some form of unlawful behavior (Baier & Wright, 2001). At the same time, controversy remains concerning the relative importance and universality of the influence of religion on adolescent misbehavior (Baier & Wright, 2001; Cochran et al., 1994; Regnerus, 2003). For example, Cochran et al. (1994) present evidence in support of their argument that the effects of religion on serious delinquency are fully mediated by more potent predictors. "When controlling for both arousal and social control indicators, the effect of religiosity is reduced to insignificance in the case of assault, theft, vandalism, illicit drug use, and truancy, although it remains significant regarding the use of legalized substances" (i.e., tobacco and alcohol) (Cochran et al., 1994, p. 92). They interpret their findings on tobacco and alcohol as supporting the "ascetic argument" that religion beliefs only deter offenses when there are clear religious proscriptions, but inconsistent and ambivalent responses from the larger society. Although there is confusion in the literature regarding what acts are ascetic offenses (e.g., truancy, vandalism), alcohol use is typically given as an example of these offenses (Evans, Cullen, Dunaway, & Burton, 1995). Alcohol consumption by adolescents is an offense toward which societal reactions are erratic and generally indulgent, whereas illicit use of other drugs and delinquency typically elicit more stable and stronger responses (Empey, Stafford, & Hay, 1999). It has been assumed in the literature that religious caregivers do not condone underage consumption of alcohol (Burkett, 1993; Ellison & Levin, 1998).

Another common stipulation on the relationship between religion and unlawful behavior is that adolescent females are more affected by religion than their male counterparts because sex-role socialization emphasizes nurture and obedience in girls and self-reliance and autonomy in boys (Bao, Whitbeck, Hoyt, & Conger, 1999; Smith, Lundquist, Faris, & Regnerus, 2002). It also has been assumed that African American youth are more influenced by religion than Caucasian youth, particularly in rural communities where the church is the center of social activity and support (Brody, Stoneman, Flor, & McCrary, 1994). This differential effect of religion could be particularly true in this investigation because rural areas in the state studied generally have homogenous populations with similar beliefs and values. Such settings have been referred to as "moral communities" in the literature (Stark & Bainbridge, 1997).

The purpose of the present study is to: (a) determine whether church attendance and religiousness are related to alcohol consumption, use of illicit drugs, and delinquency in a statewide sample of young adolescents, and (b) to determine if gender, race (Caucasians and African Americans), residence (rural and urban), and church attendance moderate–or interact with–the effects of religion on these forms of unlawful acts. The vast majority of studies of religion and unlawful behavior of adolescents use a single-item measure of church attendance, or a combination of attendance and an item measuring the importance of religion (see review, Baier & Wright, 2001). It has been argued that church attendance is a sound proxy measure of religion–that is, it has been assumed that church attendance is a good indicator of the importance of religion and of belief in God (Evans et al., 1995). However, there is evidence that religiousness—or a more direct measure of the importance of religion and belief in God—is a more potent influence on unlawful behaviors of adolescents, particularly alcohol consumption (Benda & Corwyn, 2001). Church attendance among youth often is the result of parental pressure, and in rural areas of community expectations, norms, and social opportunities (Welch, Tittle, & Petee, 1991).

Succinctly stated, church attendance can be a ritual devoid of meaning. In the present study, the relative strength of church attendance and of religiousness are compared in terms of predicting alcohol consumption, other drug use, and delinquency because it is assumed that religious beliefs and values have greater impact on behavior. A key assumption underlying this study is that the prevalent use of church attendance—as a measure of religious influence—is responsible for modest and inconsistent findings regarding the relationship between religion and various forms of unlawful behavior, especially underage consumption of alcohol. For the same reason, it is possible that there are no significant differences in the effects of religiousness on unlawful behavior between males and females, between Caucasians and African Americans, and between rural and urban youth. An interaction between church attendance and religion is examined because it is logical to assume that people who regularly attend are more likely to be religious.

METHOD

Sample

Sixty-six school districts in a southern state were approached to participate in the study, and administrators in 54 (81.1 percent) of these districts agreed to be involved in the study. The participating districts included 17,260 enrolled students. To achieve a representative sample of these students, a stratified random sample of 3,551 adolescents from grades seven through nine were selected to participate in the study. The stratification assured that 33 percent of the sample was from the urban area, and 67 percent was from rural communities, which represents the proportion in the state. A total of 156 students, or 4.4 percent of the sample, were excluded from the study due to absences, or missing data, gross inconsistencies in responses, logical errors, or range checks. Hence, statistical analyses were conducted on 3,395 students.

The majority of the rural (73 percent) and urban (64 percent) students was Caucasian, and most of the other students from those settings were African Americans (24 percent and 32 percent respectively). Seventeen percent of the rural students and seven percent of the urban pupils were from families receiving welfare.

Procedures

Consent for the study was obtained from the State Board of Education, school district superintendents, principals, and teachers involved. After receiving caregiver permission, assent was obtained from students before the survey to prevent identification of participants. The students completed the self-report form during one class within 20 to 50 minutes. All students in the selected classrooms received information on social services and hotlines for depression, drug problems, suicide, and other mental health problems. The University of Arkansas Institutional Review Board and the National Institutes of Health Office approved this protocol for the Protection of Research Resources.

The survey instrument used in this study contained 94 multiple choice questions based largely on the Health Behavior Questionnaire (HBQ), which has good reliability and validity (Jessor, Donovan, & Costa, 1991; McLennan et al., 1998).

Dependent Variables

A single item measures *alcohol use*: "Over the past 6 months, how often did you have 5 or more drinks of alcohol (liquor, wine, beer)?" A 7-point scale is used, ranging from 0 = I don't drink to 7 = daily or almost daily.

Other drug use is measured by asking respondents "how many times have you used each of the following drugs in the past month" (scaled: 0 = never, 1 = 1-2 times, 2 = 3-9 times, 3 = 10-19 times, 4 = 20 or more times): (a) marijuana; (b) uppers, downers, tranquilizers; (c) crack/cocaine; (d) LSD (acid); (e) anabolic steroids; and (f) heroin (α = .89).

Delinquency is measured with 6 items asking "In the past 6 months, how many times have you (scaled: 0 = never, 1 = once, 2 = twice, 3 = 3-4 times, 4 = 5 or more times): (a) started a fight, (b) taken something from a store without paying (shoplifting), (c) damaged or marked up public or private property, (d) stolen something from another person, (e) stayed out all night without permission, and (f) skipped school without permission (α = .86).

Measures

Church attendance is a single item with a 7-point scale, ranging from "none" to "2 or more times weekly." *Religiousness* consists of 5 items (4-point Likert scales): (1) how religious are you, (2) how religious is your family, (3) how religious do you wish your family would be, (4) how important is religion in you life and, (5) do you believe in God (3-point scale) ($\alpha = .79$).

Family relations are measured with two items (4 point scales) on closeness to caregivers ($\rho = .92$). Three items (5-point scales) asked about *caregiver supervision*: (1) friends, (2) activities, and (3) time ($\rho = .94$).

Commitment is measured by two items (3-point scales) asking about importance of doing well in school and going to college ($\alpha = .90$).

Future expectations are measured by 5 items (5-point scales) asking about chances of graduating high school, going to college, having a well paying job, having a happy family life, and staying in good health ($\alpha = .90$).

Friends' alcohol consumption is a single item asking how many of your friends drink alcohol often (1 = none, 2 = less than half, 3 = half, 4 = more than half, 5 = all).

FINDINGS

Pearson product-moment correlations between each study factor and risk behaviors are shown in Table 1. These bivariate analyses show that religiosity has higher inverse correlations than church attendance to alcohol consumption, use of other drugs, and delinquency. Only correlations for friend's alcohol use and caregiver supervision exceed the sizes of the coefficients for religiosity.

In Table 2 are shown the standardized coefficients obtained by simultaneous entry of predictors in ordinary least squares (OLS) regression procedures (Freund & Wilson, 1998). These standardized coefficients indicated that religiosity has the third strongest relationship to each dependent variable, whereas church attendance is not significantly (alpha = 0.05) related to alcohol consumption or to delinquency, and attendance has a relatively small relationship (Beta = $-.09$) to drug use.

Removing each predictor in separate OLS analyses, and comparing the amounts of variance explained with and without the predictor in the

TABLE 1. Pearson Product-Moment Corrections Between Study Factors and Illegal Behaviors

Factor	Alcohol	Drugs	Delinquency
Religiosity	−.35**	−.42**	−.30**
Church attendance	−.12*	−.17**	−.13*
Age	.25**	.27**	.15**
Gender (0 = female, 1 = male)	.18**	.24**	−.13**
Race (0 = white, 1 = person of color)	−.15**	.17**	.06
Father's education in years	−.15**	−.20**	−.09*
Welfare (0 = no, 1 = yes)	.10*	.18**	.06
Region (0 = rural, 1 = urban)	.16**	.06	.05
Family relations	−.30**	−.28**	−.26**
Caregiver supervision	−.36**	−.40**	−.39**
Commitment	−.28**	−.26**	−.25**
Future expectations	−.33**	−.36**	−.27**
Friends' alcohol use	.51**	.44**	.35**

Note: * $P < .05$; ** $P < .01$.

TABLE 2. Ordinary Least Squares Regression of Risk Behaviors on Predictors

Predictors	Alcohol	Drugs	Delinquency
Religiosity	−.28**	−.33**	−.30**
Church attendance	−.06	−.09*	−.05
Age	.12*	.20**	.09*
Gender (0 = female, 1 = male)	.10*	.21**	−.07
Race (0 = white, 1 = person of color)	−.05	.14**	.03
Father's education in years	−.11*	−.18**	−.05
Welfare (0 = no, 1 = yes)	.04	.12*	.05
Region (0 = rural, 1 = urban)	.03	.04	.02
Family relations	−.25**	−.21**	−.23**
Caregiver supervision	−.30**	−.34**	−.33**
Commitment	−.22**	−.24**	−.23**
Future expectations	−.27**	−.32**	−.26**
Friends' alcohol use	.50**	.40**	.32**
Summary Statistics			
F-test	110.32**	101.30**	65.91**
Adjusted r^2	.48	.42	.33

Note: Standardized regression coefficients shown. Predictors were simultaneously entered.
* $P < .05$; ** $P < .01$.

analysis can determine the unique amount of the variance in each risk behavior accounted for by religiosity and church attendance. The amount of unique variance explained by religiousness is 2.5 percent in alcohol use, 3 percent in use of other drugs, and 3.4 percent in delinquency. The unique variance accounted for by church attendance is far below the one percent level typically considered to be noteworthy (Freund & Wilson, 1998).

Two-way interactions also were examined between gender, race (Caucasians and African Americans), residence (rural and urban), church attendance, and religiousness for each outcome. Interactions were analyzed–one at a time–together with the factors shown in Table 2. The only significant interaction (alpha = 0.05) showed that females were more impacted by religiousness than were males in their consumption of alcohol, use of other drugs, and delinquency. These analyses of interactions were not shown owing to space limits.

DISCUSSION

Considerable research on facilitative and buffering factors related to illegal behavior among adolescents is aimed at developing prevention strategies and identifying those youth most at risk (Hawkins, 1996; Moeller, 2001). Presently, there are inconsistencies in findings regarding whether religion serves as a significant buffer to engaging in alcohol consumption, other drug use, and delinquency (Baier & Wright, 2001). A review of the literature suggests to us that a primary reason many studies fail to find religion to be significantly related to offenses is because of the pervasive the use of a single-item measure of church attendance (Benda & Corwyn, 2001). Despite assertions to the contrary, church attendance is not a good proxy measure for beliefs and convictions about religion. People attend church regularly for many reasons that are unrelated or peripheral to religious principles and values. Adolescents, in particular, are likely to be attending church because of external influences, such as parental expectations and social opportunities.

In this study, bivariate correlations indicate that religiousness has considerably stronger inverse relationships to the unlawful acts studied than church attendance. When these two aspects of religion are considered simultaneously with other established predictors of adolescent offenses, a measure of importance of religion and belief in God–not church attendance–is inversely related to alcohol consumption and to delinquency. Religiousness also is a more robust predictor of drug use than church attendance. These findings do not bode well for the oft-repeated "ascetic argument" that religion only plays a role in minor offenses that receive ambivalent reactions from the larger society–such as underage alcohol use. Alcohol use often is highlighted as the epitome of ascetic offenses. Yet, a test for equality of regression coefficients (Paternoster, Brame, Mazerolle, & Piquero 1998) shows no significant differences between the effects of religiousness on underage alcohol consumption, use of other drugs, and delinquency.

The findings also show that religiousness is more important to the behavior of girls than of boys. Developmental and sex-role theories suggest that girls develop more rapidly during adolescence than do boys, and they more readily adopt caregiver beliefs and practices because of sex-role socialization and closeness to caregivers (Bao et al., 1999; Regnerus, 2003). There is also evidence that girls are more closely monitored by caregivers (Hay, 2001).

This study does not find support for the common generalization that African American and rural youth are more affected by religion in their behavior than are Caucasians. A primary reason for the discrepancy in findings regarding race and residence between this study and previous research may be prevalent use of church attendance in measuring religious influence. Because the church often is the center of social activity and support in African American communities, especially in rural areas, it may be that youth receive closer adult monitoring and have less opportunity to engage in unlawful acts. However, church attendance is not prima facie evidence of religiousness–or religious convictions–particularly among youth who are pressured by caregivers to attend and who are drawn by social opportunities.

Personal and familial religiousness, importance of religion and belief in God are more direct measures of convictions and beliefs that likely regulate youthful behavior than church attendance. Religion, in essence, consists of principles for healthy physical, emotional, and spiritual living (Ellison, Boardman, Williams, & Jackson, 2001; Kendler et al., 2003). To remain in spiritual communion with God, people are required to shun unlawfulness (Worthington, 1993). Many religious parents prohibit underage use of alcohol, believing alcohol can be destructive to physical, emotional, and spiritual health (Mason & Windle, 2002). This study supports the logical assumption that church attendance increases the likelihood that religiousness will play a significant role in eschewing illicit acts. Church is where most people learn religion, but church attendance is not a good indicator that people made a commitment to religion.

Conclusions and Treatment Implications

In conclusion, religion often is an uncomfortable or taboo subject for practitioners because of skepticism and strident antagonism expressed by many scholars and educators (Fallot, 2001; Glenn, 1997; Hodge, 2002; Larson, Milano, & Lu, 1998). Religion, for example, has been characterized as a neurotic conflict, and optimal emotional health has been equated with being exonerated from any religious obsessions and compulsions (Hodge, 2002). An ideology exists in several professions that religion is an anachronistic set of beliefs from a less enlightened period (Fallot, 2001; Hodge, 2002). Elements of ideology include pre-conscious assumptions, presumptions that are unexamined, and emotionally charged beliefs (Guba, 1990). Omission of religion from professional discourse appears to be based far more on ideology than on logical or empirical grounds, which normally are the "holy grail" of social science (Guba, 1990). Despite this neglect, emerging evidence indicates that religion is associated with healthy living and avoidance of unlawful acts, such as underage alcohol consumption (e.g., Baier & Wright, 2001; Kendler et al., 2003; McCullough, Larson, Hoy, Koenig, & Thoreson, 2000; George et al., 2000).

Professional ethics decree that practitioners should encourage clients to use all resources at their disposal to prevent or remedy problems. A valuable resource for discouraging unlawful and unhealthy acts, according to several recent studies, is religion (see review, Johnson, De Li, Larson, & McCullough, 2000). Religion is especially beneficial to adolescents because of their struggles with identity and with the meaning and purpose of life (Lerner, Lerner, De Stefanis, & Apfel, 2001). Religious beliefs offer a coherent explanatory framework for understanding and navigating the maelstrom of temptations and experiences that characterize adolescence (Carnegie Council on Adolescent Development, 1995). Religion provides a meaning and purpose for life and for resisting temptations to engage in behavior that breaks societal rules (Fallot, 2001). The faithful believe religion proffers a recipe for relating to an omniscient and omnipotent Being that can provide guidance and solutions (Worthington, 1993).

While not all professionals can be expected to endorse religion–generally or in particular–religious beliefs should not be summarily dismissed or omitted because of ideological preferences. Most professionals are likely uncomfortable examining religious doctrines and principles, and the role of therapist is not to evangelize–with these observations few would disagree. However, when clients can benefit from religion, discussions of religious beliefs should not be disquieting or curtailed because of ideologies passed off as a professional creed. Even the hallowed "separation of church and state" argument–a discussion that must be deferred to another day–is not nearly as convincing as many professionals think. When a need is present, and there is evidence that we know what can benefit a client, it is unethical and immoral to withhold beneficial information and assistance. Professionals should discuss religion in the same respectful and supportive manner as other beliefs and information they think are useful and beneficial to clients.

REFERENCES

Baier, C. J., & Wright, B. R. E. (2001). If you love me, keep my commandments: A meta-analysis of the effect of religion on crime. *Journal of Research in Crime and Delinquency, 38*, 3-21.

Bao, W., Whitbeck, L. B., Hoyt, D. R., & Conger, R. D. (1999). Perceived parental acceptance as a moderator of religious transmission among adolescent boys and girls. *Journal of Marriage and the Family, 61*, 362-375.

Benda, B. B. (1995). The effect of religion on adolescent delinquency revisited. *Journal of Research in Crime and Delinquency, 32*, 446-466.

Benda, B. B., & Corwyn, R. F. (2001). Are the effects of religion on crime mediated, moderated, and misrepresented by inappropriate measures? *Journal of Social Service Research, 27*, 57-86.

Brody, G. H., Stoneman, Z., Flor, D., & McCrary, C. (1994). Religion's role in organizing family relationships: Family process in rural, two-parent African American families. *Journal of Marriage and the Family, 56*, 878-888.

Burkett, S. R. (1993). Perceived parents' religiosity, friends' drinking, and hellfire: A panel study of adolescent drinking. *Review of Religious Research, 35*, 136-154.

Carnegie Council on Adolescent Development (1995). Great transitions: Preparing adolescents for a new century. New York: Carnegie Corporation.

Cochran, J. K., Wood, P. K., & Arneklev, B J. (1994). Is the religiosity-delinquency relationship spurious? A test of arousal and social control theories. *Journal of Research in Crime and Delinquency, 31*, 92-123.

Ellison, C. G., Boardman, J. D., Williams. D. R., & Jackson, J. S. (2001). Religious involvement, stress, and mental health: Findings from the 1995 Detroit area study. *Social Forces, 60*, 215-249.

Ellison, C. G., & Levin, J. S. (1998). The religion-health connection: Evidence, theory, and future directions. *Health Education and Behavior, 25*, 700-720.

Empey, L.T., Stafford, M. C., & Hay, C. H. (1999). *American delinquency: Its meaning and construction* (4th ed.). Belmont, CA: Wadsworth.

Evans, D. T., Cullen, F. T., Dunaway, R. G., & Burton, V. S. (1995). Religion and crime reexamined: The impact of religion, secular controls, and social ecology on adult criminality. *Criminology, 33,* 195-217.

Fallot, R. (2001). The place of spirituality and religion in mental health services. *New Directions for Mental Health Services, 91,* 798-811.

Freund, R. J., & Wilson, W. J. (1998). *Regression analysis: Statistical modeling of a response variable.* New York: Academic Press.

George, L. K., Larson, D. B., Koeing H. G., & McCullough, M. E. (2000). Spirituality and health: What we know, what we need to know. *Journal of Social and Clinical Psychology, 19,* 102-116.

Glenn, N. (1997). *Closed hearts, closed minds: The textbook story of marriage.* New York: Institute for American Values.

Guba, E. G. (Ed.) (1990). *The paradigm dialog.* Newbury Park: Sage.

Hawkins, J. D. (Ed.) (1996) *Delinquency and crime: Current theories.* New York: Cambridge University Press.

Hodge, D. R. (2002). Does social work oppress Evangelical Christians? A "new class" analysis of society and social work. *Social Work, 47,* 401-414.

Jessor, R., Donovan, J. E., & Costa, F. M. (1991). *Beyond adolescence: Problem behavior and young adult development.* New York: Cambridge University Press.

Johnson, B. R., DeLi, S., Larson, D. B., & McCullough, M. (2000). A systematic review of the religiosity and delinquency literature. *Journal of Contemporary Criminal Justice, 16,* 32-52.

Kendler, K. S., Liu, Z, Gardner, C. O., McCullough et al. (2003). Dimensions of religiosity ad their relationship to lifetime psychiatric and substance use disorders. *American Journal of Psychiatry, 160,* 496-503.

Larson, D. B., Milano, G. M., & Lu, F. (1998). Religion and mental health: The need for cultural sensitivity and synthesis. In S. O. Okpaku (Ed.), *Clinical methods in transcultural psychiatry* (pp. 191-210). Washington, DC: American Psychiatric Association.

Lerner, R. M., Lerner, J. V., De Stefanis, I., & Apfel, A. (2001). Understanding developmental systems in adolescence: Implications for methodological strategies, data analytic approaches, and training. *Journal of Adolescent Research, 6,* 9-27.

Mason, A. W., & Windle, M. (2002). A longitudinal study of the effects of religiosity on adolescent alcohol use and alcohol-related problems. *Journal of Adolescent Research, 17,* 346-364.

McLennan, J. D., Shaw, E., Shema, S. J., Gardner, W. P., Pope, S, K., & Kelleher, K. J. (1998). Adolescents' insight in heavy drinking. *Journal of Adolescent Health, 22,* 409-416.

Moeller, T. G. (2001). *Youth aggression and violence: A psychological approach.* Mahwah, NJ: Lawrence Erlbaum.

Paternoster, R., Brame, R., Mazerolle, P., & Piquero, A. (1998). Using the correct statistical test for the equality of regression coefficients. *Criminology, 36,* 859-866.

Regnerus, M. D. (2003). Linked lives, faith, and behavior: Intergenerational religious influence on adolescent delinquency. *Journal for the Scientific Study of Religion, 42,* 189-203.

Smith, C., Lundquist, M., Faris, R., & Regnerus, M. (2002), Mapping American adolescent religious participation. *Journal for the Scientific Study of Religion, 41,* 597-613.

Stark, R., & Bainbridge, W. S. (1997). Religion, deviance, and social control. New York: Routledge.

Welch, M. R., Tittle, C. R., & Petee, T. (1991). Religiosity and deviance among adult Catholics: A test of the 'Moral Communities' hypothesis. *Journal for the Scientific Studies of Religion, 30,* 159-172.

Worthington, E. L. Jr. (Ed.) (1993). *Psychotherapy and religious values.* Grand Rapids, MI: Baker.

Dimensions of Religious Involvement and Mental Health Outcomes Among Alcohol- and Drug-Dependent Women

Nicola A. Conners, PhD
Leanne Whiteside-Mansell, EdD
Allen C. Sherman, PhD

SUMMARY. The current study examined ties between religious variables and mental health in a high-risk population: lower-income chemically dependent pregnant or parenting women participating in a residential treatment program. The primary goal of the study was to investigate the relationship between various facets of religiousness and mental health symptoms, including depression and post-traumatic stress. Negative religious coping was associated with greater PTSD symptoms, greater depressive symptoms, and greater syndromal depression after controlling for background demographic and addiction variables. Other aspects of religiousness, including positive coping and involvement with organized religion, were not associated with mental health outcomes. These

---

Nicola A. Conners is Assistant Professor and Leanne Whiteside-Mansell and Allen C. Sherman are Associate Professors, University of Arkansas for Medical Sciences.

Address correspondence to: Nicola A. Conners, University of Arkansas for Medical Sciences, Partners for Inclusive Communities, 2001 Pershing Circle, North Little Rock, AR 72114 (E-mail: connersnicolaa@uams.edu).

[Haworth co-indexing entry note]: "Dimensions of Religious Involvement and Mental Health Outcomes Among Alcohol- and Drug-Dependent Women." Conners, Nicola A., Leanne Whiteside-Mansell, and Allen C. Sherman. Co-published simultaneously in *Alcoholism Treatment Quarterly* (The Haworth Press, Inc.) Vol. 24, No. 1/2, 2006, pp. 89-108; and: *Spirituality and Religiousness and Alcohol/Other Drug Problems: Treatment and Recovery Perspectives* (ed: Brent B. Benda, and Thomas F. McGovern) The Haworth Press, Inc., 2006, pp. 89-108. Single or multiple copies of this article are available for a fee from The Haworth Document Delivery Service [1-800-HAWORTH, 9:00 a.m. - 5:00 p.m. (EST). E-mail address: docdelivery@ haworthpress.com].

Available online at http://www.haworthpress.com/web/ATQ
doi:10.1300/J020v24n01_06

results suggest that negative aspects of religiousness, particularly religious struggle, merit greater attention from clinicians and investigators. *[Article copies available for a fee from The Haworth Document Delivery Service: 1-800-HAWORTH. E-mail address: <docdelivery@haworthpress.com> Website: <http://www.HaworthPress.com> © 2006 by The Haworth Press, Inc. All rights reserved.]*

KEYWORDS. Spirituality, maternal, substance abuse, depression, post-traumatic stress disorder

An expanding body of research has focused on associations between health outcomes and various aspects of religiousness or spirituality (McCullough, Hoyt, Larson, Koenig, & Thoresen, 2000; Plante & Sherman, 2001; Powell, Shahabi, & Thoresen, 2003). A reduced incidence of alcohol and other drug abuse has been noted among more highly religious individuals (e.g., those who more frequently attend religious services or engage in private prayer) (Gartner, Larson, & Allen, 1991; Gorsuch, 1995; Koenig, George, Meador, Blazer, & Ford, 1994). Moreover, a number of epidemiological studies reported more favorable mental health outcomes among community-dwelling individuals who were more religious (e.g., Ellison, 1991; Ellison, Boardman, Williams, & Jackson, 2001; Kendler et al., 2003; Strawbridge, Shema, Cohen, & Kaplan, 2001; Wink & Dillon, 2001, 2003). Similar findings regarding improved mental health or adjustment have begun to emerge in clinical settings among patients with various medical conditions (Baider et al., 1999; Fehring, Miller, & Shaw, 1997; Koenig, Cohen, & Blazer, 1992; Pressman, Lyons, Larson, & Strain 1990). As yet, however, few clinical studies have focused on the role of religion or spirituality among patients receiving treatment for addiction (Jerusiewicz, 2000; Pardini, Plante, Sherman, & Stump, 2000; Richard, Bell, & Carlson, 2000). In particular, little is known about the potential correlates of religiousness among substance abuse populations faced with the greatest burdens, such as economically disadvantaged women who are pregnant or parenting. These patients struggle with numerous health and social problems such as psychiatric co-morbidity (e.g., depression), medical illness, extensive histories of trauma, unemployment, poverty, and criminal justice system involvement (Conners, Bradley, Whiteside-Mansell, & Crone, 2001).

The study of religious or spiritual involvement among chemically dependent individuals is of special interest, because spiritual growth and support traditionally have been thought to be an important component of recovery (Carroll, 1993; Miller, 1997; Peteet, 1993). Twelve-step programs, for example, emphasize the value of spiritual changes. Small, preliminary studies suggested that greater religiousness or religious coping was associated with longer periods of abstinence among patients receiving substance abuse treatment (Horstmann & Tenigan, 2000; Jerusiewicz, 2000). Conclusions are limited by the small samples and cross-sectional research designs, which offer few hints about causal relationships. A larger study noted that substance abuse patients with stronger religious faith experienced more favorable mental health outcomes (e.g., less anxiety, greater optimism and stress resilience), relative to their less religious peers (Pardini et al., 2000). Similarly, in a study of African American mothers enrolled in treatment, those with greater spiritual well-being reported better adjustment (e.g., more favorable self-concept, active coping, and family functioning) (Brome, Owens, Allen, & Vevaina, 2000); caution is required in interpreting these findings because the measure of spirituality may be somewhat confounded with the outcomes assessed. Finally, in a prospective investigation, increased church attendance was associated with reduced crack cocaine and alcohol use among patients who had participated in a residential treatment program (Richard et al., 2000). In contrast, patients' baseline ratings of the importance of religion (i.e., "individual religiosity") were not tied to these outcomes. Thus, there are preliminary indications that, for some individuals, various aspects of religiousness or spirituality might be linked with more successful recovery from addiction. The nature of these relationships has rarely been explored among high-risk, difficult to reach groups, such as addicted pregnant or parenting women.

   If religious or spiritual involvement is indeed associated with recovery for some addicted patients, which dimensions are most important? In general, much of the literature to date concerning religiousness and health has relied on relatively narrow indices of religiousness. There has been a growing call to move toward more differentiated measures, which better approximate the complex, multidimensional nature of religiousness or spirituality (Pargament, 1997; Sherman & Simonton, 2001b; Thoresen, Harris, & Oman, 2001). Moreover, there has been a shift from dependence on simple descriptive indices (e.g., attendance at services) toward greater use of functional measures (e.g., religious coping), which offer better information about the role that religion actually plays in patients' daily lives (Ellison & Levin, 1998; Pargament, Koenig, & Perez, 2000; Sherman & Plante, 2001). Religious coping (i.e., how one turns toward faith in response to difficulties) and religious social support (i.e., how one makes use of the religious community) are among the domains of particular interest.

Although most attention has focused on *positive* dimensions of faith, religious involvement may encompass *negative* experiences as well. In response to trying circumstances, some individuals may derive a sense of comfort or meaning from their faith; others, however, might struggle with perceived abandonment, doubt, or alienation. Investigators such as Pargament (1997; Pargament, Koenig, Tarakeshwar, & Hahn, 2001; Pargament, Zinnbauer, Scott, Butter, Zerowin, & Stanik, 1998b) have begun to examine negative aspects of religious coping, or religious struggle. In diverse studies involving multiple myeloma patients (Sherman, Simonton, Latif, Spohn, & Tricot, 2005; Sherman, Simonton, Plante, Moody, & Wells, 2001), elderly medical patients, and healthy individuals coping with the aftermath of a community tragedy (i.e., the Oklahoma City bombing) (Pargament, Smith, Koenig, & Perez, 1998a), religious struggle has been tied to greater emotional distress. Moreover, there are indications that negative religious coping is sometimes more robustly associated with outcomes than is positive religious coping, at least over the short-term (Pargament et al., 1998b; Sherman et al., 2005). Positive and negative dimensions of religious coping have rarely been investigated among substance abuse patients (Horstmann & Tonigan, 2000).

The current study examined ties between religious variables and mental health in a high-risk population: lower-income chemically dependent pregnant or parenting women participating in a residential treatment program. To build on previous investigations, we examined multiple dimensions of religiousness, including (1) organizational religious practices (e.g., church attendance), (2) religious coping, and (3) religious social support. Moreover, we examined negative as well as positive facets of religiousness. The primary goal of the study was to investigate the relationship between various facets of religiousness and mental health symptoms, including depression and post-traumatic stress. These symptoms are highly prevalent and present considerable treatment challenges among women with substance abuse difficulties. In view of prior research (Pargament et al., 1999; Sherman et al., 2005), we anticipated that *functional* aspects of faith (i.e., religious coping and religious social support) would be more strongly predictive of mental health than more *descriptive* dimensions (i.e., organizational religious behavior). Moreover, building on our previous work (Sherman et al., 2005; Sherman et al., 2001), we anticipated that *negative* religious coping might be more strongly tied to outcomes than would *positive* religious coping.

A secondary aim was to contribute additional information about the value of a measure of religiousness/spirituality in this special population. Among the instruments that have been developed to explore relationships between religiousness or spirituality and health, one of the most comprehensive was constructed by an interdisciplinary working group convened by the Fetzer Institute and the National Institute on Aging (NIA) (Fetzer Institute/NIA Working Group, 1999; Idler et al., 2003). The *Brief Multidimensional Measure of Religiousness/Spirituality* was designed to be concise and practical, while encompassing multiple domains that appear especially relevant for health outcomes. Following a series of pilot tests, the instrument was evaluated in a large (N = 1,445) nationally representative epidemiological study (1998 General Social Survey); results were promising (Idler et al., 2003). Efforts to further examine its value in diverse clinical settings are currently underway. This measure was employed in the current investigation.

METHOD

Setting

The Arkansas Center for Addictions Research, Education, and Services (Arkansas CARES) operates under the auspices of the University of Arkansas for Medical Sciences (UAMS) Department of Psychiatry. It is an accredited behavioral health provider and licensed to provide alcohol and drug treatment, adult and child mental health services, childcare, early childhood special education, and early intervention and prevention services. The program operates in two locations: (1) The Little Rock site of Arkansas CARES was established as a five-year Center for Substance Abuse Prevention (CSAP) Pregnant and Postpartum Women with their Infants (PPWI) demonstration project (1992-1997) and expanded to include a Center for Substance Abuse Treatment Residential Women with Children (RWC) project (1995-1999). Multi-family housing is provided for approximately 15 families with children aged birth to 12 years. (2) The North Little Rock location is the result of a partnership between the city of North Little Rock and UAMS Arkansas CARES, and was launched with grant funds from the Center for Substance Abuse Treatment in 2001, under their Targeted Capacity Expansion (TCE) program. The program is located within a public housing project and serves 12 women at one time with their respective children through age 18. Each woman resides in her own apartment unit with her children.

Arkansas CARES utilizes an integrated services model providing intensive services to address both mental health and substance abuse disorders. The planned length of stay is generally four to six months, though the treatment team may recommend a shorter or longer stay depending on the needs and circumstances of each client. Women's services include daily substance abuse treatment or relapse prevention; psychiatric assessment; individual, group, and family counseling; parenting education and support; medical assessment and referral; health and nutrition education; prenatal care and family planning; medical care; case management; transportation; life skills training; employment counseling; GED preparation; smoking cessation education; on- and off-site Twelve Step meetings; and aftercare. Comprehensive children's services are provided. Multi-disciplinary staff participates in weekly treatment team meetings for women and children to develop treatment plans and determine program completion.

Procedure

The participants in this study included women who were admitted to Arkansas CARES from 2001 to 2004, and who agreed to participate in a treatment evaluation study. To be admitted to Arkansas CARES, the woman must have a substance abuse disorder, and be pregnant and/or enter with dependent children. All participants admitted to treatment at Arkansas CARES were approached and asked to give written consent to participate in the treatment evaluation study. Women were excluded if they had previously participated in the evaluation study during a prior admission (n = 20), or if they left treatment before the intake process was completed and consent could be obtained (n = 21).

Once written consent was obtained, participants completed an extensive battery of tests and questionnaires collected through face-to-face interviews with a masters' level social worker and a trained research assistant. Information from the initial interview was utilized for this paper. The study was approved by the UAMS Institutional Review Board to ensure the protection of the participants.

Instruments

Brief Multidimensional Measure of Religiousness/Spirituality–Religiousness was assessed by selected subscales drawn from the Brief

Multidimensional Measure of Religiousness/Spirituality (Fetzer Institute/National Institute on Aging Workshop Group, 1999). We employed 5 of the 12 subscales. These subscales evaluated (1) Public Religious Practices (2 items, e.g., "How often do you attend religious services?"), (2) Positive Religious Coping (3 items, e.g., "I look to God for strength, support, and guidance"), (3) Negative Religious Coping (3 items, e.g., " I wonder whether God has abandoned me"), (4) Anticipated Congregation Support (2 items, e.g., "If you had a problem or were faced with a difficult situation, how much comfort would the people in your congregation be willing to give you?"), and (5) Congregation Problems or Negative Interactions (2 items, e.g., "How often are the people in your congregation critical of you?"). With the exception of the 2 Public Religious Practices items, all items were scored using a Likert scale with answers ranging from 1 to 4. Higher scores on all scales indicated greater use of those religious/spiritual resources, except for the Negative Religious Coping and Congregation Problems scales, where higher scores indicated fewer religious difficulties. The Public Religious Practices items were scored using a 6-point scale with answers ranging from 'never' to 'more than once a week.' Data from a large nationally representative investigation (1997-1998 General Social Survey) supported the psychometric performance of the instrument (Idler et al., 2003). Estimates of internal consistency reliability were .82 of the Public Religious Practices scale, .81 for Positive Religious Coping, .54 for an abbreviated 2-item version of the Negative Religious Coping scale, .86 for Congregation Support, and .64 for Congregation Problems. Factor analyses, demographic correlates, and interscale correlations supported the construct validity of the instrument in the general population.

Addiction Severity Index-Expanded, Self-Administered Version (ASI)–The ASI (McLellan et al., 1990) is a semi-structured interview which is designed to gather information about aspects of a client's life which may contribute to her substance abuse problem. The ASI covers seven areas: medical, employment/support, alcohol, drug, legal, family/social, and psychiatric. As part of the Treatment Outcomes Performance Pilot Study II (TOPPS II) funded by the Substance Abuse and Mental Health Services Administration, the Utah Consortium developed an expanded, computerized version of the ASI. Arkansas CARES used this version of the ASI to collect baseline information from clients. A research assistant worked closely with the participants to ensure that they understood how to use the computer, and to assist women with low reading abilities as needed. The computer-administered ASI has been found to be a reliable and valid measure of problem severity among addicted patients (Butler et al., 1998).

Beck Depression Inventory II (BDI-II)–The BDI-II (Beck, Brown, & Steer, 1996) is a self-report instrument for measuring the severity of symptoms of depression in adolescents and adults. It is designed to screen for DSM-IV criteria for depression. The BDI-II consists of 21 items rated on a four point scale, which patients are instructed to respond to based on their feelings over the past two weeks. A total score is obtained by summing the items, and scores can be interpreted as follows: 0-13 indicates minimal depression, 14-19 indicates mild depression, 20-28 indicates moderate depression, and 29-63 indicates severe depression (Beck, Brown, & Steer, 1996). In the present study, the BDI-II yielded a coefficient alpha of .91.

PTSD Checklist-Civilian Version (PCL-C)–The PCL (Weathers, Litz, Herman, Huska, & Keane, 1993) is a brief self-report inventory for assessing symptoms of post-traumatic stress disorder (PTSD). It includes 17 items which are rated on a 1-5 scale. The patient is instructed to indicate the degree to which they were bothered by each symptom in the past month. A total score is obtained by summing the 17 items, with a score of 50 or greater representing risk for PTSD. In the present study, the PCL yielded a coefficient alpha of .94.

Sample

As seen in Table 1, the sample included 217 women. The sample size varies slightly depending on the analysis due to missing data on various items or instruments. Sixty-six percent were white and 33% were African American. Most were unmarried (77.8%); almost all women reported incomes below the poverty line (92.3%), and most were unemployed at the time of admission. Amphetamine (primarily methamphetamine) was the most commonly reported drug of choice (42.1%), followed by crack/cocaine (33.6%) and alcohol (9.8%). A majority of women (54.2%) reported their religious preference as Protestant, and only 12.3% indicated that they had no religious preference.

RESULTS

Mental Health Outcomes

As anticipated, participants reported high levels of emotional distress. Eighty-three percent exceeded cut-offs for at least mild clinical

TABLE 1. Sample Description (N = 217)

Race	
African American	32.7%
White	65.9%
Other	1.4%
Married	18.2%
Employed	11.7%
Below Poverty Line	92.3%
Ever been arrested	86.1%
Drug of Choice	
Amphetamines	42.1%
Cocaine	33.6%
Alcohol	9.8%
Other	14.5%
Religion	
Protestant	54.2%
Catholic	4.2%
Other	28.8%
None	12.3%
Abuse History	
Sexual Abuse	53.3%
Physical Abuse	87.4%
Emotional Abuse	72.4%
At Risk for Depression[a]	82.9%
At risk for PTSD[b]	40.8%
Mean BDI II Score	25.9 (SD = 12.3)
Mean PCL Score	45.1 (SD = 16.9)
Mean Age in years	29.6 (SD = 6.5)
Mean Years of Education	11.6 (SD = 1.9)
Mean AOD treatment episodes	1.5 (SD = 2.2)

[a]Risk for depression = scores > 13 on Beck Depression Inventory II (BDI II)
[b]Risk for PTSD = scores > 50 on PTSD Checklist (PCL)

depression on the BDI, and more than one third were categorized as severely depressed. Most women reported a prior history of trauma (physical, sexual, or emotional). Many reported current symptoms of PTSD (PCL-C), and 40.8% exceeded cut-off scores for clinically meaningful symptomatology.

Religious Outcomes

We examined the psychometric performance of the religiousness/spirituality scales, because as yet they have rarely been used in this population. Descriptive statistics are noted in Table 2, and are reported for the full sample as well as separately by race. Though no racial differences were found in the present study, past studies have shown racial differences in religiousness/spirituality (Levin, Taylor, & Chatters, 1994;

TABLE 2. Brief Multidimensional Measure of Religiousnessness/Spirituality Descriptive Statistics[a] (N = 217)

Scale Item	Total Sample Mean (SD)	African American Mean (SD)	White Mean (SD)
Public Religious Practices	5.4 (2.8)	5.4 (2.9)	5.4 (2.8)
How often do you go to religious services?	3.1 (1.6)	3.2 (1.7)	3.1 (1.6)
Besides religious services, how often do you take part in other activities at a place of worship?	2.3 (1.5)	2.2 (1.6)	2.3 (1.4)
Positive Religious Coping	8.9 (2.2)	9.1 (2.2)	8.9 (2.3)
I think about how my life is part of a larger spiritual force.	2.9 (1.0)	2.9 (1.0)	2.9 (1.0)
I work together with God as partners.	2.6 (.93)	2.7 (.94)	2.6 (.93)
I look to God for strength, support and guidance.	3.4 (.84)	3.5 (.75)	3.3 (.88)
Negative Religious Coping	10.2 (1.8)	10.1 (1.8)	10.3 (1.8)
I feel God is punishing me for my sins or lack of spirituality.	3.4 (.96)	3.4 (.75)	3.4 (.95)
I wonder whether God has abandoned me.	3.6 (.74)	3.6 (.86)	3.7 (.68)
I try to make sense of the situation and decide what to do without relying on God.	3.2 (.93)	3.2 (.95)	3.2 (.93)
Anticipated Congregation Support[b]	6.8 (1.6)	6.6 (1.7)	7.0 (1.6)
If you were ill, how much would the people in your congregation help you out?	3.3 (.89)	3.3 (.92)	3.5 (.88)
If you had a problem or were faced with a difficult situation, how much comfort would the people in your congregation be willing to give you?	3.4 (.89)	3.4 (.90)	3.5 (.89)
Congregation Problems[b]	7.0 (1.3)	6.9 (1.3)	7.0 (1.3)
How often do the people in your congregation make too many demands on you?	3.5 (.72)	3.5 (.79)	3.6 (.70)
How often are the people in your congregation critical of you?	3.4 (.78)	3.4 (.82)	3.5 (.78)

[a] Higher scores indicated greater use of those religious/spiritual resources, except for the Negative Religious Coping and Congregation Problems, where higher scores indicated fewer difficulties.
[b] Excludes those who indicate they do not have a church/congregation.

Taylor, Chatters, Jakody, & Levin, 1996). All scales demonstrated good internal consistency reliability (Cronbach's alpha $\geq$ .70), with the exception of negative religious coping. The Cronbach's alpha for the negative religious coping scale was .46, and no single item appeared to be responsible for the low alpha. .With one exception, the correlations among the five religious scales were generally small ($r < .32$), indicating that each scale appeared to be measuring a distinct construct, as intended. There was a larger correlation ($r = .41$) between the anticipated religious support scale and the public religious practices scale.

In terms of involvement with organized religion, most women reported attending religious services at least once or twice a year (80.7%), though fewer attended services weekly (24.2%). Among those who were involved with a congregation, over 80% indicated that people in their congregation would provide "some" or "a great deal" of comfort in a difficult time (83.1%), and would provide "some" or "a great deal" of help if they were ill (80.3%). Few women reported that people in their congregation made too many demands (13.8% "some" or "a great deal") or were critical (18.4% "some" or "a great deal"). In terms of religious coping, results indicated that spirituality and religion played an important role in how these women thought about and dealt with their problems. For example, 58.0% of women reported that they looked to God for strength and support "a great deal" when dealing with problems, and 23.9% did so "quite a bit." However, some women also responded to their difficulties by perceiving that they were being punished by God "a great deal" (8.7%) or "quite a bit" (7.7%). Fewer reported feeling that God had abandoned them (3.4% "a great deal," 6.3% "quite a bit").

As noted, African American women did not score differently on these religious/spiritual variables than their white counterparts. However, married women scored higher on negative religious coping ($p = .05$) than single women. There were no differences based on age or years of education, though this sample was relatively homogenous on those variables.

Control Variables

In preliminary analyses, we used correlations and t-tests to examine the relationships among the mental health outcomes (symptoms of depression and PTSD) and potential covariates including demographic background (i.e., age, marital status, race, years of education) and drug severity variables (i.e., number of times in treatment for alcohol or drug

[AOD] problems, and number of days of AOD use in the past 30 days). Being older ($r = .25$; $p < .001$), was associated with higher scores on the BDI II, and was marginally associated with higher scores on the PCL ($r = .13$; $p = .06$). The number of days of AOD use in the past 30 days was associated with higher scores on both the BDI II ($r = .22$; $p = .002$) and the PCL ($r = .25$; $p < .001$).

Associations Between Religiousness and Mental Health Outcomes

Of the five religiosity scales, only negative religious coping was associated with mental health problems. Greater use of negative religious coping, or religious struggle, was significantly related to both increased depressive symptoms ($r = -.21$, $p = .003$) and increased symptoms of PTSD ($r = -.16$, $p = .02$).

We used multiple regression (OLS) models to examine the relationship between negative religious coping and mental health outcomes, controlling for demographic and substance use severity variables that had been associated with outcomes in univariate analyses ($p < .10$). For depression, results indicated that negative religious coping remained a significant independent predictor of depression even after controlling for age and past 30 day drug use ($F(1) = 7.05$, $p = .009$). Age and past 30 day drug use were also significant predictors of depression. Similarly, for symptoms of PTSD, results indicated that negative religious coping remained a significant predictor even after controlling for age and past 30 day drug use ($F(1) = 4.09$, $p = .04$). Age and past 30 day drug use were also significant predictors of symptoms of PTSD.

To further explore the clinical significance of these findings, two logistic regression analyses were conducted using cut-off scores on depression and PTSD, respectively, as the dichotomous outcomes. Negative religious coping remained a significant independent predictor of clinical levels of depression (Wald $t(1) = 6.2$, $p = .01$), after controlling for age and past 30 day drug use. Negative religious coping was marginally associated with clinical levels of PTSD symptoms (Wald $t(1) = 3.2$, $p = .07$) after controlling for age and past 30 day drug use.

DISCUSSION

This study examined multiple dimensions of religious involvement in a special population of low-income, addicted mothers with dependent children who were entering a multi-modal residential treatment program. As one might expect in this high-risk group, substance abuse was accompanied by considerable mental health difficulties. Many women had prior histories of physical (87%) and sexual (53%) abuse, and the group as a whole experienced high levels of current PTSD symptoms and depression.

Participants varied widely in their level of religious involvement. The majority reported at least some participation in public religious activity, looked to God to assist them with life's difficulties, anticipated support from the fellowship of their congregation, and experienced little sense of religious or spiritual struggle. Relative to the general US population, one might anticipate that religious expression might be higher in a sample of Southern economically-disadvantaged women, particularly one that includes a high proportion of African Americans (Levin et al., 1994; Taylor et al., 1996; Pargament, 1997). On the other hand, impoverished chemically dependent patients about to enter treatment might be expected to report relatively low levels of religiousness, because they perceive other more pressing needs and priorities, or because they feel alienated from their faith. The data that emerged in the current study suggested a relatively high level of religious engagement and, for some women, religious struggle. Specifically, the proportion of women who attended services weekly (24.2%) was similar to that noted in the 1998 General Social Survey (25.4%), a nationally representative household survey of English-speaking Americans (Idler et al., 2003; Fetzer Institute/NIA Workshop Group, 1999). Similarly, the percentage of women in the current study who perceived their fellow congregants as supportive in a difficult situation (83.1%) was comparable to that in the national survey (83.8%). However, women in the present study appeared to rely more strongly on *positive* religious coping to manage difficulties than did their counterparts in the national survey (e.g., looked to God for strength and support, 82.0% vs. 64.1%, respectively) (Fetzer Institute/NIA Workshop Group, 1999). Moreover, women in our study also reported more *negative* aspects of religiousness, including negative religious coping (e.g., felt punished by God, 16.4% vs. 5.8%, respectively) and negative religious social interactions (e.g., perceptions that the congregation is critical, 18.4% vs. 5.8%, respectively).

How are these factors related to health outcomes? We hypothesized that *functional* dimensions of religiousness (e.g., coping, social support) would be more strongly tied to mental health outcomes than would *descriptive* dimensions (e.g., attendance at services). We also expected that *negative* facets of religiousness (negative religious coping, negative interactions with the congregation) would be stronger correlates of mental health problems than would *positive* dimensions (positive religious coping, positive religious support). These assumptions received partial support. Negative religious coping was associated with greater PTSD symptoms, greater depressive symptoms, and greater syndromal depression after controlling for background demographic and addiction variables. In other words, women who struggled with their faith experienced more extensive emotional difficulties. Negative religious coping was also tied to higher levels of recent substance abuse. Overall, these findings seem consistent with results emerging among individuals coping with other stressful situations, such as cancer (Sherman et al., 2005; Sherman et al., 2001) or terrorism (Pargament et al., 1998a). It would appear that negative aspects of religiousness, particularly religious struggle, merit greater attention from clinicians and investigators (Pargament et al., 1998a, 1998b).

Religious struggle may increase vulnerability to emotional distress; however, these data are cross-sectional and preclude any conclusions about causality. It is possible that negative religious coping increases the risk for poor emotional functioning, or that emotional difficulties elicit a questioning of one's faith, or that both reflect a broader underlying characteristic (e.g., symptom reporting, neuroticism, depressogenic perceptions, etc.). Notably, it is also possible that patterns of negative religious coping may shift over time. Some individuals who initially struggle with or feel alienated by their faith may eventually emerge with stronger religious convictions and a heightened spiritual commitment. A difficult crisis that ruptures habitual perceptions of oneself and the world may lead ultimately toward personal growth and maturity (Calhoun & Tedeschi, 1998; Carver, 1998). At the same time, other individuals may continue to wrestle actively with their faith, without resolution; some may find a new religious identity (e.g., conversion); and some may become indifferently detached from religious commitments (Pargament et al., 1998a; Sherman & Simonton, 2001a). Each of these spiritual pathways might have different associations with mental health and recovery among chemically dependent individuals. Longitudinal studies are needed to examine these processes more carefully, within particular cultural contexts.

Contrary to our hypotheses, negative interactions with the congregation were not associated with the outcomes that we assessed. Nor was positive congregational support associated with these outcomes. We had anticipated that the role of religious social support might be more salient for African American women than white women, given the well-recognized importance of the church in African American communities

(Taylor et al., 1996). However, we did not find any interactions between racial/ethnic background and any of our religious variables in predicting mental health outcomes. It is possible that involvement with formal religious institutions (as reflected by attendance at services and by interactions with the congregation) was eclipsed for these women, who were about to enter residential treatment and were perhaps preoccupied by the demands of their addictions and the myriad challenges of everyday life. As noted, however, their attendance at religious services was roughly comparable to national norms (Fetzer Institute/National Institute on Aging Workshop Group, 1999). It appears that personal religiousness (e.g., coping) may be more strongly linked with mental health than is institutional religiousness (e.g., attendance at services, religious social support) at this early phase of treatment (see Hackney & Sanders, 2003 for similar findings). Nevertheless, thus far few studies have examined health correlates of religious social support (positive or negative), and clearly this is an area in need of further investigation.

The lack of findings regarding positive congregational support and positive religious coping may have another explanation as well. It is possible that positive dimensions of religiousness are more strongly tied to *beneficial* outcomes (e.g., well-being, relationship satisfaction, parenting skills, readiness for treatment) than to *negative* outcomes (e.g., depression, PTSD symptoms). Preliminary research in other settings has suggested that this may be the case (Hackney & Sanders, 2003; Pargament et al., 1998a; Tix & Frazier, 1998), though findings have been mixed (Sherman & Simonton, 2001a; Sherman et al., 2005). This would be a useful area to pursue among individuals with substance abuse difficulties.

A secondary aim of this study was to provide some additional information about the psychometric performance of the Fetzer/NIA Brief Multidimensional Measure of Religiousness/Spirituality (1999; Idler et al., 2003), which has performed well in the general population but has not been evaluated in the addictions setting. Despite their brevity, the scales we selected demonstrated good internal consistency, with the exception of negative religious coping, which had low internal consistency as well in the initial validation study (Idler et al., 2003). It appears that this scale includes conceptually related items, but that individuals often rely on one type of negative coping strategy without necessarily using the others at the same time. Similar observations have been noted with respect to other coping scales (e.g., Carver, Scheier, & Weintraub, 1989), and these measures are considered useful despite the limited internal coherence of the items. Nevertheless, additional items might enhance the reliability of this scale. As for validity, the modest correlations among the scales (r's < .32) suggest that each contributes unique information, as intended (i.e., divergent validity). A moderately high correlation (r = .41) occurred between the anticipated religious support scale and the public religious practices scale, which is not surprising as items on both scales relate to involvement with a religious institution and/or its members. Overall, results suggest that this is a promising measure for use with substance abuse populations. Future efforts to cross-validate the instrument might examine some of the subscales that were not included in the current study. It would also be helpful to evaluate social desirability response bias, sensitivity to change over time, and associations with additional established indices of religious/spiritual constructs (i.e., convergent validity).

Strengths of this study included examination of positive and negative facets of religiousness and their links with important mental health outcomes in a sample of high-risk, chemically dependent women. Among the notable limitations was the cross-sectional research design, as discussed above. Longitudinal investigations are needed to explore these relationships more fully over the course of recovery. In the current study, the assessment of mental health and substance abuse variables were derived from validated self-report and interview measures. The evaluation would have been further strengthened by the addition of clinical diagnoses of depression or PTSD, and by urinalysis measures of substance use; unfortunately these indices were not available. It is unclear whether the current findings would generalize to other addicted populations, including, for example, men, patients from higher socioeconomic backgrounds, or those from other cultural groups (e.g., Latina women, Muslims, Jews, etc.). It is also unknown whether different patterns would emerge among patients at more advanced phases of treatment and recovery. Nevertheless, current findings underscore the value of examining multiple dimensions of religious involvement, beyond simple descriptive indices of religious service attendance or self-rated religiosity. Negative religious coping, or religious struggle, in particular appears to be associated with adjustment in a number of different clinical populations.

In terms of treatment implications, it may be helpful for counselors to be sensitive to negative as well as positive aspects of faith. Obviously, it would be ethically inappropriate for addictions counselors to impose their own spiritual or religious views in an effort to help the patient develop a more benign or affirming perspective. However, counselors might assist patients to explore their own religious perceptions and coping strategies, apprise them that their spiritual experiences may shift over time, and offer referrals to clergy, as appropriate.

REFERENCES

Baider, L., Russak, S.M., Perry, S., Kash, K., Gronert, M., Fox, B., Holland, J., & Kaplan-DeNour, A. (1999). The role of religious and spiritual beliefs in coping with malignant melanoma: An Israeli sample. *Psycho-Oncology, 8*, 27-35.

Beck, A., Brown, G., & Steer, R. (1996). *Beck Depression Inventory II manual.* San Antonio, TX: The Psychological Corporation.

Brome, D.R., Owens, M.D., Allen, K., & Vevaina T. (2000). An examination of spirituality among African American women in recovery from substance abuse. *Journal of Black Psychology, 26*, 470-486.

Calhoun, L.G., & Tedeschi, R.G. (1998). Posttraumatic growth: Future directions. In Tedeschi, R.G., Park, C.L., & Calhoun, L.G. (Eds.), *Posttraumatic Growth: Positive Changes in the Aftermath of Crisis*: Mahwah, NJ: Erlbaum, pp. 215-238.

Carroll, S. (1993). Spirituality and purpose in life in alcoholism recovery. *Journal of Studies on Alcohol, 54*, 297-301.

Carver, C.S. (1998). Resilience and thriving: Issues, models, and linkages. *Journal of Social Issues, 54*, 245-266.

Carver, C.S., Scheier, M.F., & Weintraub, J.K. (1989). Assessing coping strategies: A theoretically based approach. *Journal of Personality and Social Psychology, 56*, 267-283.

Conners, N. A., Bradley, R. H., Whiteside-Mansell, L., & Crone, C. C. (2001). A comprehensive substance abuse treatment program for women and their children: An initial evaluation. *Journal of Substance Abuse Treatment, 21*, 67-75.

Ellison, C.G. (1991). Religious involvement and subjective well-being. *Journal of Health and Social Behavior, 32*, 80-99.

Ellison, C.G., Boardman, J.D., Williams, D.R., & Jackson, J.S. (2001). Religious involvement, stress, and mental health: Findings from the 1995 Detroit Area Study. *Social Forces, 80*, 215-249.

Ellison, C.G., & Levin, J.S. (1998). The religion-health connection: Evidence, theory, and future directions. *Health Education and Behavior, 25*, 700-720.

Fehring, R., J., Miller, J.F., & Shaw, C. (1997). Spiritual well-being, religiosity, hope, depression, and other mood states in elderly people coping with cancer. *Oncology Nursing Forum, 24*, 663-671.

Fetzer Institute/National Institute on Aging Working Group. (October, 1999). *Multidimensional Measurement of Religiousness/Spirituality for Use in Health Research: A Report of the Fetzer Institute/National Institute on Aging Working Group.* Kalamazoo, MI: Fetzer Institute.

Gartner, J. Larson, D.B., & Allen, G. (1991). Religious commitment and mental health: A review of the empirical literature. *Journal of Psychological Theology, 19*, 6-25.

Gorsuch, R.L. (1995). Religious aspects of substance abuse and recovery. *Journal of Social Issues, 51*, 65-83.

Hackney, C.H., & Sanders, G.S. (2003). Religiosity and mental health: A meta-analysis of recent studies. *Journal for the Scientific Study of Religion, 42*, 43-55.

Horstmann, M.J., & Tonigan, J.S. (2000). Faith development in Alcoholics Anonymous (AA): A study of two AA groups. *Alcoholism Treatment Quarterly, 18*, 75-84.

Idler, E.L., Musick, M.A., Ellison, C.G., George, L.K., Krause, N., Pargament, K.I., Powell, L.H., Underwood, L.G., & Williams, D.R. (2003). Measuring multiple dimensions of religion and spirituality for health research. *Research on Aging, 25*, 327-365.

Jarusiewicz, B. (2000). Spirituality and addiction: Relationship to recovery and relapse. *Alcoholism Treatment Quarterly, 18*, 99-109.

Kendler KS, Liu, X-Q, Gardner, C.O. McCullough, M.E., Larson, D., & Prescott, C.A. (2003). Dimensions of religiosity and their relationship to lifetime psychiatric and substance abuse disorders. *American Journal of Psychiatry, 160*, 496-503.

Koenig, H.G., Cohen, H.J., Blazer, D.G. (1992). Religious coping and depression elderly, hospitalized medically ill men. *American Journal of Psychiatry, 149*, 1693-1700.

Koenig, H.G., George, L.K., Meador, K.G., Blazer, D.G., & Ford, S.M. (1994). Religious practices and alcoholism in a Southern adult population. *Hospital and Community Psychiatry, 45*, 225-231.

Levin, J.S., Taylor, R.J., & Chatters, L.M. (1994). Race and gender differences in religiosity among older adults: Findings from four national surveys. *Journal of Gerontology: Social Sciences, 49*, S137-S145.

McLellan, A., Kushner, H., Metzger, D., Peters, R., Smith, I., Grissom, G., et al. (1990). The fifth edition of the Addiction Severity Index. *Journal of Substance Abuse Treatment, 9*, 199-213.

McCullough, M.E., Hoyt, W.T., Larson, D.B, Koenig, H.G., & Thoresen, C.E. (2000). Religious involvement and mortality: A meta-analytic review. *Health Psychology, 19*, 211-222.

Miller, W.R. (1997). Spiritual aspects of addictions treatment and research. *Mind/Body Medicine, 2*, 37-43.

Moore Strawbridge, W.J., Cohen, R.D., Shema, S.J., & Kaplan, G.A. (1997). Frequent attendance at religious services and mortality over 28 years. *American Journal of Public Health, 87*, 957-961.

Pardini, D., Plante, T.G., Sherman, A., & Stump, J.E. (2000). Strength of faith and its association with mental health outcomes among recovering alcoholics and addicts. *Journal of Substance Abuse Treatment, 19*, 347-354.

Pargament, K.I. (1997). *The Psychology of Religion and Coping: Theory, Research, and Practice.* New York: Guilford.

Pargament, K.I., Cole, B., Vandecreek L, Belavich, T., Brant, C., & Perez, L. (1999). The vigil: Religion and the search for control in the hospital waiting room. *Journal of Health Psychology, 4*, 327-341.

Pargament, K.I., Koenig, H.G., & Perez, L.M. (2000). The many methods of religious coping: Development and initial validation of the RCOPE. *Journal of Clinical Psychology, 56*, 519-543.

Pargament, K.I., Koenig, H.G., Tarakeshwar, N., & Hahn, J. (2001). Religious struggle as a predictor of mortality among medically ill elderly patients: A 2-year longitudinal study. *Archives of Internal Medicine, 161*, 1881-1885.

Pargament, K.I., Smith, B.W., Koenig, H.G., & Perez, L. (1998a). Patterns of positive and negative religious coping with major life stressors. *Journal of the Scientific Study of Religion, 37*, 711-725.

Pargament, K.I., Zinnbauer, B.J., Scott, A.B., Butter, E.M., Zerowin, J., & Stanik, P. (1998b). Red flags and religious coping: identifying some religious warning signs among people in crisis. *Journal of Clinical Psychology, 54*, 77-89.

Peteet, J.R. (1993). A closer look at the role of a spiritual approach in addictions treatment. *Journal of Substance Abuse Treatment, 10*, 263-167.

Plante, T.G., & A.C. Sherman, A.C. (Eds.) (2002). *Faith and Health: Psychological Perspectives.* New York: Guilford, pp. 381-402.

Powell, L.H., Shahabi, L., & Thoresen, C.E. (2003). Religion and spirituality: Linkages to physical health. *American Psychologist, 58*, 36-52.

Richard, A.J., Bell, D.C., & Carlson, J.W. (2000). Individual religiosity, moral community, and drug user treatment. *Journal for the Scientific Study of Religion, 39*, 240-246.

Sherman, A.C., & Plante, T.G. (2001). Conclusions and future directions for research on faith and health. In Plante, T.G., & Sherman, A.C. (Eds.), *Faith and Health: Psychological Perspectives.* New York: Guilford, pp. 381-402.

Sherman, A.C., & Simonton, S. (2001a). Religious involvement among cancer patients: Associations with adjustment and quality of life. In Plante, T.G., & Sherman, A.C. (Eds.), *Faith and Health: Psychological Perspectives.* New York: Guilford, pp. 167-194.

Sherman, A.C., & Simonton, S. (2001b). Assessment of religiousness and spirituality in health research. In Plante, T.G., & Sherman, A.C. (Eds.), *Faith and Health: Psychological Perspectives,* Guilford, New York, pp. 139-163.

Sherman, A.C., Simonton, S., Latif, U., Spohn, R., & Tricot, G. (2005). Religious struggle and religious comfort in response to illness: Health outcomes among stem cell transplant patients. *Journal of Behavioral Medicine, 28*, 359-367.

Sherman, A.C., Simonton, S., Plante, T., Moody, V.R., & Wells, P. (2001). Patterns of religious coping among multiple myeloma patients: Associations with adjustment and quality of life. [abstract]. *Psychosomatic Medicine, 63*, 124.

Strawbridge, W.J., Shema, S.J., Cohen, R.D., & Kaplan, G.A. (2001). Religious attendance increases survival by improving and maintaining good health behaviors, mental health, and social relationships. *Annals of Behavioral Medicine, 23*, 68-74.

Taylor, R., Chatters, L., Jakody, R., & Levin, J. (1996). Black and White differences in religious participation: A multisample comparison. *Journal for the Scientific Study of Religion, 35*, 403-410.

Thoresen, C.E., Harris, A.H.S., & Oman, D. (2001). Spirituality, religion, and health: Evidence, issues, and concerns. In Plante, T.G., & Sherman, A.C. (Eds.), *Faith and Health: Psychological Perspectives.* New York: Guilford, pp. 15-52.

Tix, A.P., & Frazier, P.A. (1998). The use of religious coping during stressful life events: Main effects, moderation, and mediation. *Journal of Consulting and Clinical Psychology, 66*, 411-422.

Weathers, F., Litz, B., Herman, D., Huska, J., & Keane, T. (1993). *The PTSD Check-list: Reliability, validity, and diagnostic utility.* Paper presented at the Annual Meeting of the International Society for Traumatic Stress Studies, San Antonio, TX.

Wink, P., & Dillon, M. (2001). Religious involvement and health outcomes in late adulthood: Findings from a longitudinal study of women and men. In T.G. Plante, & A.C. Sherman (Eds.), *Faith and Health: Psychological Perspectives* (pp. 75-106). New York: Guilford Press.

Wink, P., & Dillon, M. (2003). Religiousness, spirituality, and psychological functioning in late adulthood: Findings from a longitudinal study. *Psychology and Aging, 18,* 916-924.

Spiritual Well-Being, Relationships, and Work Satisfaction in the Treatment of Homeless Veterans with Alcohol/Other Drug Problems

Brent B. Benda, PhD
Frederick A. DiBlasio, PhD
Sandra K. Pope, PhD

SUMMARY. This study examined a random sample of 600 homeless male veterans, aged 46 to 65, who served in the military during the Vietnam War. The purpose of the study was to identify predictors of readmission to an inpatient treatment program for alcohol and drug abuse in a 2-year follow-up. Among the strongest predictors were comorbidity, suicidal thoughts, memory loss, and childhood sexual and physical abuse.

Improvements in family relationships, friendships, work satisfaction,

Brent B. Benda is Professor, School of Social Work, University of Arkansas at Little Rock, Little Rock, AR 72204 (E-mail: BBBENDA@ualr.edu).

Frederick A. DiBlasio is Professor, School of Social Work, University of Maryland, 525 West Redwood Street, Baltimore, MD 21201.

Sandra K. Pope is Assistant Professor, Department of Geriatrics, College of Medicine and Department of Epidemiology, College of Public Health, University of Arkansas for Medical Sciences, Little Rock, AR 72205.

Address correspondence to: Dr. Brent B. Benda at the above address.

[Haworth co-indexing entry note]: "Spiritual Well-Being, Relationships, and Work Satisfaction in the Treatment of Homeless Veterans with Alcohol/Other Drug Problems." Benda, Brent B., Frederick A. DiBlasio, and Sandra K. Pope. Co-published simultaneously in *Alcoholism Treatment Quarterly* (The Haworth Press, Inc.) Vol. 24, No. 1/2, 2006, pp. 109-124; and: *Spirituality and Religiousness and Alcohol/Other Drug Problems: Treatment and Recovery Perspectives* (ed: Brent B. Benda, and Thomas F. McGovern) The Haworth Press, Inc., 2006, pp. 109-124. Single or multiple copies of this article are available for a fee from The Haworth Document Delivery Service [1-800-HAWORTH, 9:00 a.m. - 5:00 p.m. (EST). E-mail address: docdelivery@haworthpress.com].

and spiritual well-being were positively related to length of time home-less veterans remained in the community without readmission. Discussion of these findings for service provisions was presented. *[Article copies available for a fee from The Haworth Document Delivery Service: 1-800-HAWORTH. E-mail address: <docdelivery@haworthpress.com> Website: <http://www.HaworthPress.com> © 2006 by The Haworth Press, Inc. All rights reserved.]*

KEYWORDS. Alcohol and other drug problems, homeless veterans, childhood abuse, survival in the community, work satisfaction, relationships, spiritual well-being

Among the highest costs for medical care in the United States is treatment of alcohol and other drug abuse (Murray, Anthenelli, & Maxwell, 2000; Piette, Baisden, & Moos, 1997; Virgo, Price, Spitznagel, & Ji, 1999). These costs are especially high because alcohol and drug abusers typically have comorbid psychiatric disorders (Benda, 2002a, 2002b, 2004a, 2005; Hoff & Rosenheck, 2000). Costs of treating comorbidity are elevated not only because of the complex nature of interrelated disorders, but also because, historically, substance abuse has been treated in different systems or programs than psychiatric morbidity. Alcohol and drug treatment programs have had dissimilar, even contradictory, treatment orientations and approaches compared to mental health systems. As a result of these dissimilarities, substance abuse frequently is improperly assessed or overlooked in mental health centers, whereas mental health problems generally are not appropriately diagnosed or treated in drug rehabilitation programs. Chemical abusers who suffer other psychiatric problems often are shuffled between drug rehabilitation and mental health systems, using scarce resources, without receiving adequate treatment in either system (Dixon, McNary, & Lehman, 1997; Nuttbrock et al., 1998; Rosenheck & Cicchetti, 1998). These problems are compounded by the orientation of counselors in substance abuse programs, who frequently assume that a certain degree of mental health is requisite to the recovery process. Synchronously, many mental health professionals have been socialized to believe abstinence must be achieved before psychiatric treatment is viable. The net effect of complex coexisting problems, and compartmentalized conception of treatment, is that comorbidity is one of the strongest predictors of longevity of service use and readmission to inpatient treatment (Benda, 2001; Moos, Moos, & Andrassy, 1999; Rosenheck, Bassuk, & Salomon, 1999).

While integrated programs to treat alcohol and other drug abuse, as well as various psychiatric disorders, have emerged in recently in many communities, they are still relatively scarce for homeless veterans (Hoff, & Rosenheck, 2000; Moos et al., 1999; Virgo et al., 1999). The purpose of the present study is to determine how well factors identified in, or inferred from, life-course theory (Elder, 1985, 1998) predict readmission to a Veterans Affairs medical center for alcohol and drug abuse treatment. A central tenet of life-course theory is that there are "turning points" or transforming experiences that engender social bonding to others in the larger society. The foundational assumption of life-course theory (Sampson & Laub, 1993) is that social bonding to others quells one's tendency to act on unhealthy natural desires for self-gratification. The "turning points" of interest in this study are greater satisfaction with work (Kashner et al., 2002), improved family and friend relations (Moos et al., 1999), and enhanced spiritual well-being (Ellison, Boardman, Williams, & Jackson, 2001; Kendler et al., 2003). These "turning points" or milestones are postulated to ameliorate the ill effects of adversities that occurred early in childhood, such as insecure attachments and sexual and physical abuses (Cicchetti, & Toth, 1995; Horwitz, Widom, McLaughlin, & White, 2001; Ireland, Smith, & Thornberry, 2002; Rogosch & Cicchetti, 2004). A primary research question is whether improved work satisfaction, relationships with family and friends, and spiritual well-being will reduce the longitudinal effects of these early life adversities on readmission to inpatient care at V. A. hospitals (Benda, 2004b; Benda, in press).

Only recently have studies begun to examine the relative protracted effects of early sexual and physical abuses (Ireland et al., 2002; Thornberry, Ireland, & Smith, 2001). No studies have been located that examine the longitudinal effects of these forms of abuse on undesirable outcomes in adulthood, after considering the possible ameliorating influences of factors such as improved family or friend relationships or spiritual well-being (Koegel, Melamid, & Burnam, 1995; Koegel, Sullivan, Burnam, Morton, & Wenzel, 1999; Wenzel, Koegel, & Gelberg, 2000). These ameliorating experiences may reduce the protracted effects of early abuse on outcomes such as readmission to a treatment program for substance abuse and other psychiatric disorders in adulthood. Identification of predictors of readmission to such treatment programs provides valuable clues for formulating conceptual models. Predictors also indicate possible influences on recidivism or readmission for treatment programs to target in intervention (Fontana, Schwartz, & Rosenheck, 1997; Kressin et al., 1999).

According to community surveys and studies of the general population of homeless people, the sequelae of abuses in childhood include a myriad of adversities, including, but are not limited to, depression, aggression, fearfulness, posttraumatic stress disorder (PTSD), suicidal thoughts, and various cognitive disorders (Horwitz et al., 2001; Koegel et al., 1995; Widom, 1999a, 1999b, 2001; Wenzel et al., 2000; Zlotnick et al., 2001). Childhood maltreatment and associated adversities are expected to be positive predictors of readmission to V. A. inpatient treatment for alcohol, drug, and other psychiatric problems. Diminished problems with family, friends, and work, and enhanced spiritual well-being are hypothesized to be negative predictors of readmission. Based on life-course theory, self-efficacy and ego identity also are anticipated to be negative predictors of readmission to V. A. treatment (Benda, 2004b, 2005).

METHOD

Sample

A systematic random sample of 600 homeless male veterans aged 46 to 65, who had served in the military during the Vietnam War, was selected. Those veterans were inpatients in a program for homeless substance abusers in a Veterans Affairs (V. A.) medical center in the Midwest. Only men who had no residence where they could live were included in the study. Participation in the study was voluntary, and less than 5 percent of the veterans approached declined to participate. Comparisons of race, age, marital status, employment pattern, substance abuse history, and psychiatric diagnoses of the study sample to the population at this V. A. indicated equivalence. The sample characteristics were shown in Table 1. A selective review indicates that the average (mean) years of alcohol (12.1) and other drug (10.5) use were high in this sample, as were the percentages that have been treated for substance abuse (71 percent) and psychiatric problems (40 percent).

In addition, 66.2 percent of these veterans are comorbid with substance abuse and psychiatric afflictions. There are 432 persons, or 72 percent, who returned to a hospital for substance abuse and/or psychiatric problems during the two-year follow-up period. The average number of days survived in the community without rehospitalization is 60.4, with a standard deviation of 119.65 days and a mode of 42 (7 percent) days.

TABLE 1. Characteristics of the Sample (N = 600)

	Mean	Mode (%)	SD
Age (in years)	52.3	52(20)	10.7
Education	12.0	12(76)	2:7
Years used alcohol	12.1	10(15)	25.7
Years used drugs	10.5	10(17)	22.8
Crimes committed	3.5	0(65)	1.2
Months homeless*	37.3	18(15)	118.7
Months employed*	120.1	91(12)	123.8
Race	Frequency		Percent
Caucasian	246		41.0
African American	239		39.8
Asian American	6		1.0
Hispanic American	73		12.2
Native American	30		5.0
Other	6		1.0

Family-of-origin structure most of the years before 18 years of age

Both biological parents	215		35.8
Biological and step	131		22.8
Mother only	171		28.5
Father only	21		3.5
Other	62		10.4
Prior alcohol/drug treatment			
Yes	426		71.0
No	174		39.0
Prior Psychiatric Hospitalization			
Yes	240		40.0
No	360		60.0
Crime			
Yes	222		37.0
No	360		60.0
Missing	18		3.0
Usual Employment in past 3 years			
Full-time	90		15.0
Part-time	156		26.0
Sporadic (daywork)	192		32.0
Disability	112		18.7
Other	50		8.3
Sexual Abuse			
Yes	113		18.8
No	479		79.8
Missing	8		2.4
Physical Abuse			
Yes	192		30.0
No	408		70.0

Note: *total months homeless and employed full-time since discharge from military.

Procedures

All study participants were interviewed on two separate days within the first two-weeks after arrival on the Domiciliary Unit, which was a program that followed the 30-day detoxification intervention. Interviews were done by 6 social workers that worked on the Domiciliary Unit. The Domiciliary program consisted of several components to secure employment, housing, and independent living. Veterans were assured of confidentiality of information. The length of stay in the Domiciliary varied from 6 months to a year, which was determined by the needs and the severity of problems. Aftercare consisted of various combinations of services to sustain abstinence, employment, housing, and social support.

Outcome

The outcome was the number of days in the community before readmission for alcohol, drug, or other psychiatric disorders during the two-year follow-up study. The number of days was determined by checking the computer files of all Veteran's Hospitals in the state studied and all surrounding states, as well as the Department of Veterans Affairs National Clinical Database in Austin, Texas. Also, 100 of the study participants or family members were contacted to verify readmission data. The telephone calls indicated the outcome data were 99 percent accurate.

Measures

The majority of measures of factors from came from Hudson's (1990) Multi-Problem Screening Inventory (MPSI). All of Hudson's subscales used in the present analyses had Cronbach (1951) alphas (α) of .80 or above in his samples and in the present study (Hudson & McMurtry, 1997). The subscales used were: (a) problems with family relationships, (b) problems with friends, (c) physical abuse, (d) depression, (e) fearfulness, (f) aggression, (g) confused thinking, (h) disturbing thoughts, (i) memory loss, (j) suicide thoughts, and (k) problems with work. Each of the measures had 7-point scales (ranging from "none of the time" to "all of the time"). Comorbidity was based on psychiatric diagnoses found in the records, and this condition is assessed in all cases due to the nature of the program. Point biserial correlations between summated scores on Hudson's subscales d through i and the psychiatric diagnoses were above .90, indicating solid validity. Scales measuring problems with family and with friends, problems with work, and spiritual well-being were administered a second time two months after they had been released to aftercare from the inpatient treatment to obtain changes in scores for analysis. A scale measuring problems with work was administered two weeks after they were employed while in inpatient treatment.

Sexual abuse was measured with Bentler's (1968) 21-item Sexual Behavior Scale (scaled no versus yes), modified to forced behavior and to allow for homosexual abuse ($\alpha = .88$). Posttraumatic stress disorder (PTSD) was measured with the 35-item (5-point Likert scales) Mississippi scale for combat-related PTSD, which has strong validity ($\alpha = .87$) (Keane, Caddell, & Taylor, 1988).

Self-Efficacy Scale consisted of 25-items (5-point scales) (Maddox, Mercandante, Prentice-Dunn, Jacobs, & Rogers, 1982) ($\alpha = .86$). The Ego Identity Scale (EIS) had 12 items that measure Erikson's (1968) concept of ego identity. Respondents choose between two responses, with one choice representing ego diffusion ($\alpha = .74$). Ego identity is defined as acceptance of self and a sense of direction, and the EIS has good validity (Tan, Kendis, Fine, & Porac, 1977). Both of these measures of "self" attributes have well-established concurrent, construct, and known groups validity (Fischer & Corcoran, 1994). Ellison's (1983) 20-item (6-point scales) Spiritual Well-Being Scale had solid concurrent validity as well. The scale was designed to evaluate spiritual well-being along two dimensions: (1) well-being in relation to God ($\alpha = .88$), and (2) well-being in terms of life purpose and satisfaction ($\alpha = .84$).

Finally, sociodemographic information was gathered on present age (in years), years of education, race (0 = white, 1 = persons of color), marital status (0 = married, 1 = other), and usual employment pattern over the 3 years prior to the study (coded 0 = full time, 1 = other).

Characteristics of Data and Analyses

Multicollinearity was checked with a fourfold approach: First, principal components analysis was used to identify whether similar concepts (e.g., disturbing thoughts, confused thinking, memory loss) loaded together or separately, using varimax rotation and a criteria of an eigenvalue of at least 1, loadings of > .40 on a factor, and loadings of < .15 between factors. Then, study factors were inter-correlated, and subjected to tolerance tests and the variance inflation factor (Freund & Wilson, 1998). None of these approaches indicated a problem with multicollinearity. The skew and kurtosis were in the normal range on those factors, and no variable in the study was missing more than 3 percent of the cases.

FINDINGS

The analyses are Cox's proportional hazard model because this procedure is not based on any assumption concerning the nature or shape of the underlying survival distribution–that is, about the proportion of persons that would not be readmitted or about how long people would survive on the streets after release from inpatient care (Allison, 1984; Wu & Tuma, 1994; Yamaguchi, 1991). Table 2 shows the hazard risk associated with each predictor in the study: a value greater than 1 indicates the increase in risk of readmission associated with every unit rise in the predictor, whereas a hazard rate less than 1 reflects a lower probability of readmission with every unit increase in the predictor variable. All predictors, except for discrete variables like race, are standardized (Z-scores). Hence, for example, with each standard deviation increase in age, there is a greater risk of readmission to treatment for substance abuse and other psychiatric disorders of 1.16 (Table 2). The strongest predictor shows that being comorbid with substance abuse and psychiatric disorders more than triples the risk of readmission. Predictors that more than double the risk of rehospitalization include childhood sexual abuse, early physical maltreatment, and suicidal thoughts. The only insignificant predictors are education, race, marital status, and fearfulness.

In accord with established procedures (Campbell & Kenny, 1999), residualized change scores for measures of transforming experiences are used in the Cox's proportional hazard model shown in Table 3. Adding transforming experiences to the predictors analyzed in Table 2 reduces the hazard risks of many of these predictors (Table 3). The reductions are noted with NC in Table 3, indicating noteworthy change (noteworthy change is determined by a test of equivalence of regression coefficients developed by Paternoster, Brame, Mazerolle, & Piquero, 1998). For example, being comorbid doubles the risk of readmission after considering the ameliorating experiences (Table 3), whereas it triples the risk before these experiences are considered (Table 2). The risk of readmission is lessened, by the addition of these experiences, for edu-

TABLE 2. Cox's Proportional-Hazard Model of Readmission for Alcohol, Drug, and Psychiatric Disorders Before Considering Transforming Experiences

Predictor	Beta	Hazard Ratio (HR)	(1/HR)
Age	.15*	1.16	
Education in years	−.12	0.89	1.12
Race (0 = white, 1 = other)	.05	1.05	
Usual employment (0 = full-time, 1 = other)	.17*	1.18	
Marital status (0 = married, 1 = other)	.03	1.03	
Childhood sexual abuse	.80**	2.22	
Childhood physical abuse	.76**	2.13	
Depression	.62**	1.85	
Fearfulness	.06	1.06	
Aggression	.18*	1.20	
Confused thinking	.28**	1.32	
Disturbing thoughts	.45**	1.57	
Memory loss	.51**	1.66	
Suicide thoughts	.70**	2.02	
PTSD	.64**	1.89	
Comorbidity (0 = no, 1 = yes)	1.14**	3.13	
Self-efficacy	−.73**	0.48	2.08
Ego identity	−.82**	0.44	2.27

Model χ^2 365.21, 18 df

Note: All predictors, except discrete variables, are standardized. * P < .05, ** P < .01.

cation, usual pattern of employment before the study, both forms of childhood abuse, aggression, confused thinking, disturbing thoughts, suicidal thoughts, and PTSD. Each of the ameliorating experience also is a significant predictor. The reciprocal hazard (1/HR) is shown for inverse relationships to allow a direct comparison to the more numerous positive relationships. For example, the risk of readmission declines .68 as the change in spiritual well-being increases, while that risk increases 1.47 (1/.68 = 1.47) as the change in spiritual well-being decreases.

DISCUSSION

This study of 600 homeless Vietnam veterans, who abused alcohol and other drugs, found that the majority (72 percent) was readmitted for inpatient treatment during the two-year follow-up. Many of the predic-

TABLE 3. Cox's Proportional-Hazard Model of Readmission for Alcohol, Drug, and Psychiatric Disorders After Considering Transforming Experiences

Predictor	Beta	Hazard Ratio (HR)	(1/HR)
Age	.12	1.12	
Education in years	−.04	0.96 NC	1.04
Race (0 = white, 1 = other)	.05	1.05	
Usual employment (0 = full-time, 1 = other)	.01	1.01 NC	
Marital status (0 = married, 1 = other)	.03	1.03	
Childhood sexual abuse	.53**	1.70 NC	
Childhood physical abuse	.28**	1.32 NC	
Depression	.20*	1.22	
Fearfulness	.01	1.01	
Aggression	.05	1.05 NC	
Confused thinking	.19*	1.21 NC	
Disturbing thoughts	.22**	1.25 NC	
Memory loss	.48**	1.62	
Suicide thoughts	.51**	1.67 NC	
PTSD	.27**	1.31 NC	
Comorbidity (0 = no, 1 = yes)	.72**	2.06 NC	
Self-efficacy	−.87**	0.42	2.38
Ego identity	−1.08**	0.34	2.94
(Ameliorating Experiences–Change Scores)			
Reduced family problems	−.42**	0.66	1.52
Reduced friend problems	−.51**	0.60	1.67
Less work problems	−.60**	0.55	1.82
Enhanced spiritual well-being	−.39**	0.68	1.47

Model χ^2 3142.20, 22 df

Note: All predictors, except discrete variables, are standardized. NC indicates noteworthy change in the hazard ratio after introducing the ameliorating experiences in the analysis. * P < .05, ** P < .01.

tors of readmission considered were statistically significant. In descending order of size of the hazard risk (HR) of readmission, the significant predictors of readmission were ego identity, self-efficacy, comorbidity, less work problems, childhood sexual abuse, suicide thoughts and reduced friendship problems (HRs of 1.67), memory loss, diminished family problems, enhanced spiritual well-being, childhood physical abuse, PTSD, disturbing thoughts, depression, and confused thinking. Ego identity, self-efficacy, reduced family and friend problems, less work problems, and enhanced spiritual well-being were associated with decreased risk of readmission, while the other predictors had positive relationships with that risk.

It is particularly striking that the two strongest predictors are personality assets. Ego identity is defined by the authors of the scale used (Tan et al., 1977) as an acceptance of self, and a sense of meaning and purpose in life. It is reasonable to assume that persons who have a stronger belief that they are living a worthwhile life are less likely to relapse into alcohol and drug abuse or psychiatric problems. A sense of efficacy in one's pursuits also motivates persons to remain abstinent and make efforts to avoid succumbing to psychiatric problems, such as depression, suicidal ideation, and disturbing thoughts.

Both of these personality assets are amenable to treatment. Insight therapy, learning problem-solving skills, and cognitive treatment can be used to instill a better appreciation for self-worth and successes in life, as well as a greater sense of being able to accomplish what one sets out to do. Insights can help people to understand why they do not positively value themselves and their purpose in life. Cognitive restructuring and reframing can be used to change the way people think about themselves and their approaches to life. Cognitive restructuring involves modifying erroneous or illogical beliefs, such as the road to recovery is too arduous, or suicide is the only real solution to life's difficulties. Cognitive reframing refers to altering the meaning of experiences; for example, instead of viewing substance abuse as an inevitable outcome, it can be perceived as a susceptibility that can be overcome with diligence. Learning how to solve problems by taking incremental steps can build a sense of self-efficacy or mastery.

This study suggests that resolving problems at work may be a major factor in preventing readmission of homeless male veterans. The 10 items on the measure of problems with work (Hudson, 1990) include "job is boring," "hate job," "like job," "boss is a fool," and "I work hard." In essence, these items seem to be a measure of job satisfaction. Selective job placement and resolving employment problems would appear to be essential to remaining in the community without readmission among these veterans. The critical role played by employment in the recovery process is verified in research that specifically focuses on this satisfaction with work (Kashner et al., 2002). Success in employment should enhance self-efficacy and ego identity, providing veterans with a sense of accomplishment and purpose. Because employment seems to play a major role in recovery and mental health of former homeless veterans, an important aspect of inpatient treatment should be devoted to preparing persons attitudinally for jobs they will likely obtain, and to problem-solving skills for continuing employment. These efforts will have to be continued in aftercare, and staff will need to be available to assist in resolving interpersonal and performance difficulties as they arise. Support groups, including family and friends, could be beneficial in encouraging and reinforcing problem solving on the job.

Improvements in relationships with family and friends may act in concert with satisfactory employment to deter alcohol and drug abuse and mollify angst leading to psychiatric problems. A concomitant factor in the cycle of relapse seems to be isolation and lack of social support among homeless people (Rossi, 1989; Wright, Rubin, & Devine, 1998). Family and friends can be very valuable sources of encouragement and support when harsh struggles tempt persons to revert back to using alcohol and other drugs to ease frustration and stress. For example, they can provide housing and other tangible resources that meet exigencies. At the same time, discretion has to be exercised in establishing and reinforcing these relationships because they can be dysfunctional and harmful as well. There are instances in which these relationships must be developed incrementally and therapeutically. Therefore, a comprehensive approach to aftercare for homeless veterans will entail family counseling and treatment to remedy problems in the family system that could be deleterious to recovery and mental health of veterans.

Spiritual activities and guidance also are suggested in this study. Certainly, the 12-step program is founded on spiritual principles (Laudet, Magura, Vogel, & Knight, 2000, 2003). A vast literature is emerging, which historically has been overlooked by many professionals (Hodge, 2002), that demonstrates that spirituality can have significant salubrious effects on physical and mental health, as well as recovery from substance abuse (George, Larsons, Koeing, McCullough, 2000; Gorsuch, 1993; Kendler et al., 2003; Koenig, 1997; Koenig, George, Meador, & Ford, 1994; Koenig, George, & Peterson, 1998; Worthington, Kurusu, McCullough, & Sandage, 1996). The National Institute of Healthcare Research team (Larson, Swyers, & McCullough, 1997, p. 21), based on an exhaustive search of the literature, define spirituality as "the feelings, thoughts, experiences, and behaviors that arise from a search for the sacred." The sacred is divine, which many people believe is a supreme being known as God. In addition to the 12-step programs, religious individuals and institutions need to become more involved in assisting homeless people with spiritual growth. Spirituality offers a divine sense of meaning and purpose for life that is a compelling incentive to sustain recovery from substance abuse and psychiatric problems. Spirituality also conveys that there is an omnipotent power from which to draw strength to overcome any despair or setbacks.

In conclusion, this study provides empirical support for the need to develop integrated programs that address a complex nexus of interrelated problems associated with alcohol and drug abuse and other psychiatric disorders. These programs will require the coordinated efforts of diverse professionals. Interdisciplinary teams seem to be the optimal organization of professionals to assure collaborative efforts toward problem resolution. Clients are assigned to a designed team that provides their services from the point of admission to inpatient treatment to the end of aftercare.

REFERENCES

Allison, P. D. (1984). *Event history analysis.* Newbury Park, CA: Sage.

Benda, B. B. (2001). Predictors of rehospitalization of military veterans who abuse substances. *Social Work Research, 25,* 199-212.

Benda, B. B. (2002a) Factors associated with rehospitalization among veterans in a substance abuse treatment program. *Psychiatric Services, 53,* 1176-1178.

Benda, B. B. (2002b). Test of a structural equation model of comorbidity among homeless and domiciled military veterans. *Journal of Social Service Research, 29,* 1-35.

Benda, B. B. (2004a). Life-course theory of readmission of substance abusers among homeless veterans. *Psychiatric Services, 55,* 1308-1310.

Benda, B. B. (2004b). Gender differences in the rehospitalization of substance abusers among homeless military veterans. *Journal of Drug Issues, 34,* 723-750.

Benda, B. B. (2005). Discriminators of suicide thoughts and attempts among homeless veterans who abuse substances. *Suicide & Life-Threatening Behavior, 35,* 106-116.

Benda, B. B. (in press). Survival Analyses of Social Support and Trauma among Homeless Men and Women Veterans Who Abuse Substances. *American Journal of Orthopsychiatry.*

Bentler, P. M. (1968). Heterosexual behavior. *Behavior Research and Therapy, 6,* 21-25.

Campbell, D. T., & Kenny, D. A. (1999). *A primer on regression artifact.* New York: Wiley.

Cicchetti, D., & Toth, S. L. (1995). A developmental psychopathology perspective on child abuse and neglect. *Journal of the American Academy of Child & Adolescent Psychiatry, 34,* 541-564.

Cronbach, L. J. (1951). Coefficient alpha and internal structure of tests. *Psychometrica, 16,* 297-334.

Dixon L., McNary S., & Lehman, A. (1997). One-year follow-up of secondary versus primary mental disorder in persons with comorbid substance use disorders. *American Journal of Psychiatry, 154,* 1610-1612.

Elder, G. H. Jr. (Ed.) (1985). *Life course dynamic: Transitions and trajectories.* Ithaca, NY: Cornell University Press.

Elder, G. H. Jr. (1998). The life course as developmental theory. *Child Development, 69,* 1-12.

Ellison, C. W. (1983). Spiritual well-being: Conceptualization and measurement. *Journal of Psychology and Theology, 11,* 330-340.

Ellison, C. G., Boardman, J. D., Williams. D. R., & Jackson, J. S. (2001). Religious involvement, stress, and mental health: Findings from the 1995 Detroit area study. *Social Forces, 60,* 215-249.

Erikson, E. (1968). *Identity: Youth and crisis.* New York: Norton.

Fischer J., & Corcoran, K. (1994). *Measures for clinical practice: A sourcebook* (2nd ed.) (Vol. 2). New York: Free Press.

Fontana, A., Schwartz, L. S., & Rosenheck, R. (1997). Posttraumatic stress disorder among female Vietnam veterans: A causal model of etiology. *American Journal of Public Health, 87,* 169-175.

Freund, R. J., & Wilson, W. J. (1998). *Regression analysis: Statistical modeling of a response variable.* New York: Academic Press.

George, L. K., Larsons, D. B., Koeing H. G., McCullough, M. E. (2000). Spirituality and health: What we know, what we need to know. *Journal of Social and Clinical Psychology, 19,* 102-116.

Gorsuch, R. L. (1993). Religious aspects of substance abuse and recovery. *Journal of Social Issues, 25,* 65-83.

Hodge, D. R. (2002). Does social work oppress Evangelical Christians? A "new class" analysis of society and social work. *Social Work, 47,* 401-414.

Hoff, R. A., & Rosenheck, R. A. (2000). Cross-system service use among psychiatric patients: Data from the Department of Veterans Affairs." *The Journal of Behavioral Health Services & Research, 27*(1), 98-106.

Horwitz, A. V., Widom, C. S., McLaughlin, J., & White, H. R. (2001). The impact of childhood abuse and neglect on adult mental health: A prospective study. *Journal of Health and Social Behavior, 42,* 184-201.

Hudson, W.W. (1990). *The MPSI technical manual.* Tempe, AZ: Walmer Publishing Company.

Hudson, W., W., & McMurtry, S. L (1997). Comprehensive assessment in social work practice: The Multi-Problem Screening Inventory. *Research on Social Work Practice, 7,* 79-98.

Ireland, T. O., Smith, C. A., & Thornberry, T. P. (2002). Developmental issues in the impact of child maltreatment on later delinquency and drug use. *Criminology, 40,* 359-399.

Kashner, T. M., Rosenheck, R., Campinell, A. B., Suris, A. et al. (2002). Impact of work therapy on health status among homeless, substance-dependent veterans: A randomized controlled trial. *Archives of General Psychiatry, 59,* 938-944.

Keane, T. M., Caddell, J. M., & Taylor, K. L. (1988). Mississippi Scale for Combat-Related Posttraumatic Stress Disorder: Three studies in reliability and validity. *Journal of Consulting and Clinical Psychology, 56,* 85-90.

Kendler, K. S., Liu, Z, Gardner, C. O., McCullough et al. (2003). Dimensions of religiosity and their relationship to lifetime psychiatric and substance use disorders. *American Journal of Psychiatry, 160,* 496-503.

Koegel, P., Melamid, E., & Burnam, M. A. (1995). Childhood risk factors for homelessness among homeless adults. *American Journal of Public Health, 85,* 1642-1651.

Koegel, P., Sullivan, G., Burnam, A., Morton, S., & Wenzel, S. (1999). Utilization of mental health and substance abuse services among homeless adults in Los Angeles. *Medical Care, 37,* 306-317.

Koenig, H. G. (1997). *Is religion good for your health? Effects of religion on mental and physical health.* New York: The Haworth Press, Inc.

Koenig, H. G., George, L. K., Meador, K. G., Blazer, D. G., & Ford, S. M. (1994). The relationship between religion and alcoholism in a sample of community-dwelling adults. *Hospital and Community Psychiatry, 45,* 225-231.

Koenig, H. G., George, L. K., & Peterson, B. L. (1998). Religiosity and remission from depression in medically ill older patients. *American Journal of Psychiatry, 155,* 536-542.

Kressin, N. R., Skinner, K., Sullivan, L., Miller, D. R., Frayne, S., Kazis, L., et al. (1999). Patient satisfaction with Department of Veterans Affairs health care: Do women differ from men? *Military Medicine, 164,* 283-288.

Maddox, S. M., Mercandante, J. E., Prentice-Dunn, S., Jacobs, B., & Rogers, R. W. (1982). The self-efficacy scale: Construction and validation, *Psychological Reports, 51,* 663-671.

Laudet, A. B., Magura, S.,Vogel, H. S., & Knight, E. (2000). Addictions services: Support, mutual aid and recovery from dual diagnosis. *Community Mental Health Journal, 36,* 457-476.

Laudet, A. B., Magura, S.,Vogel, H. S., & Knight, E. (2003). Participation in 12-step-based fellowships among dually-diagnosed persons. *Alcoholism Treatment Quarterly, 21,* 19-40.

Moos, R. H., Moos, B. S., & Andrassy, J. M. (1999). Outcomes of four treatment approaches in community residential programs for patients with substance use disorders. *Psychiatric Services, 50,* 1577-1583.

Murray, M. G., Anthenelli, R. M., & Maxwell, R. A. (2000). Use of health services by men with and without antisocial personality disorder who are alcohol dependent. *Psychiatric Services, 51,* 380-382.

Nuttbrock, L. A., Rahav, M., Rivera, J. J., Ng-Mak, D.S., & Link, B. G. (1998). Outcomes of homeless mentally ill chemical abusers in community residences and a therapeutic community. *Psychiatric Services, 49,* 68-76.

Paternoster, R., Brame, R., Mazerolle, P., & Piquero, A. (1998). Using the correct statistical test for the equality of regression coefficients. *Criminology, 36,* 859-866.

Piette, J. D., Baisden K. L., & Moos, R. H. (1997). *Health services for VA substance abuse and psychiatric patients: Utilization for fiscal years 1996.* Palo Alto, CA: Department of Veterans Affairs.

Rogosch, F. A., & Cicchetti, D. (2004). Child maltreatment and emergent personality organization: Perspectives from the five-factor model. *Journal of Abnormal Child Psychology, 32,* 123-136.

Rosenberg, M. J. (1979). *Conceiving the self.* New York: Basic Books.

Rosenheck, R., Bassuk, E., & Salomon, A. (1999). Special populations of homeless Americans. Retrieved June 2, 2004, http://aspe.hhs.gov/progsys/homeless/symposium/2-Spclpop.htm

Rosenheck, R. A., & Cicchetti. D. (1998). A mental health program report card: A mulitdimensional approach to performance monitoring in public sector programs. *Community Mental Health Journal, 34,* 85-106.

Rossi, P. (1989). *Down and out in America. The causes of homelessness.* Chicago: University of Chicago Press.

Sampson, R. J., & Laub, J. H. (1993). *Crime in the making: Pathways and turning points through life.* Cambridge, MA: Harvard University Press.

Tan, A. L., Kendis, R. J., Fine, J. T., & Porac, J. (1977). A Short Measure of Eriksonian Ego Identity. *Journal of Personality Assessment, 41,* 279-284.

Thornberry, T. P., Ireland, T. O., & Smith, C. A. (2001). Thee importance of time: The varying impact of childhood and adolescent maltreatment on multiple outcomes. *Development and Psychopathology, 13,* 957-979.

Virgo, K. S., Price, R. K., Spitznagel. E. L., & Ji. T. C. (1999). Substance abuse as a predictor of VA Medical Care utilization among Vietnam Veterans. *The Journal of Behavioral Health Services & Research, 26,* 126-139.

Wenzel, S. L., Koegel, P., & Gelberg, L. (2000). Antecedents of physical and sexual victimization among homeless women: A comparison to homeless men. *American Journal of Community Psychology, 28,* 367-390.

Widom, C. S. (1999a). Posttraumatic stress disorder in abused and neglected children grown up. *American Journal of Psychiatry, 156*(3), 1223-1229.

Widom, C. S. (1999b). Childhood victimization and the development of personality disorders: Commentary. *Archives of General Psychiatry, 56*(2), 607-608.

Widom, C. S. (2001). Alcohol abuse as risk factor for and consequence of child abuse. *Alcohol Research and Health, 25*(1), 52-58.

Worthington, E. L. Jr., Kurusu, T. A., McCullough; M. E., & Sandage, S. J. (1996). Empirical research on religion and psychotherapeutic processes and outcomes: A 10-year review and research prospectus: *Psychological Bulletin, 119,* 448-487.

Wright, J.D., Rubin, B.A., & Devine, J.A. (1998). *Beside the golden door: Policy, politics and the homeless.* New York: Aldine de Gruyter.

Wu, L. L., & Tuma, M. B. (1994). Assessing bias and fit of global and local hazard models. *Sociological Methods and Research, 19,* 354-87, 1994.

Yamaguchi, K. (1991). *Event history analysis.* Newbury Park, CA: Sage.

Zlotnick, C., Zimmerman, M., Wolfsdorf, B. A., & Mattia, J. I. (2001). Gender differences in patients with posttraumatic stress disorder in a general psychiatric practice. *American Journal of Psychiatry, 158,* 1923-1925.

Forgiveness in the Treatment of Persons with Alcohol Problems

Everett L. Worthington, Jr., PhD
Michael Scherer, MS
Kathryn L. Cooke, BS

SUMMARY. We describe one theoretical perspective on injustice, unforgiveness, justice, and forgiveness (i.e., an emotional-replacement model) and describe an intervention to promote forgiveness, which is applied to alcohol dependence and abuse. We identify major transgressions within families who deal with alcohol-related problems. We note risk factors related to the development of unforgiving emotions and describe ways that people typically cope with the stress of unforgiveness. Finally, an evidence-based psychoeducational group to promote for-

Everett L. Worthington, Jr. is Professor and Chair, Department of Psychology, Virginia Commonwealth University, Richmond, VA.

Michael Scherer is a recent graduate student in the Rehabilitation Counseling program and now in Counseling Psychology (APA accredited), Virginia Commonwealth University.

Kathryn L. Cooke is a graduate student in the Department of Psychology (Counseling Psychology, APA-accredited) at Virginia Commonwealth University.

Address correspondence to: Everett L. Worthington, Jr., Department of Psychology, Virginia Commonwealth University, Richmond, VA 23284-2018 (E-mail: eworth@vcu.edu).

The authors did the present work in part supported by *A Campaign for Forgiveness Research*, a 501c(3) corporation (www.forgiving.org). The authors are grateful to the 14 major donors to the *Campaign*, whose generosity made this work possible.

[Haworth co-indexing entry note]: "Forgiveness in the Treatment of Persons with Alcohol Problems." Worthington, Everett L., Michael Scherer, and Kathryn L. Cooke. Co-published simultaneously in *Alcoholism Treatment Quarterly* (The Haworth Press, Inc.) Vol. 24, No. 1/2, 2006, pp. 125-145; and: *Spirituality and Religiousness and Alcohol/Other Drug Problems: Treatment and Recovery Perspectives* (ed: Brent B. Benda, and Thomas F. McGovern) The Haworth Press, Inc., 2006, pp. 125-145. Single or multiple copies of this article are available for a fee from The Haworth Document Delivery Service [1-800-HAWORTH, 9:00 a.m. - 5:00 p.m. (EST). E-mail address: docdelivery@haworthpress.com].

Available online at http://www.haworthpress.com/web/ATQ
doi:10.1300/J020v24n01_08

giveness, derived from the emotion-replacement model of forgiveness is described and adapted to the treatment of alcohol dependence and abuse within a family context. Whereas unforgiveness seems frequent within families dealing with alcohol dependence, empirical research on unforgiveness and forgiveness within those families is sparse. *[Article copies available for a fee from The Haworth Document Delivery Service: 1-800-HAWORTH. E-mail address: <docdelivery@haworthpress.com> Website: <http://www.HaworthPress.com> © 2006 by The Haworth Press, Inc. All rights reserved.]*

KEYWORDS. Alcohol dependence, alcohol abuse, family, forgiveness, justice, intervention

Little has been written about the role of unforgiveness and forgiveness in families dealing with alcohol dependence or abuse (for a brief review, see Worthington, Mazzeo, & Kliewer, 2002). A large empirical base has developed due to the prevalence and treatment of alcohol dependence and abuse and their risk and protective factors (National Clearinghouse for Alcohol and Drug Information, 1996). When families deal with alcohol dependence or abuse in one member, transgressions are inflicted all around. These transgressions fuel defenses by the person who is dependent and constitute sources of immediate and long-term suffering and unhappiness. In this article, we assume that the readers are familiar with many of the ways that problems show up in families dealing with problems focused on alcohol abuse or dependence. We spend little time recounting those. Instead, our goals are the following:

- Articulate an established understanding of injustice, unforgiveness, justice, and forgiveness (Exline, Worthington, Hill, & McCullough, 2003), the emotional-replacement model of forgiveness (Worthington & Wade, 1999).
- Describe alternatives to forgiveness (Wade & Worthington, 2003).
- Apply those understandings to alcohol dependence and abuse.
- Describe an evidence-based intervention aimed at helping people to grant forgiveness, forgive themselves, and seek forgiveness from others (for a review, see Wade, Worthington, & Meyer, 2005; Worthington, 2003).
- Summarize research supporting the intervention (Burchard et al., 2003; Kiefer et al., 2004 McCullough & Worthington, 1995;

McCullough, Worthington, & Rachal, 1997; Ripley & Worthington, 2002; Sandage, 1997; Worthington et al., 2000).
• Describe how the intervention could be adapted to families affected by alcohol.

UNDERSTANDING INJUSTICE, UNFORGIVENESS, JUSTICE, AND FORGIVENESS

Worthington (2003; Worthington & Wade, 1999) has described a process by which transgressions eventually yield unforgiving emotions and motivations in people's lives. Transgressions, perceived as offenses and hurts, produce immediate emotional reactions such as anger and fear. Rumination elaborates the transgression, its effect on the person, and subsequent events. A sense of injustice and feelings of unforgiveness may result. Perceived injustice is related to magnitude of harm done to oneself, others, and a higher power. Unforgiveness is related to the perceived amount of injustice arising from the transgression and subsequent events. In the following sections, we describe each portion of this process of developing unforgiveness from transgressions.

TRANSGRESSIONS

What Are Transgressions?

Transgressions are violations of boundaries. Transgressions may be offenses, which are violations of moral boundaries, or may also be hurts, which are violations of physical or psychological boundaries. Most transgressions both offend and hurt the victim. People vary in their tendencies to interpret transgressions as hurts or offenses.

The severity of transgressions affects how people deal with them. Minor transgressions are easy to ignore or confront. Severe transgressions are so arousing that victims often do not even want to think about them. People may deny or psychologically project problems onto others, thus not dealing with the transgression, or people may explode in rage.

A variety of transgressions are inflicted when a member of a family is dependent on or abuses alcohol. These may be categorized as transgressions by the alcohol-dependent individual on partners, friends, family and the self. It also includes transgressions by friends and family members against the alcohol-dependent person.

In a family of a well-functioning alcohol-dependent family member, resentments are sometimes subtle. For example, a wife may feel like the husband is more interested in having a drink when he gets off from work than in being with her or the family. Sometimes this relationship with drinking can feel like infidelity–but one in which the alcohol cannot be confronted. It can feel to children as if the parent doesn't really care.

In families where abuse and dependence are more impairing, family members develop continuing fear, anger, blame, and resentment during the active dependence and abuse phase. Children and spouses can be embarrassed for their loved ones and humiliated in front of friends. Despite the widespread acceptance of alcoholism as a disease (Sheehan & Owen, 1999), family members can be stigmatized. Economic impact on their family can be devastating.

Children are likely to (a) adopt the behaviors of parents (Chassin & Ritter, 2001; Kilpatrick et al., 2000), (b) have access to alcohol in the home, (c) resent both parents (for abusing alcohol or not protecting the child from the abusing parent), (d) receive little adult supervision, so children are at risk for learning to abuse alcohol, and (e) be objects of abuse (Windom & Hiller-Sturmhofel, 2001). Furthermore, children might worry that genes for alcohol dependence have been passed onto them and that they might develop the disease themselves or pass it on to their children. Adolescents and adult children of alcoholics may blame an alcoholic parent for their own addictions or even for non-related difficulties that they reason must have come from the parent or the way the parent treated them.

Transgressions spread into the social network. Alcohol dependence can involve disciplinary actions or misconduct at work, missed days, and problems that never seem to end. Family members or friends might be asked to care for children, provide financial assistance, or expend time and resources, which can cause resentment toward the alcohol-affected family.

Transgressions spread to the spiritual. People might blame God for their difficulties, struggle to understand how God could allow such things, or question God's omnipotence or kindness. A spiritual struggle may result.

In addition, transgressions may be inflicted on the person who is alcohol dependent. A family member's attempt to help the affected member recognize the problem and its impact on the entire family, the person is often treated with a demeaning attitude, is condemned, and is castigated for low self-control.

When people do seek treatment, they often experience vicious self-loathing. They may confront themselves (Miller & Rollnick, 2002) or be confronted by others (Alcoholics Anonymous, 1976). They may accept their guilt and try to make amends for their actions (Steps 7 and 8; Alcoholics Anonymous, 1976). Sometimes they become highly unforgiving of self. They struggle to identify transgressions and forgive themselves for transgressions they inflicted. While this can provide elevation of mood, disappointment with the self and self-loathing often return. Worthington (2003) has argued that forgiveness of self is often insufficient to produce lasting mood elevation because unforgiveness of the self is not the whole problem. Rather, damage occurs to one's self-concept and self-esteem due to admitting that one is *the type of person who could inflict such transgressions.* Self-acceptance and self-forgiveness are needed.

Treatment is time-consuming and drains family resources. That can cause additional transgressions. Treatment requires family behavior patterns to be changed. Some adult spouses resent not being able to have alcohol in the house themselves if the treatment programs recommend complete abstinence for the alcohol dependent person. Some people are advised to engage in different types of therapy, such as adjunctive groups to deal with particular problems not covered in a 12-step group or individual, couple, or family therapy.

Even if a person maintains sobriety for years, many problems might still be evident. The alcohol abuser might not be aware of the pain and suffering that came from his or her drinking and might therefore be unable to make amends because he or she is not aware that amends are necessary. The alcohol-dependent person might be indebted to numerous people who have provided help over the years, but not realize that gratitude is owed.

THE INJUSTICE GAP AFTER TRANSGRESSIONS

Once a person experiences a transgression, the person will also experience an *injustice gap* (Exline et al., 2003; Witvliet et al., 2004; Witvliet et al., 2003). The injustice gap is the difference between what the person would ultimately like to see after the transgression and the current status of affairs. The size of the injustice gap is hypothesized to be directly proportional to the strength of the justice motive, the amount of unforgiveness (Worthington & Scherer, 2004), and the difficulty forgiving (Witvliet et al., 2004; Witvliet et al., 2003), and inversely proportional to the amount of forbearance (McCullough, Fincham, & Tsang, 2003) and the number of previously employed alternatives to forgiveness (Worthington, 2001). The size of this injustice gap is affected by the alcohol-dependent person's behavior. This may include making amends or aggravating the situation.

RUMINATION OVER TRANSGRESSIONS AND THEIR CONSEQUENCES

There is a considerable difference between having to deal with an alcoholic transgressor on a frequent basis versus having dealt with one in the past. For example, a teenage child who is dealing with an alcohol dependent parent in the home must experience the situation daily. An adult who is trying to cope with the memories, problems, and transgressions inflicted during childhood might need only to confront the actual person occasionally, if at all. It is intrusive rumination–angry, fearful, or depressive repetitive and intrusive memories–that keeps the resentment, anger, and bitterness alive. Over time, rumination may transform the anger and fear of daily transgressions into resentment, bitterness, hostility, hatred, seething anger, and fear. This combination is more toxic than mere anger and fear; it becomes unforgiveness (Worthington & Wade, 1999). Berry et al. (2005) have argued that consideration of rumination must involve two dimensions. First, rumination should be measured on its intrusiveness into the person's life (McCullough et al., 2001; McCullough et al., 2003). Second, the type of rumination is important. Rumination can be anxious, fearful, angry, vengeful, depressive, guilty, or shameful (Berry et al., 2005; Berry et al., 2001).

UNFORGIVENESS

The emotion of unforgiveness depends on a number of variables. First, it depends on whether transgressions are ongoing. When interactions are continuous, relationship issues are difficult to resolve through forgiveness. However, when transgressions are continuous but the person is trying to do better, it can speed repair of the relationship. On the other hand, when an alcohol-abusing person has moved away from his or her family, negative interactions with the person cease or are less frequent. This aids healing, but reduces the possibilities for seeking repentance; hence relational mending is harder. There is no easy generalization about whether unforgiveness is more or less if the alcoholic is present or absent from the family.

Second, the person who is dependent on alcohol typically does not inflict a single transgression, but several. More than the stress of any single transgression, the sheer buildup of transgressions affects the way people deal with them. Some have argued that a buildup of daily hassles is as stressful as coping with traumas (Cross, 2003). It is easier to identify a single big trauma, isolate it, and deal with it, than to remember and deal with many smaller transgressions. Unforgiveness can be large in both cases.

Third, people can become pessimistic about the future because they have experienced chronic problems arising from a family member's alcohol dependence or abuse. Hopelessness and powerlessness can be factors in depression and lack of motivation to change and can fuel unforgiving emotions.

UNFORGIVENESS IS STRESSFUL AND CAN HAVE HEALTH CONSEQUENCES

When people think about relationships characterized by transgressions, they experience stress reactions (Berry & Worthington, 2001). Those reactions can lead to health difficulties if the experiences are chronic (Tyrer, 1999). Toussaint et al. (2001) surveyed younger adult, middle adult, and older adult age range in a national probability sample in the United States. Unlike in middle-aged or younger adults, a significant relationship exists between unforgiveness as a disposition and health outcomes for elderly people. The effects of chronic unforgiveness build up over time until they manifest as health symptoms in the elderly.

Unforgiveness and stress are connected (for a review, see Worthington & Scherer, 2004; Worthington, Witvliet, Lerner, & Scherer, 2005). Berry and Worthington (2001) found that baseline cortisol and cortisol reactivity was positively correlated with dispositional measures of unforgiveness–this implicated immune-system functioning with unforgiveness. Witvliet and her colleagues (Witvliet et al., 2002; Witvliet et al., 2001; Witvliet et al., 2004; Witvliet et al., 2003) have demonstrated that merely imagining transgressions or thinking about someone towards whom unforgiveness is directed, produces physiological responses indicating stressfulness (see also Lawler et al., 2003). These researchers have also implicated involvement of the cardiovascular system in health. Altogether the conclusion is inescapable. Damage inflicted during periods of active alcohol abuse can show up much later in spouses and children and affect their health, especially as they age.

COPING WITH THE STRESS OF UNFORGIVENESS

People cope with stress in many ways. Worthington (2001) identified over 20 coping mechanisms people employ to reduce unforgiveness. McCullough (2002) and Worthington and Scherer (2004) conceptualized forgiveness as one (of many) coping mechanism for dealing with injustice and unforgiveness.

Problem-focused coping strategies are targeted at solving the problems perceived to be the source of stress. If people experience injustices due to alcohol abuse or dependence of a family member, they may confront the family member. However, coercion, control, and ostracism can as easily offend a drinker and increase drinking as it can reduce drinking. Otherwise problem-focused coping strategies may also be employed. Decisional forgiveness–deciding to control one's future behavior to release an offender from retribution–can be employed as a problem-focused coping strategy.

Meaning-focused coping strategies are attempts to put an event into perspective. They help a person who has been offended to gain emotional or behavioral equanimity. The decision either to accept an offense and move on with one's life or to decisionally forgive changes the meaning of the offense. This reduces the injustice gap and helps the person derive a sense of meaning-focused coping. People can also use meaning-focused coping to re-narrate the events of the transgression. For example, they might come to understand mitigating factors that led to a family member's harsh confrontation or comprehend that a family member cares enough to confront. Such re-narrations change the meaning of perceived transgressions.

Emotion-focused coping is an attempt to manage one's negative emotions, rather than solve the problem or finding meaning in it. For example, denial and projection are unconscious attempts to control negative emotions associated with admitting having a drinking problem.

We define *emotional forgiveness* as the emotional juxtaposition of positive other-oriented emotions against negative unforgiving emotions (Worthington & Wade, 1999). The positive other-oriented emotions that lead to forgiveness involve empathy, sympathy, compassion, or altruistic or romantic love for the transgressor. If a person can be induced to imagine a transgression and not become overly aroused, but to juxtapose against on that emotion an experience of empathy, sympathy, compassion, or love, then a reduction in the unforgiveness will result. If the experience of the other-oriented positive emotion is strong enough, it can neutralize the unforgiveness and perhaps even completely or partially replace that negative emotion with positive emotion toward the person. Emotional forgiveness, thus, can be conceptualized as an emotion-focused coping strategy (Worthington & Scherer, 2004). This is known as the emotional replacement model of forgiveness. In cases where alcohol dependency occurs within a family, love is mixed with the negative emotions of unforgiveness. Assisting family members to empathize, sympathize, feel compassionate toward, or re-experience love for the affected person can help them forgive that person.

AN EVIDENCE-BASED INTERVENTION TO PROMOTE FORGIVENESS

From the beginning, we wish to acknowledge that an intervention to promote forgiveness is not sufficient in of itself to reduce alcohol consumption or maintain sobriety. Evidence-based treatments are readily available. Alcohol addictions typically result in transgressions against the alcohol-dependent person, family members, and society. Forgiveness therapy alone cannot prevent or cure alcohol abuse, nor can it repair the entire damage antecedent to, coincident with, and subsequent to the alcohol abuse (Worthington, Mazzeo, & Kliewer, 2002). Direct treatment of the problem is necessary. Treatment for alcohol addiction needs to occur within a twelve-step or an alternative evidence-based model (e.g., McCrady & Miller, 1993; Miller & Kurtz, 1994). Forgiveness, which is secondary to the treatment of alcohol addiction or the support of members, can be taught in adjunctive psychoeducational groups.

Hart et al. (2002) have studied people in the United Kingdom who were enrolled in 12-step programs for recovery from alcohol and drug abuse. The participants attended over 200 hours of treatment based on Enright's process model for forgiveness (Enright & Fitzgibbons, 2000). This was compared to a 12-step treatment focusing on the first nine steps and emphasizing spirituality. Of 84 clients, 31 completed the Enright-based groups and 30 completed the 12-step groups. The Enright-based forgiveness approach produced equal reductions in depression and anxiety, relative to the 12-step approach, though the spiritual benefits were not as great. This study illustrates that psychoeducational intervention for promoting forgiveness with recovering addict's benefited recovery. It suggested also that forgiveness psychoeducation might succeed even better if the spiritual were integrated within the intervention (Hart, 1999).

Within Forgiveness Therapy We Must Attend to Many Aspects of Forgiveness

Most forgiveness interventions focus on granting forgiveness for past transgressions. Within families and communities affected by a member's alcohol abuse or dependence, that emphasis will likely be well received. For the alcohol-dependent person, however, more attention will likely be directed toward forgiving the self (Hall & Fincham, 2005) and seeking forgiveness. Steps 8 and 9 in the 12-step program direct a person to make amends for transgressions toward others. Making amends can be understood narrowly as offering restitution for harms done, but it can be more broadly understood as expressing contrition, regret, and sorrow for one's actions, making physical or monetary restitution, and seeking forgiveness. When one seeks forgiveness, the offended person usually feels more forgiving and less demanding of strict justice or reparation (Witvliet et al., 2004).

Worthington and Drinkard (2000) described a six-component method for reconciliation, which used a metaphor of building a bridge to reconciliation. This is the basis of our intervention named Forgiveness and Reconciliation through Experiencing Empathy (FREE). The first plank in the bridge was to decide whether one wants to reconcile and if so, how and when. In Plank 2, people learn to talk about transgressions productively. Participants learn to make reproaches (i.e., requests for explanations for the causes for one's behavior), accounts (i.e., explanations of the cause), and confessions that do not derail conversation. In Plank 3, victims consider decisional forgiveness and express the amount of emotional forgiveness they experienced through employing five steps to REACH forgiveness (see below for a description of the acrostic, REACH). The five steps, thus, are an integral part of FREE. In Plank 4, participants repair relational damage through concrete behavioral actions. In Plank 5, participants plan for relapse into unforgiveness and decide how to recover a forgiving attitude. In Plank 6, people build love back into the relationship.

TEACHING THE FIVE STEPS TO REACH FORGIVENESS

We summarize Worthington's (2003) psychoeducational group intervention derived from the emotional-replacement model. The intervention can be done individually or in a group. Because of the popularity of twelve-step and other groups, group intervention seems most useful. The groups could be used with families or as adjuncts with individuals in therapy.

Pre-Step: Motivational Interviewing

Miller and Rollnick (2002) found that self-confrontation induces a person to talk about the benefits of stopping the drinking and the costs associated with drinking. Motivational interviewing is built on the ambivalence associated with problem drinking. If one can get the person to talk and think about the side of the ambivalence that favors stopping, then the person might decide to stop without being provoked to resist.

Family members not familiar with motivational interviewing often see the alcohol abuse as an injustice that is being inflicted upon the partner or the family. Therefore, the family members might attempt to bring justice into the situation through extracting confessions, restitution, and promises the person will seek and adhere to treatment. Those attempts provoke resistance. If family members, on the other hand, express their *own* failures and ask for forgiveness, the problem drinker can be encouraged to confront himself or herself.

Motivational interviewing can guide people to discover different ways of coping with injustices and unforgiveness. Whereas we have not used motivational interviewing in our protocol, its principles of guided self-discovery are congruent with our approach.

Pre-Step: Define Crucial Terms

When conducting a session that attempts to promote forgiveness, it is necessary to help participants agree on a working definition. Blindly assuming that people understand forgiveness will result in ineffective treatment. Wade, Worthington, and Meyer (2005) have conducted a meta-analysis of the existing intervention studies examining forgiveness. One of the largest effect sizes for any component in the studies was the time spent discussing and agreeing on a working definition of forgiveness. This is true across different therapeutic perspectives.

We try to help participants understand (a) unforgiveness as a negative emotion and forgiveness as (b) a decision, and (c) an emotional change. *Decisional forgiveness* is a statement of behavioral intention not to seek harm to the person and to relieve them of their debt. *Emotional forgiveness* is the experience of forgiveness one has when negative emotions are replaced by positive other-oriented emotions. These definitions are taken as the group's working definitions, and the goal of the group is stated explicitly: to experience emotional forgiveness by experiencing more positive emotions toward the offender. We then help people express decisional forgiveness, hence, foregoing revenge and unhealthy avoidance. We encourage people to focus on the emotional experience of forgiving by generating positive other-oriented emotions in the context of examining and trying to forgive the grudge.

Pre-Step: Declare Decisional Forgiveness

We invite people to indicate the degree to which they wish to forgive the person. We do not try to coerce people into forgiveness, but give them the opportunity to state that they will try to control revenge and avoidance motivations (to the extent that continued interaction is safe).

Step R: Recall the Hurts

We invite people to identify what we call an "index hurt." This index hurt is a symbolic event in their life that can stand for many of the hurts they have experienced at the hands of the person. In families characterized by alcohol dependence, there are often numerous hurts that could be the index hurt. People should select a particular event and write an account of what happened. This event will be referred to, talked about, analyzed, and shared with others. People, therefore, should not select an event that they are unwilling to talk about in front of others.

After group members write the account of the transgression, they talk with a dyadic partner about the index hurt. If they become angry and emotional, we support them; we do not attempt to inhibit negative emotional expression. However, after people have catharted, we suggest that forgiveness involves replacing negative emotions with positive emotions. We observe that when negative emotions are stirred up, it is hard to replace them. So, we ask group members to describe the hurt again to their dyadic partner. This time, they should objectively describe it–without excessively blaming the transgressor or without appealing to their own victimization. People reflect, as a group, on the differences in their experiences when recalling emotionally versus objectively.

Step E:
Empathize (Including Sympathize, Show Compassion, and Experience Love)

Because we define emotional forgiveness as emotional replacement, this is the key step. Forgiveness will not happen quickly. When people use the symbolic index hurt and empathize with the transgressor, they can gradually experience lessened unforgiveness.

We encourage empathy by having each person talk in a dyad about the index hurt as if he or she were the offending person. They write a letter from the offender's viewpoint. They engage in an empty-chair exercise. Each exercise promotes perspective taking and deepens empathy, edging out additional unforgiveness.

After experiences of empathy, group members try to sympathize with the transgressor. Perhaps they can feel sympathy by reflecting on a person's background–exposed to alcohol, and swept into its use until it becomes destructive. Sympathy might further reduce unforgiveness and even begin to yield some positive feelings toward the transgressor.

People then try to experience compassion for the offender. We define compassion as sympathy plus a desire to help the person. We carefully avoid enabling any person to continue in a destructive lifestyle of alcohol abuse. The group discusses practical ways they can be truly helpful in a sympathetic way.

Finally, we talk about how a person can love their transgressor. We solicit ways that they loved this person in the past and encourage them to again act lovingly.

Step A: Altruistic Gift of Forgiveness

Forgiveness can be motivated by self-enhancement or altruism. People might want to forgive because they anticipate benefits to their own physical health (Worthington & Scherer, 2004), mental health (Enright & Fitzgibbons, 2000), relationships (Fincham, 2000), or spiritual or religious health (Rye et al., 2000). Some sense that unforgiveness harms themselves but not the offender. We term these self-enhancement motives (McCullough et al., 1997).

One may also forgive for altruistic motives–to bless a needy offender (McCullough et al., 1997)–or out of humility (Shults & Sandage, 2003).

Hart (1999) has championed a resurgence of a classic view of the 12-step AA model as being based on humility (see also Tiebout, 1944).

We seek to promote an altruistic, humble motive for forgiving through three steps. First, group facilitators induce people to identify, describe, reflect on, and then talk with a dyadic partner and the group about a time when they transgressed and received forgiveness. Second, we elicit descriptions of their emotions when they were forgiven–usually feelings of freedom, lightness, and joy. Third, they consider whether they wish to give that gift to their offender.

Appeal to self-enhancement motives typically boosts forgiveness quickly. Altruistic forgiveness builds slowly and eventually produces deeper emotional forgiveness. If one had less than two hours for a forgiveness intervention, one should stress self-enhancement. If one had two to four hours or more, best outcomes result from altruistic forgiveness (Worthington et al., 2000).

Step C: Commit to the Forgiveness You Experience

It is important to make public some statement of one's emotional forgiveness once it is experienced. That public statement helps the person hold on to forgiveness at a later time. The commitment might be in a form of a written letter, certificate, or simply telling someone that he or she has experienced emotional forgiveness.

Step H: Hold on to Forgiveness in the Face of Doubts

A public commitment reassures the individual that he or she has forgiven when this is in doubt. A typical scenario is a person who works through a lot of deep-seated unforgiveness and after much effort, wins freedom from unforgiveness and blame. Then the person comes face-to-face with the transgressor. That meeting may generate anger and fear as a result of the past. The individual may doubt that he or she has truly forgiven.

This is often because the person has bought into the cultural idea that, if one forgives, then one must necessarily forget. Realistically, a wound is rarely forgotten. One usually still has a conditioned reaction to the painful or angering experience. Understanding this helps people deal with doubts that their experience of emotional experience was genuine.

Post-Step: Relapse Prevention

Inarguably, self-control takes energy and effort. People strengthen self-control by the practice of self-control behavior. Self-control is weakened when people have too many temptations to deal with (Baumeister & Exline, 2000). Programs that aim at preventing relapse, once sobriety is attained, can help people to reduce the number of temptations that they experience and can also help them stay motivated to remain sober (Marlatt & Gordon, 1985).

Dealing with past hurts and offenses can also contribute to effective self-control. Self-righteous justifications for relapsing may be minimized as people forgive old wounds and make relationships with previous transgressors more positive. If family members can forgive, they place less pressure on the person who is alcohol dependent by not continually condemning the person, which is crucial after the person has become sober. A person's resources for self-control are stronger if the person does not continually experience rejection from those who are in a position to give the best support.

In families characterized by alcohol dependence and abuse, the number of transgressions is usually great. It takes little expression of unforgiveness to catapult family members back into familiar patterns of rejection, resentment, and sometimes relapse into drinking. Unforgiveness is seen as an uninvestigated risk factor for relapse. Forgiveness can be a protective factor.

Post-Step: Teach How to Talk About Transgressions

Much relapse into resentment is due to ways family members talk about the past, confront each other about past transgressions, and deal with new transgressions. FREE (which includes the five steps to REACH forgiveness) includes training in making sensitive requests for family members to explain perceived wrongdoing. We highlight do's and don'ts. We encourage frank admission of responsibility for wrongdoing by teaching an eight-step method to confess. We teach people to respond sensitively to confessions, and if time is needed to navigate the five steps to REACH emotional forgiveness, to ask for it.

Reconciliation–rebuilding trust–requires more than deciding to forgive and experiencing emotional forgiveness. It requires requesting forgiveness by wrongdoers and not expecting immediate absolution. It requires apologies and restitution made from a sincere desire to restore the relationship, and not made from mere guilt or duty. Reconciliation also requires the offended party to extend mercy without giving up standards of accountability. Finally, the wrongdoer must be able to accept forgiveness when it is offered.

TIMING OF FORGIVENESS INTERVENTIONS

DiClemente (1999) argued that, "changing addictive behaviors is a dynamic process requiring differential use of multiple processes of change at different points or stages in the cycle of change. Successful outcome results not from doing more, but from doing the right thing at the right time" (p. 101). The question naturally arises, at what points are forgiveness interventions most likely to be successful? The empirical study of forgiveness in alcohol treatment is embryonic. Without any empirical basis, we logically suggest that forgiveness interventions might best succeed with the alcohol dependent person in four places.

First, in the motivational phase, perhaps following motivational interviewing, people might be ready to address transgressions. Our rationale is that many people who are alcohol dependent subvert treatment by blaming family members or people who have wronged them. Forgiving transgressors up-front might make treatment smoother.

Second, forgiveness of self might be addressed during or shortly after detoxification. People often become convinced of their unworthiness and failures as they suffer the vulnerability of detoxification. Expressions of self-loathing are frequent, and people may not benefit from a self-forgiveness treatment until some self-loathing subsides. Success seems more likely when self-image and self-esteem rebound. Assessment of readiness to forgive is crucial.

Third, family members can benefit from forgiveness interventions at any point. However, prior to an alcohol dependent person's entry into treatment, family members often are focused on justice than on forgiveness. We suggest that practitioners promote forgiveness in families when the alcohol-dependent person enters detoxification. This would allow the alcohol-dependent person to re-enter the family with a reduced backlog of condemnation.

Fourth, after staying abstinent for a prolonged period, people might be willing to reconsider transgressions against them from childhood, from pre-treatment, or even post-treatment. Successful abstinence can release people in the battle for self-control. That freed-up energy can be applied to considering the past (Baumeister & Exline, 2000).

CONCLUSION

In the present article, we appeal to the readers' experience with families involving alcohol problems. Since studies of forgiveness have only recently gained acceptance in empirical behavioral science, our experience has not been put to empirical test with adjunctive treatments in an alcoholic family. However, research supports the efficacy of the psychoeducational forgiveness intervention with individuals, couples, and parents.

We have focused on the psychological and social aspects of alcohol dependence and abuse that are related to common experiences of transgressions throughout family systems. We claimed that these could fuel justifications for family members' behaviors and contribute to maintenance and relapse of dependent and abusive behaviors. Thus, they deserve empirical investigation as potential risk factors. We appealed to stress-and-coping theory to understand unforgiveness as an emotion (i.e., Worthington & Wade, 1999), which is contextualized inside of violations of justice (Exline et al., 2003), and emotional forgiveness as emotion-focused coping that juxtaposes positive emotions against negative ones (Worthington & Wade, 1999).

Since it would be impossible to recall all transgressions inflicted by all parties and deal with them, we recommend dealing with the most symbolic transgressions as they come to the psychological or social foreground. We have provided a psychoeducational treatment outline, which employed the FREE and REACH models by Worthington (2003) and Worthington and Drinkard (2000) and is supported by at least nine empirical studies (for a review, see Wade, Worthington, & Meyer, 2005). Forgiveness groups can supplement the more important direct treatment of alcohol dependence and abuse that use model programs or those with Tier 2 or Tier 3 research support. We have put forth a hypothesis regarding recommended protocol; empirical investigation should be conducted to assess the viability of our suggestions.

REFERENCES

Alcoholics Anonymous (1976). New York: Alcoholics Anonymous General Service Office.

Baumeister R. F., & Exline, J. J. (2000). Self-control, morality, and human strength. *Journal of Social and Clinical Psychology, 19,* 29-42.

Berry, J.W., & Worthington, E.L., Jr. (2001). Forgiveness, relationship quality, stress while imagining relationship events, and physical and mental health. *Journal of Counseling Psychology, 48,* 447-455.

Berry, J.W., Worthington, E. L., Jr., O'Connor, L. E., Parrott, L., III, & Wade, N. G. (2005). Forgivingness, vengeful rumination, and affective traits. *Journal of Personality, 73,* 1-43.

Berry, J.W., Worthington, E.L., Jr., Parrott, L., III, O'Connor, L., & Wade, N.G. (2001). Dispositional forgivingness: Development and construct validity of the Transgression Narrative Test of Forgivingness (TNTF). *Personality and Social Psychology Bulletin, 27*, 1277-1290.

Burchard, G.A., Yarhouse, M.A., Kilian, M.K., Worthington, E.L., Jr., Berry, J.W., & Canter, D.E. (2003). A study of two marital enrichment programs and couples' quality of life. *Journal of Psychology and Theology, 31*, 240-252.

Chassin, L., & Ritter, J. (2001). Vulnerability to substance use disorders in childhood and adolescence. In R.E. Ingram & J.M. Price (Eds.), *Vulnerability to psychopathology: Risk across the lifespan* (pp. 107-134). New York: Guilford Press.

Cross, M.R. (2003). The relationship between trauma history, daily hassles, and physical symptoms. *Dissertation Abstracts International, 63*, 4364.

DiClemente, C.C. (1999). Motivation for change: Implications for substance abuse treatment. *Psychological Science, 10*, 209-213.

Enright, R.D., & Fitzgibbons, R.P. (2000). *Helping clients forgive: An empirical guide for resolving anger and restoring hope.* Washington, DC: American Psychological Association.

Exline, J.J., Worthington, E.L., Jr., Hill, P.C., & McCullough, M.E. (2003). Forgiveness and justice: A research agenda for social and personality psychology. *Personality and Social Psychology Review, 7*, 337-348.

Fincham, F.D. (2000). The kiss of the porcupines: From attributing responsibility to forgiving. *Personal Relationships, 7*, 1-23.

Hall, J.H., & Fincham, F.D. (2005). Self-forgiveness: The stepchild of forgiveness research. *Journal of Social and Clinical Psychology, 24*, 621-637.

Hart, K.E. (1999). A spiritual interpretation of the 12-steps of Alcoholics Anonymous: From resentment to forgiveness to love. *Journal of Ministry in Addiction and Recovery, 6*, 25-39.

Hart, K.E., Shapiro, D.A., Gervais, N., Wilkie, H., & Wilson, T. (2002, November). *Facilitating stage two recovery among sober members of Alcoholics Anonymous who harbor grudges: A randomized clinical trial testing two forgiveness interventions.* Poster presentation of the meeting of the Association for the Advancement of Behavior Therapy, Reno, NV.

Heather, N., Rollnick, S., Bell, A., & Richmond, R. (1996). Effects of brief counseling among male heavy drinkers identified on general hospital wards. *Drug and Alcohol Review, 15*, 29-38.

Kiefer, R.P., Worthington, E.L., Jr., Myers, B.J., Kliewer, W.L., Kilgour, J.M., Jr., & Berry, J.W. (2004). *Training parents in forgiving and reconciling.* Unpublished manuscript submitted for publication. Virginia Commonwealth University, Richmond, VA.

Kilpatrick, D.G., Acierno, R., Baunders, B., Resnick, H., Best, C.L., & Schnurr, P.P. (2000). Risk factors for adolescent substance abuse and dependence: Data from a national sample. *Journal of Consulting and Clinical Psychology, 68*, 19-30.

Lawler, K.A., Younger, J.W., Piferi, R.L., Billington, E., Jobe, R., Edmondson, K., & Jones, W.H. (2003). A change of heart: Cardiovascular correlates of forgiveness in response to interpersonal conflict. *Journal of Behavioral Medicine, 26*, 373-393.

Marlatt, G.A., & Gordon, J.R. (1985). *Relapse prevention: Maintenance strategies in the treatment of addictive behaviors.* New York: Guilford Press.

McCrady, B.S., & Miller, W.R. (1993). *Research on Alcoholics Anonymous: Opportunities and alternatives.* New Brunswick, NJ: Rutgers University Press.

McCullough, M.E. (2002). Savoring life, past and present: Explaining what hope and gratitude share in common. *Psychological Inquiry, 13,* 302-304.

McCullough, M. E., Bellah, C. G., Kilpatrick, S. D., & Johnson, J. L. (2001). Vengefulness: Relationships with forgiveness, rumination, well-being, and the Big Five. *Personality and Social Psychology Bulletin, 27,* 601-610.

McCullough, M.E., Fincham, F.D., & Tsang, J-A. (2003). Forgiveness, forbearance, and time: The temporal unfolding of transgression-related interpersonal motivations. *Journal of Personality and Social Psychology, 84,* 540-557.

McCullough, M.E., & Worthington, E.L., Jr. (1995). Promoting forgiveness: A comparison of two psychoeducational group interventions with a waiting-list control. *Counseling and Values, 40,* 55-68.

McCullough, M.E., Worthington, E.L., Jr., & Rachal, K.C. (1997). Interpersonal forgiveness in close relationships. *Journal of Personality and Social Psychology, 75,* 321-326.

Miller, W.R., & Bennett, M.E. (1997). Addictions: Alcohol/drug problems. In D.B. Larson, J.P. Swyers, & M.E. McCullough (Eds.), *Scientific research on spirituality and health: A consensus report* (pp. 68-82). Rockville, MD: National Institute for Healthcare Research.

Miller, W.R., & Kurtz. E. (1994). Models of alcoholism used in treatment: Contrasting AA & other perspectives with which it is often confused. *Journal of Studies on Alcohol, 55,* 159-166.

Miller, W.R., & Rollnick, S. (Eds.). (2002). *Motivational interviewing: Preparing people to change.* New York: Guilford Press.

National Clearinghouse for Alcohol and Drug Information (1996). *National expenditures for mental health, alcohol, and other drug abuse treatment.* [Online]. Available: http://www.health.org/mhaod/spending.htm.

Ripley, J.S., & Worthington, E.L., Jr. (2002). Hope-focused and forgiveness group interventions to promote marital enrichment. *Journal of Counseling and Development, 80,* 452-463.

Rye, M.S., Pargament, K.I., Ali, M.A., Beck, G.L., Dorff, E.N., Hallisey, C., Narayanan, V., & Williams, J.G. (2000). Religious perspectives on forgiveness. In M.E. McCullough, K.I. Pargament, & C.E. Thoresen (Eds.), *Forgiveness: Theory, research and practice* (pp. 17-40). New York: Guilford Press.

Sandage, S.J. (1997). *An ego-humility model of forgiveness: A theory-driven empirical test of group interventions.* Unpublished doctoral dissertation, Virginia Commonwealth University, Richmond, VA.

Sheehan, T., & Owen, P. (1999). The disease model. In B. S. McCrady, & E. E. Epstein (Eds.), *Addictions: A comprehensive guidebook* (pp. 268-286). Oxford, UK: Oxford University Press.

Shults, F.L., & Sandage, S.J. (2003). *The faces of forgiveness: Searching for wholeness and salvation.* Grand Rapids, MI: Baker Book House.

Tiebout, H.A. (1944). Therapeutic mechanisms of Alcoholics Anonymous. *American Journal of Psychiatry, 100*, 468-473.

Toussaint, L.L.,Williams, D.R., Musick, M.A., & Everson, S.A. (2001). Forgiveness and health: Age differences in a U.S. probability sample. *Journal of Adult Development, 8*, 249-257.

Tyrer, P. (1999). Stress diathesis and pharmacological dependence. *Journal of Psychopharmacology, 13*, 294-295.

Wade, N.G., & Worthington, E.L., Jr. (2003). Overcoming interpersonal offenses: Is forgiveness the only way to deal with unforgiveness? *Journal of Counseling and Development, 81*, 343-353.

Wade, N.G., Worthington, E.L., Jr., & Meyer, J.E. (2005). But do they really work? A meta-analysis of group interventions to promote forgiveness. In E.L. Worthington, Jr. (Ed.), *Handbook of forgiveness* (pp. 423-439). New York: Brunner-Routledge.

Windom, C.S., & Hiller-Sturmhofel, S. (2001). Alcohol abuse as a risk factor for and consequence of child abuse. *Alcohol Research and Health, 25*, 52-57.

Witvliet, C. v. O., Ludwig, T.E., & Bauer, D.J. (2002). Please forgive me: Transgressors' emotions and physiology during imagery of seeking forgiveness and victim responses. *Journal of Psychology and Christianity, 21*, 219-233.

Witvliet, C. v. O., Ludwig, T. E., & Vander Laan, K. L. (2001). Granting forgiveness or harboring grudges: Implications for emotion, physiology, and health. *Psychological Science, 12*, 117-123.

Witvliet, C.v.O., Wade, N.G., Worthington, E.L., Jr., & Berry, J.W. (2004). *Effects of apology and restitution on victims' unforgiveness, empathy, forgiveness, and psychophysiology: Words can speak as loudly as actions.* Unpublished manuscript under editorial review, Hope College, Holland, MI.

Witvliet, C.v.O., Worthington, E.L., Jr., Root, L.M., Sato, A.F., Ludwig, T.E., & Exline, J.J. (2003). *Justice, forgiveness, and emotion: A psychophysiological analysis.* Unpublished manuscript under editorial review, Hope College, Holland, MI.

Worthington, E.L., Jr. (2001). Unforgiveness, forgiveness, and reconciliation in societies. In R. G. Helmick & R.L. Petersen (Eds.), *Forgiveness and reconciliation: Religion, public policy, and conflict transformation* (pp. 161-182). Philadelphia: Templeton Foundation Press.

Worthington, E. L., Jr. (2003). *Forgiving and reconciling: Bridges to wholeness and hope.* Downer's Grove, IL: InterVarsity Press.

Worthington, E.L., Jr.,& Drinkard, D.T. (2000). Promoting reconciliation through psychoeducational and therapeutic interventions. *Journal of Marital and Family Therapy, 26*, 93-101.

Worthington, E. L., Jr., Mazzeo, S.E., & Kliewer, W. L. (2002). Addictive and eating disorders, unforgiveness, and forgiveness. *Journal of Psychology and Christianity, 21*, 257-261.

Worthington, E. L., Jr., Sandage, S. J., & Berry, J.W. (2000). Group interventions to promote forgiveness: What researchers and clinicians ought to know. In M.E. McCullough, K.I. Pargament, & C.E. Thoresen (Eds.), *Forgiveness: Theory, research and practice* (pp. 228-253). New York: Guilford Press.

Worthington, E. L., Jr., & Scherer, M. (2004). Forgiveness is an emotion-focused coping strategy that can reduce health risks and promote health resilience: Theory, review, & hypotheses. *Psychology and Health, 19*, 385-405.

Worthington, E. L., Jr., & Wade, N.G. (1999). The psychology of unforgiveness and forgiveness and implications for clinical practice. *Journal of Social and Clinical Psychology, 18*, 385-418.

Worthington, E.L., Jr., Witvliet, C.v.O., Lerner, A.J., & Scherer, M. (2005). Forgiveness in health research and medical practice. *EXPLORE: The Journal of Science and Healing, 1*, 169-176.

Alcohol and Other Drug Problems Among Homeless Veterans: A Life-Course Theory of Forgiveness

Brent B. Benda, PhD
John R. Belcher, MDiv, PhD, LCSW-C

SUMMARY. This study of 310 women and 315 men is one of the first investigations of a theoretical model of alcohol and other drug abuse among homeless veterans. The sample consists of inpatients in a Domiciliary program at Veterans Affairs Medical Center. Using structural equation modeling, it is observed that forgiveness amplifies the inverse relationships of caregiver attachment and spiritual well-being to alcohol and other drug abuse. In contrast, forgiveness reduces the relationships of abuse, distress, and depression to alcohol and other drug abuse.

The treatment implications for homeless veterans are discussed. Spiritual issues and forgiveness are long-neglected topics in treatment programs for substance abusers. *[Article copies available for a fee from The Haworth Document Delivery Service: 1-800-HAWORTH. E-mail address: <docdelivery@haworthpress.com> Website: <http://www.HaworthPress.com> © 2006 by The Haworth Press, Inc. All rights reserved.]*

Brent B. Benda is Professor, School of Social Work, University of Arkansas at Little Rock, Little Rock, AR 72204 (E-mail: BBBENDA@ualr.edu).

John R. Belcher is Professor, School of Social Work, University of Maryland, 525 West Redwood Street, Baltimore, MD 21201 (E-mail: Jbelcher@ssw.umaryland.edu).

Address correspondence to: Dr. Brent B. Benda at the above address.

[Haworth co-indexing entry note]: "Alcohol and Other Drug Problems Among Homeless Veterans: A Life-Course Theory of Forgiveness." Benda, Brent B. and John R. Belcher. Co-published simultaneously in *Alcoholism Treatment Quarterly* (The Haworth Press, Inc.) Vol. 24, No. 1/2, 2006, pp. 147-170; and: *Spirituality and Religiousness and Alcohol/Other Drug Problems: Treatment and Recovery Perspectives* (ed: Brent B. Benda, and Thomas F. McGovern) The Haworth Press, Inc., 2006, pp. 147-170. Single or multiple copies of this article are available for a fee from The Haworth Document Delivery Service [1-800-HAWORTH, 9:00 a.m. - 5:00 p.m. (EST). E-mail address: docdelivery@haworthpress.com].

doi:10.1300/J020v24n01_09

KEYWORDS. Alcohol and other drug abusers, homeless veterans, psychiatric problems, nuisance and felony offenses

The Judeo-Christian religion serves as the embryonic origin of much of contemporary Western culture. Central to this religion is the practice of forgiveness, which is viewed as essential to personal, interpersonal, and societal well-being (George, Larsons, Koeing, & McCullough, 2000; Kendler et al., 2003; Worthington, 1998; Worthington & Wade, 1999). The TANAKH, or Holy Scriptures according to the traditional Hebrew text, emphasize that forgiveness is requisite to, although not synonymous with, reconciliation (1 Samuel 15:22, Hosea. 6:6, Isaiah, 1:18-19, Joel 2:13). The basic message is that violation, without atonement, engenders estrangement. Forgiveness has been defined from different vantage points; for example, Pingleton (1989, 1997) conceptualizes forgiveness as the voluntary letting go of the right to retaliate after injury. Similarly, North (1997) defines forgiveness as the relinquishing of anger and resentment in response to grievance. From a more direct interpersonal perspective, Hargrave (1994) posits that forgiveness is releasing resentment toward an offender, whereas Fitzgibbons (1986) views forgiveness as releasing the perpetrator of injury from deserved potential retaliation. Enright and The Human Development Study Group (1991) postulate that forgiveness requires the person who is violated to develop beneficence and compassion for the violator.

Worthington (1998a, 1998b) has formulated a pyramid model of forgiveness, which involves five sequential steps. In the first step, a person recalls the experience that precipitated ill feelings toward another individual or group of people. The second step involves expressing an empathic understanding of the motives of the offender(s). A third step involves realizing that forgiveness ultimately is an altruistic gift, or an unmerited favor extended to another or others; then, the next step is commitment to forgive. One must make a conscious choice or commitment to forgive rather than hold a grudge or to feel malice toward the offender(s). Finally, since hurts and offenses will inevitably be recalled, a distinction must be made between remembering the painful memory without ill feelings and lack of forgiveness manifested as bitterness and hatred.

Mutually loving and altruistic relationships rely on forgiveness because interpersonal offenses are inherent to humanity. Even the most self-sacrificing among us err due to lack of understanding or insensitivity, lapses into self-absorption, and unintentional slights or affronts. Other offenses are intentional and can be egregious.

Forgiveness is a potential liberating and restoring willful human response to violation (DiBlasio, 1998, 2000); it is requisite to reconciliation and the mitigation of estrangement. Estrangement is a stressful human condition. The psycho-neuroimmunology literature supports that stress is associated with diminished immunity and altered physiological and psychological functioning (Festa & Tuck, 2000; Worthington & Wade, 1999). Forgiveness can be understood as prevention in terms of the potential stresses of interpersonal insults, and health promotion in terms of tension associated with pathophysiology and psychopathology. With a keener awareness of the adverse effects of resentments and hostilities, professionals can embrace the relevance of forgiveness to well-being and health maintenance and appreciate the healing contributions forgiveness can offer psychological and physiological health. Traumatic or persistent interpersonal problems induce stress that leads to physical and psychological disorders (Ellison, Boardman, Williams, & Jackson, 2001).

It is assumed in this study that forgiveness is a potent interpersonal choice that can assuage the stress that accompanies natural ill feelings that emanate from offenses. Therefore, forgiveness offers immense therapeutic potential in ameliorating and remedying interpersonal difficulties and unhealthy psychological states (McCullough, Worthington, & Rachal, 1997; McCullough et al., 1998; McCullough, Exline, & Baumeister, 1998; Worthington & Drinkard, 2000). Often researchers and others who write about forgiveness have conceptualized and operationalized it as the absence of malice or desire for revenge and retaliation (see review, McCullough, Worthington, & Rachal, 1997). In actuality, however, forgiveness is only one way of diminishing or eradicating ill feelings and intentions; indeed, these ill-fated feelings and motivations may also be reduced or managed through exacting revenge, seeking punitive damages, violence, suicidal thoughts, substance abuse and other psychiatric disorders (Molnar, Buka, & Kessler, 2001; Mulder, Beautrais, Joyce, & Fergusson, 1998; Wenzel, Koegel, & Gelberg, 2000).

PRESENT STUDY

The purpose of the present study is to examine a theoretical model of alcohol and other drug abuse among homeless veterans comprised of elements from life-course theory (Elder, 1985, 1998; Sampson & Laub,

1993) and forgiveness (Worthington, 1998c). Actually, the concept and practice of forgiveness is synchronous with the primary tenets of life-course theory. A principal tenet of life-course theory (Elder, 1985; Sampson & Laub, 1993) states that adversities suffered early in life can be ameliorated or eradicated by salubrious experiences later in life. Traditionally, these salubrious experiences have been identified as finding satisfaction in parenthood, marriage, and employment (Benda, 2002; Benda, 2003, 2004, 2005; Benda, Toombs, & Peacock, 2003; Kruttschnitt, Uggen, & Shelton, 2000; Piquero, Brame, Mazerolle, & Haapanen, 2002; Wright, Caspi, Moffitt, & Silva, 2001). A major assumption underlying this study is that forgiveness is one of the most salubrious experiences in the life-course.

Forgiveness should not be confused with denial of victimization or with a Pollyannaish idea that the victim is to ignore the egregious nature of an offense or one's true feelings toward the transgression. To the contrary, the choice to forgive is a decision to release the perpetrator(s) and victim from the oppression of harmful feelings (DiBlasio, 2000; DiBlasio & Benda, 2002; Hargrave, 1994; Pingleton, 1997; Worthington, 1998b). Instead of being tethered to the offender emotionally or spiritually, one is liberated to seek viable reconciliation (Worthington, 1998b). While reconciliation is optimal, it may not be attainable. However, the personal liberation is in the willingness to pursue reconciliation, not in the achievement of it. The tranquility lies in the inner resolve to "give up" one's entitlement to ill will so everyone involved in a natural transgression can be free emotionally and spiritually to pursue self-actualization, unhindered by past mistakes. In other words, there is serenity in knowing that one removed a barrier to others' and one's own development of self-identity (Clinton & Sibcy, 2002). Willingness to forgive is thought to be fostered by close attachments to caregivers and spiritual well-being, both of which promote an empathic identification with others that facilitate forgiveness (McCullough, Worthington, & Rachal, 1997; Worthington & Wade, 1999). Attachment to caregivers (Bowlby, 1980, 1988) and spiritual well-being (Ellison, 1983) are thought to be reciprocal experiences, mutually reinforcing each other, and the primary origins of vital personal assets such as self-efficacy and healthy ego identity (Kirkpatrick & Shaver, 1990).

In contrast, a highly prevalent experience among homeless substance abusers, especially women, that kindles adverse feelings, thoughts, and behaviors is abuse during childhood (Bassuk et al., 1997; Bassuk, Melnick, & Browne, 1998; Benda, 2004, 2005; Koegel, Melamid, & Burnam, 1995; Wenzel et al., 2000). Sexual and physical abuses violate every aspect of humanity, including physical, psychological and spiritual. Early maltreatment fractures the formation of attachment so essential to feelings of security and the healthy development of self-identity (Bowlby, 1980, 1988; Crittenden, 2000; Hanson & Spratt, 2000). A reciprocal relationship is expected to exist between abuse and attachment because it is assumed that maltreatment also results from an unhealthy attachment (Hanson & Spratt, 2000). A plethora of destructive emotions, thoughts and behaviors are associated with early abuses, including, but not limited to, depression, suicidal thoughts and attempts, and stress (Bassuk et al., 1998; Bassuk et al., 1997; Benda, 2001, 2002; Geissler, Bormann, Kwiatkowski, Braucht, & Reichardt, 1995; Horwitz, Widom, McLaughlin, & White, 2001; Link et al., 1995; Zlotnick et al., 2001).

According to life-course theory (Elder, 1985, 1998), there are vitalizing experiences and relationships that can attenuate or eradicate the adversities resulting from early abuse (Cicchetti & Toth, 1995; Ireland, Smith, & Thornberry, 2002). Two ameliorating occurrences typically identified in homeless people lives are closer family ties and friendships and employment (Kashner et al., 2002; Koegel, Sullivan, Burnam, Morton, & Wenzel, 1999; Lam & Rosenheck, 1999; Rosenheck, Bassuk, & Salomon, 1999). It is assumed in this study that another potent attenuating experience is the act of forgiveness (DiBlasio, 2000; Worthington, 1998a, 1998b).

Although forgiveness is a simple act of asking God to forgive us (1 John 1:9), it can be complicated for those who have become encumbered emotionally, cognitively, and spiritually by addictions, psychiatric disorders, and social isolation (Belcher, Scholler-Jaquish, & Drummond, 1991; Belcher, Green, McAlpine, & Ball, 2001). These encumbrances typically induce feelings of hopelessness and despair, and a loss of a sense of meaning and purpose to one's life. Homeless persons who feel despondent and a lack of "social capital," worsen their social isolation and fail to perceive a need for forgiveness or to forgive (Belcher, Zanis, & DeForge, 2003). Social isolation and despondency often are exacerbated by lack of forgiveness and rejection by family and former friends due to a history of pathological interactions. In some instances, homeless people have alienated family and friends with their pathology and incessant demands and other offenses, whereas other individuals are homeless, in part at least, because of others' offenses. Familial relations and friendships can be pathological. Pathology lessens the likelihood of forgiveness being given or received by all, except God (Worthington, 1998a, 1998b).

The theoretical model being proposed is shown in Figure 1. To summarize, the conceptualization is that two diametrically opposing experiences are of preeminent importance to feelings, thoughts and behaviors that are associated with alcohol and drug abuse among homeless veterans. Loving and secure attachments and spiritual well-being are posited to encourage a healthy sense of self-efficacy and ego identity, and to buffer one from adverse feelings such as depression and stress, and destructive thoughts and behaviors such as suicide ideation and substance abuse (Cairns & Cairns, 1994; Carnegie Council on Adolescent Development, 1995). Sexual and physical exploitation in childhood, in contrast, undermines a sense of efficacy and healthy identity, and engender the adverse reactions, such as depression, distress, and relationship problems (Figure 1). The model without forgiveness (Figure 1) is then

FIGURE 1. Model of Alcohol and Drug Abuse Without Forgiveness

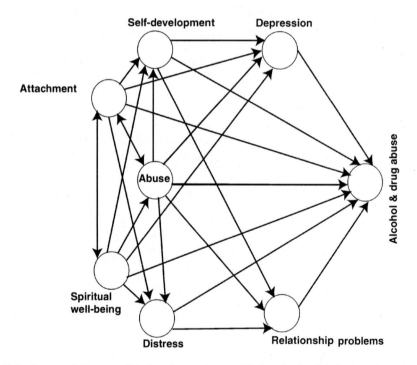

Note: Arrows point from predictor to outcome. Arrows at both ends of path indicate reciprocal relationship.

compared to a model with forgiveness included (Figure 2) to determine if forgiveness adds to the explanation of alcohol and other drug abuse.

METHOD

Samples

Because of their relatively small admission rate, a convenience sample of all homeless female veterans that entered an inpatient Veterans Affairs' (V. A.) program for comorbid substance abuse and other psychiatric disorders over a 3-year period was selected. Only 13 women, or 4 percent, who entered this program declined to participate in the study,

FIGURE 2. Model of Alcohol and Drug Abuse With Forgiveness

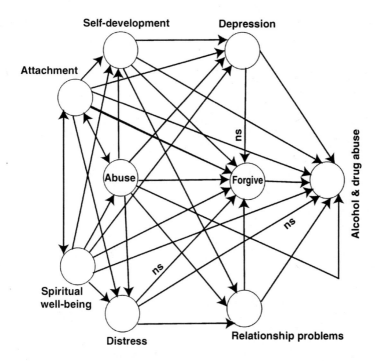

Note: Arrows point from predictor to outcome. Arrows at both ends of path indicate reciprocal relationship. ns is not significant at alpha = 0.05.

leaving 310 women who responded to the survey. A systematic random sample of every 4th homeless male veteran who entered the same program over the same 3-year period was selected to have an equivalent number of men. Of the 330 men approached to participate in the study, 15 veterans declined (4.5 percent). Only persons who had no residence where they could live were classified as homeless. Persons were considered homeless if they had spent at least a week in the 30 days preceding the present admission to the V. A. in unconventional places such as abandoned buildings or houses, cars, tents, or on the streets, a shelter, or hotel or motel room paid for by voucher.

Sociodemographics of the samples were shown in Table 1. Women were more likely to be married, to have children, and to have been sexually and physically abused in the past 2 years before the study interviews than were men. Homeless male veterans were more likely than females to have been in a substance abuse program before the study, to be arrested for a felony in the past 5 years, and to be comorbid with chemical abuse and at least one other psychiatric disorder.

Procedures

The institutional human subjects review board approved the study. Written consent to participate in the study was obtained from all veterans before four social workers conducted two intake interviews: one interview was conducted in the first week after entry in a domiciliary program, and the other interview took place in the second week of that program. All interviewers were professionals that worked in the domiciliary studied, and they received extensive training in the use of the scales shown in Table 2. The inpatient domiciliary program followed a 30-day period on a detoxification unit of the same hospital.

Measures

The Inventory of Parent and Peer Attachment (IPPA) (Armsden & Greenberg, 1987) was used to assess veterans' perceived attachment to their parents during childhood. This instrument consisted of three subscales (3-point Likert scales) measuring parental communication (3 items), trust (3 items), and alienation (4-items). A principal components (PC) analysis (Freund & Wilson, 1998), with varimax rotation, indicated these subscales measured separate factors. These three factors were used as parceled variables measuring the latent construct of *attachment* in model shown in Figure 1. The IPPA has good test-retest reliability

TABLE 1. Characteristics of Veterans in a V. A. Inpatient Program

	Women (n = 310)		Men (n = 315)	
Predictor	Persons	Percent	Persons	Percent
Race				
White	176	56.9	182	57.8
Person of color	96	41.4	133	42.2
Marital status				
Married	161	51.9	91	28.9
Other	149	48.1	224	71.1
Dependent children				
Yes	220	71.0	66	21.0
No	90	29.0	249	79.0
Prior psychiatric hospitalizations*				
Yes	93	30.0	98	31.1
No	217	70.0	217	68.9
Prior substance abuse treatment*				
Yes	99	31.9	163	51.8
No	211	68.1	152	48.2
Childhood Abuse				
Abused sexually	130	41.9	79	25.1
Abused physically	109	35.2	101	32.1

Note: * Psychiatric hospitalizations and drug treatment prior to the current hospitalization in which persons are interviewed.

and predictive validity (Paterson, Pryor, & Field, 1995), and this measure had a Cronbach's (1951) alpha (α) of .88 in the present study (α's for the present study are shown in parentheses in the remaining discussion). PC analyses, with varimax rotation, supported that all of the parceled variables were separated factors that measured latent constructs in

TABLE 2. Means and Standard Deviations (SD) of Age and Measures

	Women		Men	
	Mean	SD	Mean	SD
First interview after entry into domiciliary (first week)				
Age	36.5	8.3	45.9	10.6
Attachment to caregivers	14.2	3.1	12.9	2.9
Ego identity	6.1	1.2	8.1	1.3
Self-efficacy	49.2	5.4	35.1	3.7
Child sexual abuse	15.1	2.7	8.2	2.4
Child physical abuse	40.9	10.1	32.9	9.2
Alcohol abuse	38.7	15.1	49.1	13.9
Drug abuse	39.1	10.8	50.2	11.8
Second interview after entry into domiciliary (second week)				
Spiritual well-being	29.2	8.3	20.3	8.1
Family relations	33.9	9.9	38.7	7.5
Friend relations	44.6	8.3	32.1	9.2
Stress	45.2	7.1	40.6	7.4
Fearfulness	42.7	5.3	37.2	5.6
Depression	46.5	9.3	39.1	3.2

Note: SD is standard deviation

this study. PC analyses included the criteria of an eigenvalue of at least 1, loadings of $> .40$ within factors, and of $< .15$ between factors.

Ellison's (1983) 20-item (6-point scales) Spiritual Well-Being Scale had solid concurrent validity as well. The scale was designed to evaluate spiritual well-being along two dimensions: (1) well-being in relation to God ($\alpha = .87$), and (2) well-being in terms of life purpose and satisfaction ($\alpha = .85$). These dimensions were considered parceled variables that measure the latent construct of *spiritual well-being*. The 12-item (5-point scales) Transgression-Related Interpersonal Motivations (TRIM) Inventory (McCullough et al., 1997; McCullough et al., 1998) was used to measure *forgiveness*. McCullough et al. (1997) have conceptualized forgiveness as the absence of revenge (5 items) and avoidance (7 items), and they offer evidence of construct and discriminant validity (McCullough et al., 1998). The subscales of revenge ($\alpha = .89$) and of avoidance ($\alpha = .90$) were considered two parceled variables.

The Ego Identity Scale (EIS) (Tan, Kendis, Fine, & Porac, 1977) had 12 items that measured Erikson's (1968) concept of ego identity (α = .74). Respondents chose between two responses, with one choice representing ego diffusion. Ego identity was defined as acceptance of self and having a sense of direction. The EIS has strong construct validity (Fischer & Corcoran, 1994). Self-Efficacy Scale (α = .85) (Maddox, Mercandante, Prentice-Dunn, Jacobs, & Rogers, 1982) was measured with 25-items (5-point scales) that have strong concurrent validity (Fischer & Corcoran, 1994). These two factors were considered parceled variables measuring the latent construct of *self-development*.

Five items of the sexual abuse subscale (5-point scales) of the Childhood Trauma Questionnaire was used, which has strong validity as a measure of both child and adult sexual abuse (Bernstein & Fink, 1998) (α = .88). The 12-item (7-point scales) physical abuse subscale from Hudson's (1990) Multi-Problem Screening Inventory (MPSI) was used, which has strong concurrent validity (Hudson & McMurtry, 1997) (α = .86). These two scales were considered parceled variables measuring the latent construct of *abuse*.

The latent construct of *depression* is measured with the 12-item depression subscale and the 11-item suicidal thoughts subscale of Hudson's MPSI. The subscales of the MPSI have solid validity established, and they have alphas of .80 or above in his research (Hudson & McMurtry, 1997) and the present study. These two subscales were considered parceled variables measuring depression. The latent construct of *distress* is measured with the 12-item stress subscale and 12 items from the fearfulness subscale of the MPSI. The PC analysis indicated that 7 of the original 19 items measuring fearfulness did not load above the criterion of > .40. Dropping these 7 items does mean the validity of the fearfulness subscale is not known. The latent construct of *relationship problems* was measured with the 13-item problems with friends and the 13-item problems with family subscales of the MPSI.

Finally, the 15-item alcohol abuse and 10-item drug abuse subscales of the MPSI measured the latent construct of substance abuse, which was the outcome in this study. All subscales of the MPSI have 7-point Likert scales, ranging from "none of the time" to "all of the time."

Data Analysis

The factors shown in Table 2 were examined for multicollinearity, using a correlation matrix, tolerance tests, and the variance in inflation factor (Freund & Wilson, 1998). The analyses, which were not shown owing to space limitations, did not show problems with multicollinearity. Also, skew and kurtosis were not problems, and no variable was missing more than 5 percent of the cases.

The first step in structural equation modeling (Maruyama, 1998) was to examine the fit of the proposed theoretical model, using maximum likelihood estimation (MLE) in LISREL (Joreskog & Sorbom, 1996). The comparative fit index (CFI = .88), adjusted goodness of fit (AGFI = .87), and root mean square of approximation (RMSEA = .08) each indicated a moderate fit of the model shown in Figure 1. These respective fit indices for Model 2, which includes forgiveness, are CFI = .90, ACFI = .91, and RMSEA = .03. These indices indicate that Model 2 is a better fit than Model 1. Both models fit the data, and so the paths between latent constructs, shown in these models, can be tested to see if predictors are significantly related to outcomes.

FINDINGS

The arrows in Figure 1 point to the outcome that is thought to be predicted by the construct from which the path originates. For example, attachment is thought to predict enhanced spiritual well-being, self-development, and forgiveness, and to predict less depression, abuse, distress, relationship problems, and alcohol and other drug abuse. The paths between attachment and spiritual well being, and between attachment and abuse, have arrows at both ends, which signify a reciprocal relationship: that is, attachment is assumed to augment and be augmented by spiritual well being. In similar fashion, dysfunction attachment is thought to be associated with greater abuse, and abuse is assumed to diminish attachment between caregiver and child. The standardized regression coefficients for these relationships are presented in Table 3. As one example, it may be observed in Table 3 that spiritual well being is positively related to attachment, whereas abuse is negatively related to attachment, and these two predictors account for 10 percent (R^2) of variance in attachment. In the row below these findings, we see that attachment also is positively related to spiritual well being, which supports the expectation that there would be a reciprocal relationship between these two constructs. Attachment is inversely related to abuse, so there is a reciprocal relationship between these constructs as well. At the bottom of Table 3, it is seen that all constructs in the study are significantly (alpha = 0.05) related to abuse of alcohol and drugs. In fact, attachment and spiri-

TABLE 3. Summary of Direct and Indirect Relationships for Model in Figure 1

Outcome	Predictor	Direct	Indirect	Total
Attachment	Spiritual well-being	.30**		.30**
(R^2 = .10)	Abuse	−.20**		.20**
Spiritual well-being	Attachment	.32**		.32**
(R^2 = .05)				
Abuse	Attachment	−.44**		−.44**
(R^2 = .12)	Spiritual well-being	−.36**		−.36**
Self-development	Attachment	.25**		.25**
(R^2 = .09)	Spiritual well-being	.28**		.28**
	Abuse	−.17*	−.01	−.18*
Distress	Attachment	−.18*	−.06	−.24**
	Spiritual well-being	−.22**		−.22**
	Abuse	.20*	.00	.20*
Depression	Attachment	−.19*	−.10	−.29**
(R^2 = .13)	Spiritual well-being	−.24**	−.07	−.31**
	Self-development	−.30**		−.30**
	Abuse	.44**	.02	.46**
Alcohol/drug abuse	Attachment	−.21**	−.15*	−.34**
(R^2 = .44)	Spiritual well-being	−.36**	−.17*	−.53**
	Self-development	−.20*	−.11	−.31**
	Abuse	.32**	.16*	.48**
	Distress	.18*	.07	.25**
	Depression	.30**	.13	.43**
	Relation problems	.23**	.10	.33**

Note: R^2 is the amount of variance accounted for by predictors. Standardized path coefficients shown. *P < .05; **P < .01.

tual well-being not only have direct significant inverse relations with alcohol and drug abuse, these two constructs also have significant indirect negative relations with substance abuse as well (i.e., indirect through path to other constructs that are associated with chemical abuse).

The construct of forgiveness is added to the model in Figure 2. Several additional paths are expected to predict forgiveness. The test of the model in Figure 2 is shown in Table 4, and it can be seen that distress (i.e., stress and fearfulness) and depression (i.e., depression and suicidal thoughts) do not significantly predict forgiveness. Attachment, spiritual

TABLE 4. Summary of Direct and Indirect Relationships for Model in Figure 2

Outcome	Predictor	Direct	Indirect	Total
Attachment	Spiritual well-being	.28**		.28**
(R² = .08)	Abuse	−.16*		.16*
Spiritual well-being	Attachment	.36**		.36**
(R² = .06)				
Abuse	Attachment	−.38**		−.38**
(R² = .10)	Spiritual well-being	−.32**		−.36**
Self-development	Attachment	.22**		.22**
(R² = .07)	Spiritual well-being	.27**		.27**
	Abuse	−.14	−.00	.14
Distress	Attachment	−.12	−.04	−.16*
	Spiritual well-being	−.22**		-.22**
	Abuse	.17*	.01	.18*
Depression	Attachment	−.19*	−.10	−.29**
(R² = .13)	Spiritual well-being	−.24**	−.07	−.31**
	Self-development	−.30**		−.30**
	Abuse	.44**	.02	.46**
Forgiveness	Attachment	.30**	.10	.40**
(R² = .24)	Spiritual well-being	.40**	.11	.51**
	Self-development	.22**	.01	.23**
	Abuse	−.26**	−.05	−.31**
	Distress	−.04	−.00	−.04
	Depression	−.10		−.10
	Relation problems	−.22**		−.22**
Alcohol/drug abuse	Attachment	−.24**	−.19*	.43** SC
(R² = .56)	Spiritual well-being	−.34**	−.26**	−.60** SC
	Self-development	−.18*	−.12	−.30**
	Abuse	.12	.02	.14 SC
	Distress	.12	.03	.15 SC
	Depression	.14	.02	.16* SC
	Forgiveness	−.44**		−.44**
	Relation problems	.17*	.08	.24**

Note: R² is the amount of variance accounted for by predictors. Standardized path coefficients shown. SC means adding forgiveness to the model shown in Figure 1 significantly changes or reduces these relationships. *P < .05; **P < .01.

well-being, and self-development (i.e., self-efficacy and ego identity) are strong positive predictors of forgiveness, whereas childhood abuse (i.e., sexual and physical) and relational problems (i.e., family and friends) are negative predictors of this outcome.

The essence of this study, however, are the findings shown at the bottom of Table 4 on predictors of alcohol and drug abuse: indeed, adding forgiveness (model in Figure 2) to the original model (Figure 1) and the associated paths significantly changed (SC in Table 4) several relationships between predictors of alcohol and drug abuse. For instance, the direct relationship between attachment and substance abuse is enhanced from a standardized coefficient of $-.21$ to $-.24$, and the indirect relationship is amplified from $-.15$ to an insignificant $-.19$–the total effect of attachment rises from $-.34$ to $-.43$. The total of the direct and indirect relationships are significant for all predictors of alcohol and drug abuse except for childhood abuse and distress. Self-development is the only predictor where the total effect is not significantly changed by the addition of forgiveness (Figure 2). The model in Figure 2 accounts for 56 percent of the variance in alcohol and drug abuse, which is commensurate with the variance explained by the model in Figure 1.

DISCUSSION

It is the meaning of these rather complicated statistics that is important to alcohol and drug treatment. The findings of this study indicate that adding forgiveness to a theoretical model of alcohol and drug abuse significantly affects the relationships between factors in the model. For example, these findings suggest that including forgiveness (Figure 2) in the original model (Figure 1) amplifies the direct, indirect, and total relationships of caregiver attachment and spiritual well being to alcohol and drug abuse. In contrast, the addition of forgiveness reduces the direct, indirect, and total relationships of abuse, distress, and depression to substance abuse. Indirect relationships are the effects through other constructs; attachment, for instance, is directly related to alcohol and drug abuse, but it is also associated with several other constructs in Figure 2 that are related to this abuse.

Furthermore, introducing forgiveness in the original model diminished the relationships of abuse and distress to insignificance in this study. These findings need to be confirmed in future research. Meanwhile, they suggest that forgiveness is a potent exercise for ameliorating or alleviating painful feelings and memories associated with childhood abuse, and for mitigating present feelings of distress and depression. There is some indication that forgiveness relieves problems with relating to family and friends. The assumption in this study is that some people simply are disposed to be vengeful or avoidant instead of forgiving when they are offended (McCullough et al., 1997, 1998). When people forgive, they relinquish their motivation to seek vengeance and to avoid the offender(s), in favor of motivation to seek viable positive relationships. Conciliatory relations are sought with the offender(s) despite recognition that the offenses are an injustice. However, forgiveness is not tantamount to lack of punishment. In many cases, felonious behavior by a homeless person should be dealt with by the justice system. Forgiveness is conceptualized in this study as a willingness of individuals who are offended to release vengeful feelings and desires to avoid offenders.

In accord with life-course theory, the findings suggest that forgiveness is a salubrious experience in later life that ameliorates adverse feelings such as distress and depression, which may result from insecure caregiver attachments and childhood maltreatment that lead to alcohol and drug abuse. Perhaps alcohol and other drugs are used to anesthetize one to the painful memories of early sexual and physical abuses and the resulting agonizing emotions. However, this sequence of interrelationships must be established in longitudinal research before conclusive statements can be made about the evolution of alcohol and drug abuse among homeless veterans. This study is limited not only in its cross-sectional design, but in retrospective self-reports, which may be affected by current relationships and recall, especially among persons who could have cognitive impairments as a consequence of substance abuse (Hommer, Momenan, Kaiser, & Rawlings, 2001).

The findings of this study suggest that those homeless people who experience victimization in childhood are more likely to have severe substance abuse and other problems as adults. This suggests that there is a sub-set of homeless adults, those who have experienced maladaptive early child hood experiences, who will most likely benefit from intensive interventions designed to address their current social disconnectedness.

Treatment Implications

A thorough discussion of services needed by both men and women who enter the V. A. system lies beyond the scope of this study of a theoretical model of alcohol and drug abuse among homeless veterans. However, some concluding observations are made to add to the dialog concerning specialized services designed specifically to address needs presented by current clientele at V. A. medical centers. Two primary characteristics of the clientele have been overlooked or neglected at many of these centers, and yet both are mounting problems.

First, historically, services at V. A. medical centers have not been specifically designed for women because of the disproportionate number of men and the assumption that the minute number of female veterans seeking services could be accommodated by programs created for men (Fontana, Schwartz, & Rosenheck, 1997). There is research that suggests that substance abuse treatment should be gender specific (Greene, Ball, Belcher, & McAlpine (2003). The orientation of services for veterans toward men is likely a major reason that only one in five eligible women feel comfortable going to a V. A. for any type of assistance (Kressin et al., 1999). It is also the case that many V. A. medical centers do not have services needed by women, or staff does not have an appreciation of all the adversities a significant percentage of women suffer. For example, studies show that a large proportion of homeless women veterans have a long history of victimization, including abuses while in the military and living on the streets, and are more likely than homeless men to be suffering from depression, posttraumatic stress disorder, and suicidal tendencies (Benda, 2004, 2005; Koegel et al., 1995; Lambert, Griffith, Hendrickse, 1996; Salgado, Vogy, King, & King, 2002; Wenzel et al., 2000). Existing services typically do not address the extent of these interrelated problems.

However, the proportion of active-duty military personnel that are women has risen from 2 percent to 15 percent between 1970 and 2000 (Quester & Gilroy, 2002). The ascending number of women that serve in the military, and the rises in costs of alternative care, means that there will be greater demand for V. A. services that are specific to women in upcoming years. Services specifically designed for women are needed at V. A, medical centers, and some existing interventions will require modifications for some women. For example, confrontational techniques often used in 12-step programs (Chappel & DuPont, 1999; Laudet, Magura, Vogel, & Knight, 2000) can be detrimental for women veterans who have recently been abused and are experiencing self-deprecating feelings and suicidal thoughts. Instead, these women would need more empathic and supportive approaches to the 12-step program, and they need to be in groups where other members have had similar experiences and are more advanced in their progression through the steps to share their success for encouragement, support, and informative purposes. There is research suggesting that women and men develop their spirituality differently (Brome, Owens, Allen, & Vevanina, 2000).

Therefore, interventions with women need to take into consideration the different ways women go about developing spirituality.

Another increasing characteristic of homeless male and female substance abusers seen at the V. A. is that they are comorbid with substance abuse and a variety of other psychiatric disorders (see review, Rosenheck et al., 1999). Integrated treatment for comorbid disorders is in an embryonic stage in most V. A. medical centers. What is needed is an administrative restructuring of staff to form teams comprised of diverse specialties, such as psychiatrists, social workers, nurses, alcohol and drug counselors, and occupational therapists. While such teams are being formed in many V. A. medical centers, a more collaborative–rather than hierarchical–decision-making process needs to be implemented to realize the full potential of having a seamless coordination of services. As long as the value of opinions is appraised according to professional status, partial participation will likely characterize the actual functioning of the team. A more democratic style of collaboration, however, must be balanced with particular expertise at times. For example, there are instances when medical or cognitive impairments must remain paramount over all other considerations. An optimal arrangement would seem to be hire a collaboration-minded psychiatrist as the ultimate team leader, with another professional as the onsite leader, who oversees the daily operation of the team. Each team should provide services to assigned clients from the time they enter detoxification into aftercare to have continuity of care longitudinally as well as simultaneously. This structure means the team is comprised of persons who are specialized in detoxification, inpatient treatment, and aftercare services.

Features of this proposed structuring of treatment are already in place in some V. A. medical centers; however, the full implementation seems to be heavily dependent on how willing diverse specialists are to openly share authority, information, and decision-making. Also, professionals must be willing to learn from each other: psychiatrists and drug counselors need an understanding of current employment and housing opportunities, and occupational and housing specialists need to have clear appreciation of the medical and psychiatric problems. The 12-step programs should become more oriented to the complexities on interlocking problems most substance abusers are experiencing (Laudet, Magura, Vogel, & Knight, 2003). This study also indicates that there should be persons on the team that can offer spiritual guidance, especially leaning how to forgive offenses that have occurred. There are specific steps that people can learn in forgiving other persons (Ellison, Boardman, Williams, & Jackson, 2001; DiBlasio, 2000; Worthington, 1998a, 1998b). Despite their origin in religious teachings, Alcoholics Anonymous meetings and the 12-step programs often are only peripherally interested in the spiritual relationship to God that is the essence of the 12 steps. Instead of relating to a personal God who actually responds and loves and forgives, members discuss an abstract higher power that is devoid of intimacy and one-to-one communion. Yet, it is God who is the higher power that desires an intimate relationship with us, and Who can liberate persons from addictions that rob them of spiritual well being (Belcher & Benda, 2005). Moreover, it is important to take into account the individual's view of God and how that view affects their ultimate healing (Belcher, 2003).

In conclusion, a long-standing limitation in all professional schools with which the authors are familiar is the lack of courses that specifically teach knowledge and skills concerning how to treat diverse comorbid problems. There are courses that cover content about the various problems being experienced by homeless veterans, but knowledge and skills are almost ubiquitously taught in a compartmentalized fashion, with no real efforts at integration. Content on alcohol and drug abuse and treatment typically includes only peripheral discussion of accompanying physiological problems. Internships often do offer exposure to interdisciplinary team assessments and meetings. However, teaching and training of the intern almost always remains discipline-specific, and the emphasis is how to work with other disciplines rather than on how to treat comorbidity. Certainly, the carrying out of certain treatments, such as medication, must remain the province of certified professionals. At the same time, a more efficacious treatment can be offered if all team members have an understanding of problems and services needed. In regard to this study, most professionals not only do not teach or practice spiritual guidance and approaches to forgiveness; they are opposed to these treatments (Belcher & Benda, 2005; Hodge, 2002). Very rarely does an interdisciplinary team meeting include a pastor or Chaplin. However, there is mounting evidence that spiritual well being and forgiveness play a major role in attaining freedom from addiction (Ellison et al., 2001; Kendler et al., 2003).

REFERENCES

Armsden, G. C., & Greenberg, M. T. (1987). The inventory of parent and peer attachment: Individual differences and their relationship to psychological well-being in adolescence. *Journal of Youth and Adolescence, 16,* 427-454.

Bassuk, E. L., Buckner, J. C., Weinreb, L. F., Browne, A., Bassuk, S. S., Dawson, R., & Perloff, J. N. (1997). Homelessness in female-headed families: Childhood and adult risk and protective factors. *American Journal of Public Health, 87,* 249-255.

Bassuk, E. L., Melnick, S., & Browne, A. (1998). Responding to the needs of low-income and homeless women who are survivors of family violence. *Journal of the American Medical Women's Association, 53,* 57-64.

Belcher, J. R. (2003). Helping the homeless: Where is the Holy Spirit? *Pastoral Psychology, 51,* 179-188.

Belcher, J. R., & Benda, B. B. (2005). Issues of divine healing in psychotherapy: Opening a dialog. *Journal of Religion & Spiritualilty in Social Work,* 24, 21-38.

Belcher, J.R., Greene, J., McAlpine, C., & Ball, K. (2001) Considering pathways into homelessness: Mothers, addictions and trauma. *Journal of Addictions Nursing, 13,* 199-208.

Belcher, J.R., Scholler-Jaquish, A., & Drummond, M. (1991). Three states of homelessness: A conceptual model for social workers in health care. *Health and Social Work, 6,* 87-93.

Benda, B. B. (2001). Predictors of rehospitalization of military veterans who abuse. substances. *Social Work Research, 25,* 199-212.

Benda, B. B. (2002a). Factors associated with rehospitalization among veterans in a substance abuse treatment program. *Psychiatric Services, 53,* 1176-1178.

Benda, B. B. (2002b). Test of a structural equation model of comorbidity among homeless and domiciled military veterans. *Journal of Social Service Research, 29,* 1-35.

Benda, B. B. (2003). Survival analysis of criminal recidivism of boot camp graduates using elements from general and developmental explanatory models. *International Journal of Offender Therapy and Comparative Criminology, 47,* 89-101.

Benda, B. B. (2004). Gender differences in the rehospitalization of substance abusers among homeless military veterans. *Journal of Drug Issues, 34,* 723-750.

Benda, B. B. (2005). Discriminators of suicide thoughts and attempts among homeless veterans who abuse substances. *Suicide & Life-Threatening Behavior, 35,* 106-116.

Benda, B. B., Toombs, N. J., & Peacock, M. (2003). An examination of competing theories in predicting recidivism of adult offenders five years after graduation from boot camp. *Journal of Offender Rehabilitation, 37,* 43-75.

Bernstein, D. P., & Fink, L. (1998). *Childhood Trauma Questionnaire: A retrospective self-report questionnaire and manual.* San Antonio, TX: The Psychological Corporation.

Bowlby, J. (1980). *Attachment and loss. Vol 3: Loss, sadness and depression.* New York: Basic Books.

Bowlby J. (1988). Developmental psychiatry comes of age. *American Journal of Psychiatry, 145,* 1-10.

Brome, D.R., Owens, M.D., Allen, K., & Vevanina, T. (2000). An examination of spirituality among African-American women in recovery from substance abuse. *Journal of Black Psychology, 26,* 470-486.

Cairns, R. B., & Cairns, B. D. (1994). *Lifelines and risks: Pathways of youth in our time.* New York: Cambridge University Press.

Carnegie Council on Adolescent Development (1995). *Great transitions: Preparing adolescents for a new century.* New York, Carnegie Corporation.

Chappel, J., & DuPont, R. (1999). Twelve-step and mutual-help programs for addictive disorders. *Addictive Disorders, 22,* 425-446.

Cicchetti, D., & Toth, S. L. (1995). A developmental psychopathology perspective on child abuse and neglect. *Journal of the American Academy of Child & Adolescent Psychiatry, 34,* 541-564.

Clinton, T., & Sibcy, G. (2002). Attachments: Why you love, feel, and act the way you do. Brentwood, TN: Integrity Publishers.

Crittenden, P.M. (2000). A dynamic-maturational approach to continuity and change in patterns of attachment. In P. M. Crittenden & A. H. Clausson (Eds.), *The organization of attachment relationships: Maturation, culture and context* (pp. 343-357). New York: Cambridge University Press.

Cronbach, L. J. (1951). Coefficient alpha and internal structure of tests. *Psychometrica, 16,* 297-334.

DiBlasio, F. A. (1998). The use of a decision-based forgiveness intervention within intergenerational family therapy. *Journal of Family Therapy, 20,* 77-94.

DiBlasio, F.A. (2000). Decision-based forgiveness treatment in cases of marital infidelity. *Psychotherapy, 37,* 149-158.

DiBlasio, F. A., & Benda, B. B. (2002). The effect of forgiveness treatment on self-esteem of spouses: Initial experimental results. *Marriage and Family: A Christian Journal, 5,* 511-524.

Elder, G. H. Jr. (Ed.) (1985). *Life course dynamic: Transitions and trajectories.* Ithaca, NY: Cornell University Press.

Elder, G. H. Jr. (1998). The life course as developmental theory. *Child Development, 69*(1), 1-12.

Ellison, C. W. (1983). Spiritual well-being: Conceptualization and measurement. *Journal of Psychology and Theology, 11,* 330-340.

Ellison, C. G., Boardman, J. D., Williams. D. R., & Jackson, J. S. (2001). Religious involvement, stress, and mental health: Findings from the 1995 Detroit area study. *Social Forces, 60,* 215-249.

Enright, R. D., & The Human Development Study Group (1991). The moral development of forgiveness. In: Kurtines W, Gewirtz J, (Eds.), *Moral behavior and development, Vol. 1,* (pp. 123-152.). Hillsdale, NJ: Erlbaum.

Erikson, E. (1968). *Identity: Youth and crisis.* New York: Norton.

Festa, L. M., & Tuck, I. (2000). A review of forgiveness literature with implications for nursing practice. *Holistic Nursing Practice, 14,* 77-86.

Fischer J., & Corcoran, K. (1994). *Measures for clinical practice: A sourcebook* (2nd ed.) (Vol. 2). New York: Free Press.

Fontana, A., Schwartz, L. S., & Rosenheck, R. (1997). Posttraumatic stress disorder among female Vietnam veterans: A causal model of etiology. *American Journal of Public Health, 87,* 169-175.

Freund, R. J., & Wilson, W. J. (1998). *Regression analysis: Statistical modeling of a response variable.* New York: Academic Press.

Geissler, L. J., Bormann, C. A., Kwiatkowski, C. F., Braucht, G. N., & Reichardt, C. S. (1995). Women, homelessness, and substance abuse: Moving beyond the stereotypes. *Psychology of Women Quarterly, 19,* 65-83.

George, L. K., Larsons, D. B., Koeing H. G., & McCullough, M. E. (2000). Spirituality and health: What we know, what we need to know. *Journal of Social and Clinical Psychology, 19,* 102-116.

Greene, J., Ball, K., Belcher, J., & McAlpine, C. (2003). Addictions, homelessness, spirituality: A women's health issue. *Journal of Social Work Practice in Addictions, 3*, 39-56.

Hanson, R. F., & Spratt, E. G. (2000). Reactive attachment disorder: What we know about the disorder and implications for treatment. *Child Maltreatment, 5*, 137-145.

Hargrave, T. D. (1994). *Families and forgiveness: Healing wounds in the intergenerational family.* New York: Brunner/Mazel.

Hodge, D. R. (2002). Does social work oppress Evangelical Christians? A "new class" analysis of society and social work. *Social Work, 47*, 401-414.

Hommer, D. W., Momenan, R., Kaiser, E., Rawlings, R. R. (2001). Evidence for a gender-related effect of alcoholism on brain volumes. *American Journal of Psychiatry, 158*, 198-603.

Horwitz, A. V., Widom, C. S., McLaughlin, J., & White, H. R. (2001). The impact of childhood abuse and neglect on adult mental health: A prospective study. *Journal of Health and Social Behavior, 42*, 184-201.

Hudson, W.W. (1990). *The MPSI technical manual.* Tempe, AZ: Walmer Publishing Company.

Hudson, W. W., & McMurtry, S. L (1997). Comprehensive assessment in social work practice: The Multi-Problem Screening Inventory. *Research on Social Work Practice, 7*, 79-98.

Ireland, T. O., Smith, C. A., & Thornberry, T. P. (2002). Developmental issues in the impact of child maltreatment on later delinquency and drug use. *Criminology, 40*, 359-399.

Joreskog, K. G., & D. Sorbom. (1996). *LISREL 8: A guide to the program and applications* (3rd ed). Chicago, IL: SPSS Inc.

Kashner, T. M., Rosenheck, R., Campinell, A. B., Suris, A. et al. (2002). Impact of work therapy on health status among homeless, substance-dependent veterans: A randomized controlled trial. *Archives of General Psychiatry, 59*, 938-944.

Kendler, K. S., Liu, Z., Gardner, C. O., McCullough, M. E. et al., (2003). Dimensions of religiosity and their relationship to lifetime psychiatric and substance use disorders. *American Journal of Psychiatry, 160*, 496-504.

Kirkpatrick, L. A., & Shaver, P. R. (1990). Attachment theory and religion: Childhood attachments, religious beliefs, and conversion. *Journal for the Scientific Study of Religion, 29*, 315-334.

Koegel, P., Melamid, E., & Burnam, M. A. (1995). Childhood risk factors for homelessness among homeless adults. *American Journal of Public Health, 85*, 1642-1651.

Koegel, P., Sullivan, G., Burnam, A., Morton, S., & Wenzel, S. (1999). Utilization of mental health and substance abuse services among homeless adults in Los Angeles. *Medical Care, 37*, 306-317.

Kressin, N. R., Skinner, K., Sullivan, L., Miller, D. R., Frayne, S., Kazis, L. et al. (1999). Patient satisfaction with Department of Veterans Affairs health care: Do women differ from men? *Military Medicine, 164*, 283-288.

Kruttschnitt, C., Uggen, C., & Shelton, K. (2000). Predictors of desistance among sex offenders: The interaction of formal and informal social controls. *Justice Quarterly, 17*, 61-88.

Lam, J. A., & Rosenheck, R. A. (1999). Social support and service use among homeless persons with serious mental illness. *The International Journal of Social Psychiatry, 45*, 13-28.

Lambert M.T., Griffith J.M., Hendrickse W. (1996). Characteristics of patients with substance abuse diagnoses on a general psychiatry unit in a VA medical center. *Psychiatric Services, 47*:1104-1107.

Laudet, A. B., Magura, S.,Vogel, H. S., & Knight, E. (2000). Addictions services: Support, mutual aid and recovery from dual diagnosis. *Community Mental Health Journal, 36*, 457-476.

Laudet, A. B., Magura, S.,Vogel, H. S., & Knight, E. (2003). Participation in 12-step-based fellowships among dually-diagnosed persons. *Alcoholism Treatment Quarterly, 21*, 19-40.

Link, B., Phelan, J., Bresnahan, M., Stueve, A., Moore, R., & Susser, E. (1995). Lifetime and five-year prevalence of homelessness in the United States: New evidence on an old debate. *American Journal of Orthopsychiatry, 65*, 347-354.

Maddox, S. M., Mercandante, J. E., Prentice-Dunn, S., Jacobs, B., & Rogers, R. W. (1982). The self-efficacy scale: Construction and validation, *Psychological Reports, 51*, 663-671.

Maruyama, G. M. (1998). *Basics of structural equation modeling.* Thousand Oaks, CA: Sage.

McCullough, M. E., Worthington, E. L. Jr., & Rachal, K. C. (1997). Interpersonal forgiving in close relationships. *Journal of Personality and Social Psychology, 73*, 321-336.

McCullough, M. E., Rachal, K. C., Sandage, S. J., Worthington, E. L., Jr., Brown, S. W., & Hight, T. L. (1998). Interpersonal forgiving in close relationships.Theoretical elaboration and measurement. *Journal of Personality and Social Psychology, 75*, 1586-1603.

McCullough, M. E., Exline, J. J., & Baumeister, R. E (1998). An annotated bibliography of research on forgiveness and related concepts. In E. L. Worthington, Jr. (Ed.), *Dimensions of forgiveness: Psychological research and theological perspectives* (pp. 193-318). Philadelphia: Templeton Foundation.

Molnar, B. E., Buka, S. L., & Kessler, R. C. (2001). Child sexual abuse and subsequent psychopathology: Results from the National Comorbidity Survey. *American Journal of Public Health, 91*(2), 753-760.

Moos, R. H., Moos, B. S., & Andrassy, J. M. (1999). Outcomes of four treatment approaches in community residential programs for patients with substance use disorders. *Psychiatric Services, 50*, 1577-1583.

North, J. (1997). Wrongdoing and forgiveness. *Philosophy, 61*, 499-508.

Mulder, R. T., Beautrais, A. L., Joyce, P. R., & Fergusson, D. M. (1998). Relationship between dissociation, childhood sexual abuse, childhood physical abuse, and mental illness in a general population sample. *American Journal of Psychiatry, 155*, 806-811.

Paterson, J., Pryor, J., & Field, J. (1995). Adolescent attachment to parents and friends in relation to aspects of self-esteem. *Journal of Youth and Adolescent, 24*, 365-376.

Piquero, A. R., Brame, R., Mazerolle, P., & Haapanen, R. (2002). Crime in emerging adulthood, *Criminology, 40*, 137-169.

Pingleton, J. P. (1989). The role of forgiveness in the psychotherapeutic process. *Journal of Psychology and Theology, 17,* 27-35.

Pingleton, J. P. (1997). Why we don't forgive: A Biblical and object relations theoretical model for understanding failures in the forgiveness process. *Journal of Psychology and Theology, 25,* 403-413.

Quester, A. O., & Gilroy, C. L. (2002). Women and minorities in America's volunteer military. *Contemporary Economic Policy, 20,* 111-121.

Rosenheck, R., Bassuk, E., & Salomon, A. (1999). Special populations of homeless Americans. Retrieved June 2, 2003, http://aspe.hhs.gov/progsys/homeless/symposium/2-Spclpop.htm

Sampson, R. J., & Laub, J. H. (1993). *Crime in the making: Pathways and turning points through life.* Cambridge, MA: Harvard University Press.

Salgado, D. M., Vogy, D. S., King, L. A., & King, D. W. (2002). Gender awareness inventory-VA: A measure of ideology, sensitivity, and knowledge related to women veteran's health care. *Sex Role, 46,* 247-262.

Tan, A. L., Kendis, R. J., Fine, J. T., & Porac, J. (1977). A Short Measure of Eriksonian Ego Identity. *Journal of Personality Assessment, 41,* 279-284.

Wenzel, S. L., Koegel, P., & Gelberg, L. (2000). Antecedents of physical and sexual victimization among homeless women: A comparison to homeless men. *American Journal of Community Psychology, 28,* 367-390.

Widom, C. S. (1999a). Posttraumatic stress disorder in abused and neglected children grown up. *American Journal of Psychiatry, 156*(3), 1223-1229.

Widom, C. S. (1999b). Childhood victimization and the development of personality disorders: Commentary. *Archives of General Psychiatry, 56*(2), 607-608.

Widom, C. S. (2001). Alcohol abuse as risk factor for and consequence of child abuse. *Alcohol Research and Health, 25*(1), 52-58.

Worthington, E. L., Jr. (1998a) An empathy-humility-commitment model of forgiveness applied with family dyads. *Journal of Family Therapy, 20,* 59-76.

Worthington, E. L., Jr. (1998b). The Pyramid Model of Forgiveness: Some interdisciplinary speculations about unforgiveness and the promotion of forgiveness. In E. L. Worthington, Jr. (Ed.), *Dimensions of forgiveness: Psychological research and theological perspectives* (pp. 107-137). Philadelphia: Templeton Foundation.

Worthington, E. L., Jr. (Ed.) (1998c). *Dimensions of forgiveness: Psychological research and theological perspectives.* Philadelphia: Templeton Foundation.

Worthington, E. R., Jr., & Drinkard, D. T. (2000). Therapeutic interventions. *Journal of Marital and Family Therapy, 26,* 93-101.

Worthington, E. L., Jr., & Wade, N. G. (1999). The social psychology of unforgiveness and forgiveness and implications for clinical practice. *Journal of Social and Clinical Psychology, 18,* 385-418.

Wright, B. R. E., Caspi, A., Moffitt, T. E., & Silva, P. A. (2001). The effects of social ties on crime vary by criminal propensity: A life-course model of interdependence. *Criminology, 39,* 321-351.

Zlotnick, C., Zimmerman, M., Wolfsdorf, B. A., & Mattia, J. I. (2001). Gender differences in patients with posttraumatic stress disorder in a general psychiatric practice. *The American Journal of Psychiatry, 158,* 1923-1925.

Alcohol Abuse in Marriage and Family Contexts: Relational Pathways to Recovery ·

Jennifer S. Ripley, PhD
April Cunion, MA
Nicole Noble, MA

SUMMARY. Alcohol problems have pervasive effects on family functioning, with negative effects on the marriage relationship and children. In addition, family members and family relationships have a powerful positive or negative effect on treatment. This article provides a model for understanding the relationship between alcohol abusers' traits and situations, at-risk behaviors which include alcohol abuse, and family functioning. The most promising family-oriented treatments are then described with an emphasis on the empirical support for these treatments. *[Article copies available for a fee from The Haworth Document Delivery Service: 1-800-HAWORTH. E-mail address: <docdelivery@haworthpress.com> Website: <http://www.HaworthPress.com> © 2006 by The Haworth Press, Inc. All rights reserved.]*

Jennifer S. Ripley is Associate Professor of Psychology, Regent University, School of Psychology and Counseling, 1000 Regent Drive, Virginia Beach, VA 23464-9956 (E-mail: jennrip@regent.edu).

April Cunion and Nicole Noble are doctoral candidates, Regent University's Clinical Psychology program (APA-accredited), Virginia Beach, VA 23464.

Address correspondence to: Jennifer S. Ripley at the above address.

The authors wish to thank Mark Blagen, PhD, for his comments and suggestions on this article.

[Haworth co-indexing entry note]: "Alcohol Abuse in Marriage and Family Contexts: Relational Pathways to Recovery." Ripley, Jennifer S., April Cunion, and Nicole Noble. Co-published simultaneously in *Alcoholism Treatment Quarterly* (The Haworth Press, Inc.) Vol. 24, No. 1/2, 2006, pp. 171-184; and: *Spirituality and Religiousness and Alcohol/Other Drug Problems: Treatment and Recovery Perspectives* (ed: Brent B. Benda, and Thomas F. McGovern) The Haworth Press, Inc., 2006, pp. 171-184. Single or multiple copies of this article are available for a fee from The Haworth Document Delivery Service [1-800-HAWORTH, 9:00 a.m. - 5:00 p.m. (EST). E-mail address: docdelivery@haworthpress.com].

KEYWORDS. Alcohol problems, marriage, alcohol and other drug treatment, couples and family therapy

The detrimental effects of alcohol problems on the marital and family unit have been documented in multiple sources (e.g., see McCrady & Epstein, 1995; Epstein & McCrady, 2002). In fact, familial functioning is so essential that a clinical diagnosis of alcohol abuse can be assigned to an individual who consumes enough alcohol to disrupt major role obligations in the home (APA, 1994). The effects of alcohol problems on family functioning have been a focus in both family therapy (Edwards & Steinglass, 1995) and alcohol and other drug treatment (Lewis & Allen-Byrd, 2001). There have been significant gains in the treatment of alcohol problems through family and marital therapy in the last decade (Liddle & Dakof, 2002); some of the most promising treatment options will be described in this article.

There are many correlates associated with alcohol problems and family functioning, with limited information about "causes." Alcohol abuse can lead to impairments, such as reduced inhibitions, legal problems, and various risky behaviors which then cause family problems. Alternatively, dispositional factors can encourage alcohol abuse and family problems simultaneously. Family problems or dysfunction can feed backwards into this model with increased use of alcohol in reaction to family problems, or be supportive or disruptive of commitments to treatment and abstinence.

ALCOHOL ABUSING FAMILY FUNCTIONING

Alcohol and the couple. The literature linking alcohol abuse and couples problems is well-defined. Common couples problems identified by alcohol abusing populations include reports of greater dyadic disagreements and disputes (Epstein & McCrady, 2002; O'Farrell, Murphy, Neavins, & Van Hutton, 2000), greater avoidance of effective communication strategies, and less effort towards working cooperatively than those strategies evidenced by non-alcohol abusing couples (McCrady & Epstein, 1995). In addition, alcohol abusing men tend to note dissatisfying sexual relationships as presenting concerns, typically citing more disagreements about sexual relations than non-alcohol abusing counterparts (Epstein & McCrady, 2002). Alcohol abusing couples tend to exhibit significantly greater levels of physical and verbal violence. In some cases, alcohol abusing couples reported partner assault and violence rates five to seven times greater than non-alcoholic, demographically-matched controls (O'Farrell, Murphy, Neavins, & Van Hutton, 2000).

Clearly, empirical research has documented the detrimental effects of alcohol abuse on the marital unit. Research trends provide some support for the embedded negative effects of alcohol abuse on the spouses of alcoholic mates and on the family functioning of children of alcoholics. Spouses of alcoholic mates often report elevated levels of psychological distress and health problems when compared to normative populations. For instance, Moos and Moos (1984) reported trends wherein wives of alcoholic mates reported heightened levels of depression, anxiety, and psychosomatic complaints when compared to those reports provided by the general population.

Marital relationships can be a catalyst towards retaining or disrupting commitments to abstinence. Among alcohol abusing populations, marital problems have been cited as a leading cause of relapse (Epstein & McCrady, 2002). Conversely, marital and family problems, accompanied with successful problem resolution, have also been reported to increase the alcoholic family member's chances of resuming abstinence following relapse (Maisto, McKay, & O'Farrell, 1995). These findings together highlight the importance of considering the intimate relationship in the treatment of alcohol abuse in order to facilitate long-term abstinence.

Alcohol abuse and children. The level of functioning of alcoholic parents affect the development of children within the home. Much clinical attention has been given to the functioning of adult children of alcoholics (e.g., see Ohannessian & Hesselbrock, 2004; Campbell, Masters, & Johnson, 1998), and empirical investigations document the daily effects of parental alcohol abuse on developing children, resulting in higher risks for psychological, behavioral, relational, and academic difficulties (Moos & Moos, 1984).

A PROPOSED MODEL OF ALCOHOL ABUSE AND COUPLE/FAMILY FUNCTIONING

In response to this issue, we propose a model for couple and/or family functioning and alcohol abuse.[1] This model has bio-psycho-social components as well as person-situation contributions to problems taken into consideration. Problems addressed in treatment may primarily be alcohol or may primarily be relational, depending on the role of the therapy and the severity of each problem. It is empirically untested at this time but would be ripe for direct tests. Figure 1 is a display of the model. There are causal and bi-directional influences of each of the clusters of factors, which themselves represent a large number of variables. Dispositional trait factors are those factors that individuals possess, such as health, personality factors, and demographic variables. Situational factors are those variables that are outside of individuals such as economic opportunity, societal attitudes towards alcohol and the family, arousal, or environmental cues for alcohol abuse or family violence.

Trait-based correlates. There are a number of trait-based family-related correlates with alcohol abuse that are important to understand before looking specifically at the effects of alcohol abuse on the family and treatments of alcohol abuse. These correlates are difficult to disentangle from alcohol abuse in their effects on the couple and family relationships. For example, the personality traits of impulsivity and sensation-seeking correlate with alcohol abuse. These constructs also have unique detrimental effects on family relationships (Newcomb & Earleywine, 1996; Wills, Vaccaro, & McNamara, 1994). The biologically-based traits of cognitive deficits and resultant impaired judgment correlate with both alcohol abuse (Yohman & Parsons, 1987) and marital problems. Some at-risk traits are amenable to therapy, such as psychopathology (Pan, Neidig, & O'Leary, 1994) and social skills (Holtzworth-Munroe, 2000); others are not, such as cognitive deficits, or age (Pan et al., 1994).

FIGURE 1. Proposed causal model for alcohol abuse and marital or family dysfunction.

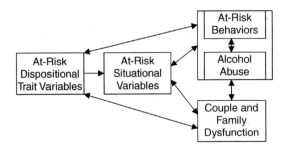

Situation-based correlates. In addition to the traits that individuals possess, specific situations put couples and family at-risk for both alcohol abuse and family dysfunction. Situations related to poverty or lack of opportunity (McLaughlin, Leonard, & Senchak, 1992), social attitudes such as gender inequity (Goodrich, 1991), or general emotional arousal (Zillmann, 1989) all create situations that are endemic towards both alcohol abuse and couple and family dysfunction.

The role of alcohol abuse. Alcohol abuse can have a feedback-type effect by exacerbating situational variables such as difficulty maintaining employment. Alcohol abuse, particularly chronic alcohol abuse or alcohol dependence, can create additional at-risk dispositional variables such as poor physical health.

Alcohol abuse as a sub-type of at-risk behaviors. Various risky behaviors, promoted by substance use, can lead to unhealthy family functioning such as affairs (Curtain, Patrick, Lang, Cacioppo, & Birnaumer, 2001), unplanned pregnancies which can lead to difficult marriages (Dozier & Barnes, 1997), and violence and social deviance (Simon, Sussman, Dent, Burton, & Flay, 1995). Therefore, alcohol abuse must be understood as a particular type of risky behavior, with a probable interaction between alcohol abuse and other at-risk behaviors.

COUPLES AND FAMILY TREATMENTS
FOR ALCOHOL ABUSE:
TRANS-THEORETICAL FACTORS

Treatment interventions for alcohol abusing couples have been conceptualized from multiple viewpoints, with the most pertinent clinical debate focusing on the dichotomous benefits of individual treatment for an alcoholic mate versus couple or family treatment for the entire family system (Epstein & McCrady, 2002). This debate is complex, with some experimental designs documenting the superiority of family therapy in achieving sobriety (e.g., Edwards & Steinglass, 1995), and some designs detailing no significant differences between treatment modalities (e.g., Longabaugh, Beattie, Noel, Stout, & Malloy, 1993).

Level of family involvement. Treatment entitled "family" or "couples" treatment can vary in the involvement level of non-abusing family members. Some situations warrant separate treatment such as the additional presence of intimate partner violence (Holtzworth-Munroe, Meehan, Rehman, & Marshall, 2002) or Antisocial Personality Disorder (Longabaugh, Rubin, Malloy, Beattie, Clifford, & Noel, 1994); in other contexts, systemic theorists typically support the use of couple and family interventions as the first approach to treatment with alcoholic populations.

Treating relationship as a causal factor. Marital relationships can be a catalyst towards retaining or disrupting commitments to abstinence, thus creating the feedback loop from couples' dysfunction to alcohol abuse. Among alcohol abusing populations, marital problems have been cited as a leading cause of relapse (Epstein & McCrady, 2002). Conversely, marital and family problems, accompanied with successful problem resolution, have also been reported to increase the alcoholic family member's chances of resuming abstinence following relapse (Maisto, McKay, & O'Farrell, 1995). These findings together highlight the importance of the marital relationship in facilitating long-term gains towards remaining abstinent.

In a meta-analysis of family approaches to alcohol abuse treatment, three factors–gender (with female alcoholics reporting greater effectiveness of couple/family interventions), investment in the relationship, and perceived support from one's spouse–mediated the effects of treatment in maintaining abstinent gains (Edwards & Steinglass, 1995). In addition, general research highlights the importance of family interventions at the initial stage of the recovery process, regardless of the selected treatment modality or intervention approach (Edwards & Steinglass, 1995). Lastly, willingness to confront an alcohol abusing mate and spousal education on the addictive effects of alcohol have been documented to lead to more substantial gains when assessing the effects of family approaches to treating alcohol abuse (Nichols & Schwartz, 2001).

COUPLES AND FAMILY TREATMENT FOR ALCOHOL ABUSE: MODELS OF TREATMENT

The major models of treatment for alcoholic families addressed in the literature include various traditional therapy formats, programmatic types of treatment, and community-based treatment.

TRADITIONAL FAMILY THERAPY APPROACHES

Various traditional family therapy approaches have been used in the treatment of alcohol abuse. Most treatments have some support, with behavioral couples' and family therapy having being more researched than other traditional family therapy approaches.

Behavioral couples and family therapy. The most common, and only extensively researched, clinical approach to couple treatment addressing alcohol abuse is behavioral couples' therapy (BCT; e.g., see Epstein & McCrady, 2002). BCT primarily focuses on the current factors maintaining drinking behaviors within the family by assessing external precipitants to drinking, cognitions regarding drinking behaviors, expectancies concerning the positive effects of alcohol, and behavioral consequences of drinking. Utilizing a ten to twenty session protocol, the goals of BCT are to facilitate motivation to change drinking behaviors, to enhance self-efficacy for both the alcoholic mate and their spouse regarding their ability to change maladaptive behaviors, to increase positive reinforcement for abstinence, and to teach new cognitive and behavioral coping skills in the maintenance of treatment gains (Epstein & McCrady, 2002). Successful completion of these goals typically includes documentation of abstinence throughout the clinical treatment protocol.

It can be difficult for a clinician to involve family members, when alcohol abuse is the goal of treatment. In Epstein and McCrady's (2002) Alcohol Behavioral Couples Therapy (ABCT) approach, the spouse is involved in all stages of treatment. In early stages, the spouse gives their feedback on the problem, gives their assessment of the extent and severity of the problem, will give input on the antecedents of abusing, and both positive and negative affects of drinking. The assigned therapist begins with the partner in enhancing motivation towards treatment, using readiness for change models as a means for engaging the spouse in treatment (Prochaska, DiClemente, & Norcross, 1992). They also employ a self-recording worksheet with the non-abusing spouse, as well as the abusing spouse. This technique involves planning on how to address high-risk situations with abusing or engaging in negative coping strategies.

Research on the efficacy of BCT has documented both significant reductions in alcohol consumption and improvements in couple functioning as typical outcomes of treatment (e.g., O'Farrell, Cutter, & Floyd, 1985; O'Farrell, Choquette, & Cutter, 1998). Greater treatment effects have been documented when assessing BCT with relapse prevention components, with treatment gains retained at up to three years posttreatment (O'Farrell, Choquette, & Cutter, 1998).

Family systems therapy. Family systems therapy, as the classic general treatment modality for families, focuses on the system of relationships in which problem drinking is entrenched (Shoham, Rohrbaugh, Stickle, & Jacob, 1998). Rather than requiring abstinence, family systems tends to begin with a consultation phase in which the therapist remains neutral about the alcoholics drinking behavior until the family chooses to pursue a goal to addressing the drinking. (Shoham, Rohrbaugh, Stickle, & Jacob, 1998). An addition goal of this approach includes altering interactions that may maintain drinking (Shoham, Rohrbaugh, Stickle, & Jacob, 1998). Research on family systems theory and treatment is complex with studies tending to indicate no difference between family systems approach and other approaches (Karno, Beutler, & Harwood, 2002). Many approaches demonstrate the efficacy of integrating family systems approaches with behavioral approaches to treatment (Barrett Waldron, Brody, & Slesnick, 2001; Vetere & Henley, 2001).

UNILATERAL FAMILY THERAPY

In the UFT model, the therapist works solely with the spouse/family of the alcoholic (Edwards & Steinglass, 1995). UFT supports the non-abusing spouse by strengthening his or her coping abilities, improving family functioning, and facilitating greater sobriety on the part of the alcohol abuser (Thomas & Ager, 1993). UFT aids families in plans to implement at home to change the drinking behavior and to motivate the abuser towards change (Miller, Meyers, Tonigan, 1999). Additional elements of UFT include disenabling, alcohol education, confrontation of the alcoholic family member, and relapse prevention training (Edwards & Steinglass, 1995). In a pilot study that assessed the effectiveness of the UFT program, 61% of the alcoholics whose spouses participated in the UFT were classified as "improved" (Thomas, Santa, Bronson, and Oyserman, 1987). In a follow-up study, 53% reduction in drinking in alcoholics with UFT spouses was found (Thomas, Santa, Bronson, and Oyserman, 1987).

Structural-Strategic family therapy. Structural-Strategic family therapy has historically been concerned with problems in substance abuse. A strength of this approach is that it is action-oriented and therefore more likely to produce good results with families and problems surrounding alcohol abuse (Wycoff & Cameron, 2000). The results of studies examining structural-strategic approach to treatment with alcohol abuse have been positive for adolescent users (Colon, 1998); however, studies with adult abusers are lacking.

Bowenian family therapy. Bowenian family therapy has not been adequately investigated for efficacy with alcohol-abuse. Some work supports Bowenian treatment to address what is commonly called "codependency" (Gibson & Donigan, 1993). With the emphasis on differentiation of self, the family member of an alcohol abuser is encouraged towards balance in issues of responsibility in the family, intimacy and individuality.

PROGRAMMATIC APPROACHES TO FAMILY TREATMENT OF ALCOHOL ABUSE

Project CALM. Counseling for Alcoholic Marriages Project (Project CALM; Rotunda & O'Farrell, 1997) has well-documented efficacy utilizing behavioral couples therapy in a long-term treatment protocol format. The primary goal of Project CALM is to increase relationship stability, thereby aiding families in maintaining sobriety. This treatment approach utilizes behavioral techniques with interventions designed to change maladaptive behavioral patterns. Project CALM involves 10-12 weekly couple sessions followed by 10 weekly couples group sessions, and quarterly follow-up visits for up to two years post-treatment (Rotunda & O'Farrell, 1997). The effectiveness of Project CALM has been consistently established empirically, despite the need for couples to commit to long-term treatment (O'Farrell & Fals-Stewart, 2000).

The CRAFT program. The Community Reinforcement and Family Training (CRAFT) is a program for teaching non-abusing family members to encourage sobriety by reinforcing non-drinking, extinguishing drinking, planning competing non-drinking activities, increasing positive relationship communication, and by encouraging treatment engagement (Meyers, Smith, & Miller, 1998). In an initial CRAFT study, Sisson and Azrin (1986) found that after a relative started CRAFT, alcoholics showed more than a 50% reduction in average consumption prior to treatment entry and nearly total abstinence in the 3 months after entering treatment. In a follow-up study that used a larger sample size and improved additional methodological weaknesses, findings showed that the CRAFT approach was significantly more effective in engaging initially unmotivated alcohol abusing adults in alcohol treatment as compared with the Johnson Intervention or Al-Anon (Miller, Meyers, & Tonigan, 1999). Research has been consistently supportive of the CRAFT approach as an effective method of family-based alcohol abuse treatment (Meyers & Miller, 2001; Meyers, Smith, & Miller, 1998; Miller, Meyers, & Tonigan, 1999; Smith, Meyers, & Miller, 2001).

COMMUNITY-BASED INTERVENTIONS

Community referrals. Often times, marital and family treatment is coupled with a referral to an individual or family-directed community-based self-help organizations, such as Alcoholics Anonymous or Al-Anon. Al-Anon was developed to provide support for individuals with alcoholic family members (Al-Anon Family Groups, 1984). Through the use of support groups, the Al-Anon approach advocates loving detachment and acceptance of the family member's helplessness to control the alcoholic behavior (Miller, Meyers, & Tonigan, 1999). Al-Anon groups can improve adaptive coping by providing a chance for the expression of negative feelings while apart from the drinking family member (Rotunda, Scherer, & Imm, 1995). Researchers studying the influence of Al-Anon on drinking behavior found that referral of family members to the group resulted in no behavior change or treatment engagement among the drinkers about whom the family was concerned (Barber & Gilbertson, 1996; Humphreys et al., 2004; Sisson & Azrin, 1986). As a result, Al-Anon appears to be more of a support network for the family, rather than the alcoholic family member.

The Johnson Intervention. The Johnson Intervention involves educational training that prepares the family members for a confrontation, often referred to as an "intervention" (O'Farrell & Fals-Stewart, 2003). The goal of confrontation is to increase the drinker's insight into the scope of the drinking problem, overcome the denial, and promote treatment engagement (O'Farrell & Fals-Stewart, 2003). Two different studies of the Johnson Intervention find some support for the intervention, although not strong support. In one study, clients referred following a Johnson intervention were significantly more likely to engage in (but not more likely to complete) treatment than those in other referral categories (Loneck, Garrett, & Banks, 1996a, 1996b). Another study found that the Johnson Intervention was more effective than four other methods for referring clients to treatment (Loneck et al., 1996a&b). While the effects of the Johnson Intervention towards engagement in therapy have the beginning of empirical support, the effects appear to lack the power on their own to effect lasting change.

CONCLUSIONS

- The causal pathways between individual traits, at-risk behaviors, and family functioning are causal and are proposed to include feedback loops. This emphasizes the importance of addressing marriage and family issues in alcohol abuse treatment.
- Multiple formats of intervention have been researched for treating alcoholism in marriages and families with behavioral or integrated behavior-systems treatments garnering the largest empirical investigation and support.
- Overall, more structured approaches to treatment have been reported to provide greater lasting benefits than community interventions, despite the overwhelming popularity of the latter.
- Research supports the use of direct family-oriented therapeutic interventions with supplemental community interventions in order to best reach this objective.

NOTE

1. Throughout this article we will refer to alcohol abuse, instead of the more general term of substance abuse. While much of the research for other abusing substances is similar to that of alcohol abuse, this article is focusing more directly on alcohol abuse, rather than including various other substances.

REFERENCES

Al-Anon Family Groups. (1984). Al-Anon faces alcohol abuse. New York: Author.

American Psychiatric Association (1994). *Diagnostic and Statistical Manual of Mental Disorders (4th ed.)*. Washington, DC: Author.

Barber, J. G., & Gilbertson, R. (1996). An experimental study of brief unilateral intervention for the partners of heavy drinkers. *Research on Social Work Practice, 6,* 325-336.

Barrett Waldron, H., Brody, J. L., & Slesnick, N. (2001). Integrative behavioral and family therapy for adolescent substance abuse. In P. Monti, & S. Colby, et al. (Eds.), *Adolescents, alcohol, and substance abuse: Reaching teens through brief interventions* (pp. 216-243). New York, NY: Guilford Press.

Campbell, J.L., Masters, M.A., & Johnson, M.E. (1998). Relationship of parental alcohol abuse to family-of-origin functioning and current marital satisfaction. *Journal of Addictions and Offender Counseling, 19,* 7-14.

Colon, R. M. (1998). *Causal relationships of familial influence and adolescents' attitude toward substance use in the theory of planned behavior: A social impact model.* Unpublished doctoral dissertation, University of Houston.

Curtain, J. J., Patrick, C. J., Lang, A. R., Cacioppo, J. T., & Birnaumer, N. (2001). Alcohol affects emotion through cognition. *Psychological Science, 12,* 527-531.

Dozier, A. L., & Barnes, M. J. (1997). Ethnicity, drug user status, and academic performance. *Adolescence, 32,* 825-837.

Edwards, M.E., & Steinglass, P. (1995). Meta-analytic review of marital therapy outcome research. *Journal of Marital and Family Therapy, 21,* 475-510.

Epstein, E.E., & McCrady, B.S. (2002). Couple therapy in the treatment of alcohol problems. In A.S. Gurman and N.S. Jacobson (Eds.), *Clinical handbook of couple therapy (3rd ed.)* (pp. 597-628). New York: Guilford Press.

Gibson, J. M., & Donigan, J. (1993). Use of bowen theory. *Journal of Addictions & Offender Counseling, 14,* 25-35.

Goodrich, T. J. (1991). *Women and power: Perspectives for family therapy.* New York: W.W. Norton.

Holtzworth-Munroe, A. (2000). Social information processing skills deficits in maritally violent men: Summary of a research program. In J. P. Vincent & E. N. Jouriles (Eds.), *Domestic violence: Guidelines for research-informed practice* (pp. 13-36). London: Jessica Kingsley. W.W. Norton and Company.

Holtzworth-Munroe, A., Meehan, J.C., Rehman, U., & Marshall, A.D. (2002). Intimate partner violence: An introduction for couple therapists. In A.S. Gurman and N.S. Jacobson (Eds.), *Clinical handbook of couple therapy (3rd ed.)* (pp. 441-465). New York: Guilford Press.

Humphreys, K., Wing, S., McCarty, D., Chappel, J., Gallant, L., Haberle, B., Horvath, A. T., Kaskutas, L. A., Kirk, T., Kivlahan, D., Laudet, A., McCrady, B. S., McLellan, A. T., Morgenstern, J., Townsend, M., & Weiss, R. (2004). Self-help organizations for alcohol and drug problems: Toward evidence-based practice and policy. *Journal of Substance Abuse Treatment, 26,* 151-158.

Karno, M. P., Beutler, L. E., & Harwood, T. (2002). Interactions between psychotherapy procedures and patient attributes that predict alcohol treatment effectiveness: A preliminary report. *Addictive Behaviors, 27,* 779-797.

Lewis, V., & Allen-Byrd, L. (2001). The alcoholic family recovery typology: A new theoretical model. *Alcoholism Treatment Quarterly, 19,* 1-17.

Liddle, H.A., & Dakof, G.A. (1995). Efficacy of family therapy for drug abuse: Promising but not definitive. *Journal of Marital and Family Therapy, 21,* 511-544.

Loneck, B., Garrett, J.A., & Banks, S. M. (1996a). A comparison of the Johnson intervention with four other methods of referral to outpatient treatment. *American Journal of Drug and Alcohol Abuse, 22,* 233-246.

Loneck, B., Garrett, J. A., & Banks, S. M. (1996b). The Johnson Intervention and relapse during outpatient treatment. *American Journal of Drug & Alcohol Abuse, 22,* 363-375.

Longabaugh, R., Beattie, M., Noel, N., Stout, R., & Malloy, P. (1993). The effect of social investment on treatment outcome. *Journal of Studies on Alcohol, 54,* 465-478.

Longabaugh, R., Rubin, A., Malloy, P., Beattie, M., Clifford, P.R., & Noel, N. (1994). Drinking outcomes of alcohol abusers diagnosed as antisocial personality disorder. *Alcohol abuse: Clinical and Experimental Research, 18,* 778-785.

Maisto, S.A., McKay, J.R., & O'Farrell, T.J. (1995). Relapse precipitants and behavioral marital therapy. *Addictive Behaviors, 20,* 383-393.

McCrady, B.S., & Epstein, E.E. (1995). Directions for research on alcoholic relationships: Marital- and individual-based models of heterogeneity. *Psychology of Addictive Behaviors, 9*, 157-166.

McLaughlin, I. G., Leonard, K., & Senchak, M. (1992). Prevalence and distribution of premarital aggression among couples applying for a marriage license. *Journal of Family Violence, 7*, 309-319.

Meyers, R. J., & Miller, W. R. (Eds.) (2001). *A community reinforcement approach to addiction treatment.* New York, NY: Cambridge University Press.

Meyers, R. J., Smith, J. E., & Miller E. J. (1998). Working through the concerned other: Community reinforcement and family training. In W. R. Miller & N. Heather (Eds.), *Treating addictive behaviors: Processes of change* (2nd ed.) New York: Plenum Press.

Miller, W. R., Meyers, R. J., & Tonigan, J. S. (1999). Engaging the unmotivated in treatment for alcohol problems: A comparison of three strategies for intervention through family members. *Journal of Consulting and Clinical Psychology, 67*, 688-697.

Moos, R.H., & Moos, B.S. (1984). The process of recovery from alcoholism III: Comparing functioning of families of alcoholics and matched control families. *Journal of Studies on Alcohol, 45*, 111-118.

Newcomb, M. D., & Earleywine, M. (1996). Intrapersonal contributors to drug use: The willing host. *American Behavioral Scientist, 39*, 823-837.

Nichols, M.P., & Schwartz, R.C. (2001). *Family Therapy: Concepts and Methods (5th ed.).* Boston, MA: Allyn and Bacon.

O'Farrell, T.J., Choquette, K.A., & Cutter, H.S.G. (1998). Couples relapse prevention sessions after behavioral marital therapy for male alcoholics: Outcomes during the three years after starting treatment. *Journal of Studies on Alcohol, 59*, 357-370.

O'Farrell, T.J., Cutter, H.S.G., & Floyd, F. (1985). Evaluating behavioral and marital therapy for male alcoholics: Effects on marital adjustment and communication from before to after therapy. *Behavior Therapy, 16*, 147-167.

O'Farrell, T.J., & Fals-Stewart, W. (2000). Behavioral couples therapy for alcohol abuse and drug abuse. *Behavior Therapist, 23*, 49-54.

O'Farrell, T.J., Murphy, C.M., Neavins, T.M., & Van Hutton, V. (2000). Verbal aggression among male alcoholic patients and their wives in the year before and two years after alcohol abuse treatment. *Journal of Family Violence, 15*, 295-310.

Ohannessian, C.M., & Hesselbrock, V.M. (2004). Do alcohol expectancies moderate the relationship between parental alcohol abuse and adult drinking behaviors? *Addictive Behaviors, 29*, 901-909.

Pan, H., Neidig, P., & O'Leary, K. D. (1994). Predicting mild and severe husband-to-wife physical aggression. *Journal of Consulting and Clinical Psychology, 62*, 975-981.

Prochaska, J. O., DiClemente, C. C., & Norcross, J. C. (1992). In search of how people change: Applications to addictive behaviors. *American Psychologist, 47*, 1102-1114.

Rotunda, R.J., & O'Farrell, T.J. (1997). Marital and family therapy of alcohol use disorders: Bridging the gap between research and practice. *Professional Psychology: Research and Practice, 28*, 246-252.

Rotunda, R. J., Scherer, D. G., & Imm, P.S. (1995). Family systems and alcohol mis-use: Research on the effects of alcohol abuse on family functioning and effective family interventions. *Professional Psychology: Research and Practice*, *26*, 95-104.

Shoham, V, Rohrbaugh, M. J., Stickle, T. R., & Jacob, T. (1998). Demand-withdraw couple interaction moderates retention in cognitive behavioral versus family-sys-tems treatments for alcohol abuse. *Journal of Family Psychology*, *12*, 557-577.

Simon, T. R., Sussman, S., Dent, C. W., Burton, D., & Flay, B. R. (1995). Prospective correlates of exclusive or combined adolescent use of cigarettes and smokeless to-bacco: A replication-extension. *Addictive Behaviors*, *20*, 517-524.

Sisson, R. W., & Azrin, N. H. (1986). Family-member involvement to initiate and pro-mote treatment of problem drinkers. *Behavior Therapy and Experimental Psychia-try*, *17*, 15-21.

Thomas E. J., & Ager, R. D. (1993). Unilateral family therapy with spouses of uncoop-erative alcohol abusers. In T. J. O'Farrell (Ed.), *Treating alcohol problems: Marital and family interventions* (pp. 3-33). New York: Guilford Press.

Thomas, E. J., Santa, C. A., Bronson, D., & Oyserman, D. (1987). Unilateral family therapy with spouses of alcoholics. *Journal of Social Service Research*, *10*, 145-162.

Vetere, A., & Henley, M. (2001). Integrating couples and family therapy into a com-munity alcohol service: A pantheoretical approach. *Journal of Family Therapy*, *23*, 85-101.

Wills, T.A., Vaccaro, D., & McNamara, G. (1994). Novelty seeking and related con-structs as predictors of adolescent substance use. *Journal of Substance Abuse*, *6*, 1-20.

Wycoff, S., & Cameron, S. C. (2000). The Garcia family: Using a structural systems approach with an alcohol-dependent family. *Family Journal-Counseling & Therapy for Couples & Families*, *8*, 47-57.

Yohman, J., & Parsons, O. A. (1987). Verbal reasoning deficits in alcoholics. *Journal of Nervous & Mental Disease*, *175*, 219-223.

Zillmann, D. (1989). Aggression and sex: Independent and joint operations. In H. L. Wagner & A. S. R. Manstead (Eds.), *Handbook of psychophysiology: Emotion and social behavior* (pp. 407-440). Chichester, England: John Wiley.

Recovery Across the Life Cycle from Alcohol/Other Drug Problems: Pathways, Styles, and Developmental Stages

William L. White, MA

SUMMARY. There is a growing body of literature on addiction recovery, but the effects of age of recovery initiation on the prospects and patterns of addiction recovery remain relatively unexplored. The purpose of this article is to explore the prevalence of, and the qualitative differences in, addiction recovery across the developmental life cycle. The review will include the influence of age of recovery initiation on differences in recovery pathways, styles of recovery, developmental stages and recovery stability. *[Article copies available for a fee from The Haworth Document Delivery Service: 1-800-HAWORTH. E-mail address: <docdelivery@haworthpress.com> Website: <http://www.HaworthPress.com> © 2006 by The Haworth Press, Inc. All rights reserved.]*

KEYWORDS. Alcoholism, addiction, age, life cycle, early onset, late onset

William L. White is a Senior Research Consultant, Chestnut Health Systems, Bloomington, IL.

Address correspondence to: William L. White, Chestnut Health Systems, 3479 Shawn Street, Port Charlotte, FL 33980 (E-mail: bwhite@chestnut.org).

Support for this article was provided by grants from the National Institute on Drug Abuse (Grants R01 DA15523, R01 DA014409, R01 DA015133) and the Illinois Department of Human Services (Office of Alcoholism and Substance Abuse Services) via the Behavioral Health Recovery Management project. The opinions expressed here are those of the author and do not reflect the opinions or policies of these agencies.

[Haworth co-indexing entry note]: "Recovery Across the Life Cycle from Alcohol/Other Drug Problems: Pathways, Styles, and Developmental Stages." White, William L. Co-published simultaneously in *Alcoholism Treatment Quarterly* (The Haworth Press, Inc.) Vol. 24, No. 1/2, 2006, pp. 185-201; and: *Spirituality and Religiousness and Alcohol/Other Drug Problems: Treatment and Recovery Perspectives* (ed: Brent B. Benda, and Thomas F. McGovern) The Haworth Press, Inc., 2006, pp. 185-201. Single or multiple copies of this article are available for a fee from The Haworth Document Delivery Service [1-800-HAWORTH, 9:00 a.m. - 5:00 p.m. (EST). E-mail address: docdelivery@haworthpress.com].

INTRODUCTION

Addiction-related scholarship has historically been either pathology-focused or intervention-focused. Only recently has there been focused attention on the study of individuals who have achieved long-term resolution of alcohol and other drug problems. The pursuit of a recovery research agenda holds great promise, but the sheer volume of questions to be answered regarding the processes of recovery initiation, consolidation, and maintenance is quite daunting (White, 2004). One sphere of such questions involves the effects of age of recovery initiation on the prospects and processes of addiction recovery. This article discusses what is currently known about recovery and developmental age and identifies key issues for continued research in this area. The article addresses the role of age of recovery initiation on the prospects of long-term recovery from alcohol and other drug problems, pathways and styles of long-term recovery, and the durability and quality of long-term recovery.

AGE AND THE PROSPECTS OF RECOVERY

People develop alcohol and other drug (AOD) problems across the developmental life cycle. Two patterns of age-related onset of AOD problems have dominated the history of addiction treatment in the United States. The first pattern is marked by late adolescent onset of drinking, a slow acceleration of alcohol consumption and alcohol-related problems, and a maturing of those problems into a point of crisis and help-seeking at mid-life. The second pattern was the adolescent onset of narcotic use, the progression of that use to physical dependence, and the rise of opiate-related problems that brought one to treatment during early adulthood. Most of what we know about addiction, treatment and recovery is based on the onset of alcohol and other drug use in mid-to-late adolescence and the flowering of that use into clinical disorders during early adulthood to mid-life (White, 1998). Two new patterns challenge this knowledge base: the early (pre-adolescent) onset of AOD use and subsequent problems and the growth of late-onset AOD-related problems.

Does early age of onset of AOD use and related problems affect the prognosis for long-term recovery? The age of onset of AOD experimentation and regular use has progressively declined (Dennis, Babor, Roebuck, & Donaldson, 2002; Stoltenberg, Hill, Mudd, Blow, & Zucker,

1999; Presley, Meilman, & Lyerla, 1991) for both adolescent males and females (Substance Abuse and Mental Health Services Administration, 1999). Pre-adolescent onset of AOD use is particularly evident in youth entering juvenile justice and addiction treatment facilities (U.S. Department of Justice, 1994). More than 80% of the 600 youth admitted to the recently completed Cannabis Youth Treatment study began regular substance use between the ages of 12 and 14 (Dennis, Titus et al., 2002). Such early onset has many clinical consequences (White, Godley, & Dennis, 2003). The National Longitudinal Alcohol Epidemiological Survey found that the risk of adult alcohol dependence was directly related to age of onset: before age 15 (40%), age 17 (24.5%), ages 18-19 (16.5%), ages 20-22 (10%). The risk of adult alcohol dependence increased an average of 9% for each decreasing year of age of onset (Grant & Dawson, 1997). Similar findings have been found on the relationship of age of onset of use of other drugs on the risk of adult drug dependence (Dennis, Babor et al., 2002).

In addition to increasing the risk of developing a substance use disorder, early age of onset of regular AOD use is associated with rapid problem development (Kreichbaun & Zering, 2000), greater problem severity and complexity (e.g., psychiatric comorbidity) (National Institute on Alcohol Abuse and Alcoholism, 2003; Arria, Dohey, Mezzich, Bukstein, & Van Thiel, 1995), less social support for subsequent recovery (Sobell, Sobell, Cunningham, & Agrawal, 1998), and poorer treatment outcomes as measured by rates of post-intervention relapse (Keller et al., 1992; Kessler et al., 2001; Chen & Millar, 1998). More studies are needed to confirm this relationship between lowered age of onset and reduced prognosis for long-term recovery and to identify the precise mechanisms that compromise these recovery outcomes (Chou & Pickering, 1992). Several mechanisms could be at work here, e.g., increased biological vulnerability of pre-adolescents to drug effects, developmental deficits resulting from early onset, lack of family/social support contributing both to problem onset and reduced recovery support resources. Those with late adolescent to young adulthood onset of AOD use who go on to develop AOD problems may have better recovery outcomes than those with early onset because of lower cumulative consumption, less psychiatric comorbidity, and greater social supports (Brennan & Moos, 1995; Sobell et al., 1998).

If the long-term effects of precocious substance experimentation are confirmed by additional studies, the lowered age of onset of substance use may stand as one of the most socially and clinically significant drug trends of the past century. If poorer long-term recovery outcomes are confirmed, identifying the precise mechanisms that increase risks of problem development and compromise recovery outcomes will be crucial to the development of more effective prevention, early intervention and treatment strategies. Isolating those mechanisms and testing strategies for amelioration of their effects is an important research agenda.

Does recovery prognosis for late-onset AOD problems differ from the recovery prognoses for other patterns of onset? Alcohol consumption declines in adulthood with advancing age, but alcohol exposure remains high (60% of adults between age 60-94 consume alcohol), and heavy drinking is reported in 13% of men and 2% of women over 60. Some 15% of older alcoholics also suffer from concurrent drug dependence (often related to prescribed medication). About two-thirds of older adults who drink heavily are alcoholics who began drinking in adolescence and whose alcohol problems progress into old age. The remaining third are characterized by a lack of risk factors (e.g., family history of alcoholism), a non-problematic relationship with alcohol through early and midlife, and the emergence of identifiable problems and consequences related to drinking late in life (Rigler, 2000).

Sometimes referred to as "late onset alcoholism," these patterns of problematic drinking are spawned by different vulnerabilities: age-related alterations in biological sensitivities to alcohol, self-medication of acute and chronic pain, use of alcohol as a balm for stressful life events (e.g., deaths, separations, retirement), or enmeshment in drinking social groups following retirement. Those elderly persons with shorter heavy drinking histories have better outcomes than those with longer heavy drinking histories (Rigler, 2000; Schutte, Brennan, & Moos, 1994; Atkinson, Tolson, & Tuner, 1990). Somewhat counter-intuitive is the finding that recovery among late-onset heavy drinkers is associated with increased stressors, suggesting that the continued presence of financial and health-related stressors may actually serve to enhance motivation for recovery maintenance (Moos, 1994).

Escalating life expectancies and shorter work lives will exert an unknown effect on the future prevalence of substance use disorders. What is clear is that new patterns of late-onset alcohol problems spring from complex etiological sources, unfold in diverse patterns and seem to respond to different treatment and support strategies. Without further refinements in the treatment of older adults, the misapplication of adult treatment philosophies and techniques may become as marked as the earlier misapplication of such technologies to adolescents. Assuring that this does not occur is an important research and clinical practice agenda.

Does one's prognosis for successful long-term recovery differ depending on the age at which that recovery is initiated (separate from the issue of the age at which problems developed)? There are two emerging bodies of data that shed some light on this question.

The first body of data encompasses outcome studies of adolescent treatment. Some of the key findings of these studies include the following (see Risberg & White, 2003; White, Dennis, & Godley, 2002; Godley, Godley, Dennis, Funk, & Passetti, 2002):

- Many adolescents mature out of substance-related problems in the transition into adult role responsibilities (see later discussion of styles of recovery).
- For other adolescents, substance use develops into a chronic, debilitating disorder, recovery from which is often proceeded by multiple treatment episodes spanning years.
- Most adolescents are precariously balanced between recovery and relapse in the months following treatment. The period of greatest vulnerability for relapse is in the first 30 days following treatment.
- The most common outcomes of adolescent treatment are enhancements in global functioning (increased emotional health and improved functioning in the family, school, and community) and reduced substance use (to approximately 50% of pre-treatment levels) rather than complete and enduring cessation of alcohol and other drug use.
- The stability of recovery is enhanced by post-treatment monitoring and periodic recovery checkups.

One of the most significant findings emerging from adolescent treatment outcome studies is the finding that the earlier the intervention (in terms of age and months/years of use) with a substance use disorder, the better the clinical outcomes, the shorter the addiction career, and the longer and more stable the recovery career (Risberg & White, 2003).

The second source of information is that collected on treatment/recovery outcomes for older adults. Findings from this data include the following:

- Remission rates for older problem drinkers are comparable to those achieved by younger adults at short term (1-4 years) follow-up (Schutte, Brennan, & Moos, 1994), but older adults have lower remission rates than younger adults at long-term (10 years) follow-up (Schutte, Byrne, Brennan, & Moos, 2001).
- Remission in older problem drinkers is associated with less alcohol use, gender (female), marital status (married), employment status (unemployed), social support (less than that of unremitted drinkers) and presence of depression and acute and chronic

health problems (Schutte, Brennan, & Moos, 1994; Schutte, Bryne, Brennan, & Moos, 2001).

• Goldman (1983), in a review of the cognitive impairments associ- ated with alcoholism, concluded that most of the enduring deficits related to alcoholism following recovery were associated with older alcoholics with lengthy drinking histories. Most of the studies re- viewed by Goldman found that cognitive functioning returned with sustained abstinence. While simple areas of cognitive functioning may be quickly regained in recovery, other areas such as tasks re- quiring more novel and rapid information processing are the last to return. The differences in findings across studies could well reflect differences in the ages of onset of addiction and recovery.

In summary, existing studies suggest that recovery rates are low among adolescents, increase through adulthood, and then decline in late life. Granfield and Cloud's (1999) concept of *recovery capital* may help interpret these findings. Recovery capital is the amount and quality of resources that one can bring to bear to initiate and sustain recovery from addiction. What most distinguishes adolescents and older adults from adult populations is the failure to have developed sufficient recovery capital among adolescents and the loss of recovery capital among older adults. The adult rehabilitation model that seeks to resolve problems so that prior levels of functioning can be naturally assumed may be inap- propriate for both adolescents and older adults. A shift in focus from problem elimination to building recovery capital for these groups might prove highly beneficial in enhancing recovery outcomes.

There is a body of literature of addiction and treatment careers (Frykholm, 1985; Hser, Anglin, Grella, Longshore, & Prendergast, 1997), but no comparable body of literature on recovery careers. A re- search-generated cartography of addiction recovery could plot the in- fluence of multiple dimensions on the prospects and processes of long-term recovery, including the influences of age of problem onset and the age of recovery initiation.

STYLES AND PATHWAYS OF RECOVERY

Are there qualitative differences in the process of recovery initiation across the life cycle? There is a growing body of literature describing the varieties of recovery experience.

Incremental versus Climactic Change. Recovery from alcohol and other drug problems may be achieved through a process of incremental change over a considerable period of time (Prochaska, Norcross, & DiClemente, 1994), or by a sudden, life-transforming experience that is unplanned, vivid, positive and permanent (Miller & C'de Baca, 2001). Variations in such styles across the life cycle have not been rigorously evaluated. Early studies of conversion-like transformations of personal identity noted that most such climactic experiences occurred during the adolescent years (Starbuck, 1901; James, 1902/1985), but modern studies of sobriety-inducing transformative change find such experiences happening primarily in adulthood (Loder, 1989; Miller & C'de Baca, 2001). In short, we know very little about differences in patterns of recovery initiation across the developmental life cycle.

Abstinence-Based Recovery versus Moderated Recovery (Problem Resolution). There is evidence that individuals resolve AOD problems through a variety of styles:

- Complete and enduring abstinence from those psychoactive substances previously associated with life problems with the substitution of other secondary drugs (e.g., alcohol, cannabis, caffeine) at sub-clinical levels (moderated use that does not meet DSM-IV criteria for substance abuse or substance dependence).
- Complete and enduring abstinence from all traditional "drugs of abuse."
- Deceleration of AOD use to sub-clinical levels.
- Prolonged abstinence followed by initiation of sub-clinical levels of AOD use (White, 1996).

There is further evidence that the viability of these strategies differs considerably across the categories of personal vulnerability (e.g., family history of AOD problems), problem severity, problem complexity, and family and social supports. What is not clear is the prevalence of these styles across age groups and the degree to which shifts in these styles can occur over time in the same individuals. Many adolescents shift from use to non-use or from problematic to non-problematic use as they move through their teens and twenties into their thirties (Chen & Kandel, 1995), but the cultural stand of "zero tolerance" towards adolescent AOD use makes even the acknowledgement of this latter potential a "third rail" issue often avoided because of the potential damage to one's professional career.

There is evidence that some elderly people with alcohol-related problems resolve such problems by reducing the frequency, intensity and circumstances of their drinking (Heather & Robertson, 1983). In a 16-20 year treatment follow-up study, Nordstrom and Berglund (1987) found that active alcohol dependence declined and stable recovery (defined as sustained abstinence or sub-clinical social drinking) increased over time. As for transitions in recovery style, they found that 40% of the sample initially abstinent in the first six years following treatment later consumed alcohol at subclinical levels (no longer meeting diagnostic criteria for abuse or dependence) during the second decade of follow-up. In a ten-year follow-up study of older problem drinkers, Schutte and colleagues (2003) found that 63% of former problem drinkers were consuming alcohol without identifiable problems. The majority of this non-abstinent remission group did not have severe problem drinking histories. In a sixty-year follow-up of alcoholic men, Vaillant (2003) found 32% of his original sample abstinent and only 1% who had sustained controlled drinking. The differences in the two studies suggests that the likelihood of successful controlled drinking among older former problem drinkers declines in relationship to the severity of their original drinking problem, a finding consistent with earlier research (Hermos, Locastro, Glynn, Bouchard, & Labry, 1988). The most frequent patterns in the Vaillant (2003) study were the movement from problem drinking to abstinence and the movement from problem drinking to experiments with controlled drinking followed by abstinence.

The findings of a 33-year follow-up study of heroin addicts (Hser, Hoffman, Grella, & Anglin, 2001) challenges the theory of an inevitable age-related maturing out of drug problems. Hser and her colleagues found very stable patterns of heroin use over more than three decades. While many of those studied had achieved some periods of abstinence, only 46% were able to achieve five years of abstinence within the 33-year period studied, and the group as a whole showed high past-year rates for multiple drugs (heroin, 40.5%; marijuana, 35.5%; cocaine, 19.4%; and daily alcohol use, 21.1%). These findings suggest that addiction can span the aging process and constitute a lifelong condition. Recovery is not an inevitable product of aging.

Treatment-Assisted versus Natural Recovery. Most people with AOD problems do not seek treatment and most people who resolve such problems do so without treatment (Cunningham, Sobell, Sobell, & Kapur, 1995; Cunningham, Koski-Jannes, & Toneatto, 1999). There is a growing body of literature on this self-managed style of problem resolution known as natural recovery. A pattern of age-related "maturing out" of narcotic addiction was first described by Winick in 1962. Winick theorized that a maturation process within the life cycle of addiction led to cessation of drug use without intervention in a large portion of addicts. Subsequent studies confirmed that drug cessation increased with age but at a much lower rate than that predicted by Winick (Vaillant, 1966; Snow, 1973). Simpson and Sells (1990) found that opiate use did not cease simply as a function of age, but instead required an accumulation of consequences or a loss of energy required to sustain the opiate lifestyle.

In their review of 38 studies of natural recovery, Sobell, Ellingstad, and Sobell (2000) found two age-related patterns of natural recovery: (1) a young adult pattern of recovery associated with maturation and the assumption of adult role responsibilities, and (2) a later-life pattern of recovery associated with cumulative consequences of alcohol and other drug use. Natural resolution of alcohol problems in young adults is associated with getting married, remaining married, and becoming a parent; the failure to achieve natural resolution is associated with selection of and participation in a heavy-drinking social network (Labouvie, 1996). Those successful in natural recovery are also reported in some studies to be younger and to have had shorter duration of AOD problems than those with treatment-assisted recovery (Cunningham et al., 1995; Saunders, Phil, & Kershaw, 1979). Studies of older problem drinkers note that more than 70% resolve their drinking problems without professional help (Schutte, Nichols, Brennan, & Moos, 2003).

Fillmore and colleagues (1988) found age-related differences in the factors promoting natural recovery. They found that natural recovery among late adolescents and young adults occurred primarily due to a shift in group norms, whereas maturing out of middle-age drinking problems was much more linked to individual life events. In the latter category, remission in the 30s and 40s was often attributed to the influence of spouse or friends, where remission after that was more likely to be associated with concerns about health. Watson and Sher (1998) noted in their review of the natural recovery literature that adults with late onset alcoholism were more likely to achieve natural recovery than were those older adults with early onset alcoholism (see also Atkinson et al., 1990). Age-related maturing out may differ among African Americans and Hispanics who are more likely to develop alcohol problems later in life. There is also evidence of gender differences in age-related remission patterns, with men achieving remission at higher rates than women from the late 20s to the mid-40s and women achieving higher rates of remission than men after the mid-40s (Fillmore, Hartka, Johnstone, Speiglman, & Temple, 1988).

Recovery and Personal Identity. Persons who resolve AOD problems may do so with a pro-recovery (defining themselves as an "alcoholic"/"addict" in "recovery") or recovery-neutral identity (defining AOD problems in terms of a transient experience rather than in terms of their identity) (White, 1996). The degree to which such styles vary by age of recovery initiation has not been scientifically studied, but one would suspect such variations for adolescent-initiated recoveries and for recoveries initiated among older adults.

Peer-Supported Recovery versus Solo Recovery. Persons with AOD problems may resolve these problems with active support from other recovering people or with little or no contact with recovering people (White, 1996). Participation in mutual aid groups is associated with enhanced recovery rates (Emrick, Tonigan, Montgomery, & Little, 1993; Humphreys, Wing, McCarty, Chappel, Gallant, Haberle et al., 2004). Such participation produces an additive effect to professional treatment of AOD problems (Fiorentine & Hillhouse, 2000), but these effects are limited by failure to affiliate with mutual aid groups such as Alcoholics Anonymous and Narcotics Anonymous following treatment and high dropout rates following initial exposure (see McIntyre, 2000 for a detailed analysis; Mäkelä et al., 1996; Kelly & Moss, 2003). There is little data on differences in recovery mutual aid group affiliation rates by age. There are studies confirming that adolescent participation in recovery mutual aid groups is associated with improved recovery outcomes following treatment (Johnson & Herringer, 1993; Margolis, Kilpatrick, & Mooney, 2000; Kelly, Myers, & Brown, 2002), but this finding is tempered by reports that failure to affiliate and high attrition rates following exposure to self-help groups is the norm among adolescents (Godley & Payton, 2004). A recent membership survey of AA noted that 2% of AA members were under age 21 and that 13% of AA members were aged 61 or over (Alcoholics Anonymous, 1999). There are reports of attrition of older AA members due to the influx of younger members with different lifestyles and drug choices (Chappel, 1993). McIntyre (2000) also notes that many AA members stop regularly attending meetings after achieving stable sobriety, although they continue to see themselves as AA members and may attend occasional AA celebrations. Studies finding that self-help participation increases in the months immediately following treatment but then rapidly erodes–from 71% to 43% in one recent study of adults (Kissin, McLeod, & McKay, 2003)–have yet to be replicated in multiple studies with populations of adolescents and older adults. Studies have confirmed that intensity of self-help participation (e.g., number of meetings, having a sponsor, sponsoring others, reading program literature, etc.) enhances recovery outcomes (Montgomery, Miller, & Tonigan, 1995; Humphreys, Moos, & Cohen, 1997). This intensity of mutual aid involvement has been found in at least one study to apply to adolescents as well as adults (Margolis, Kilpatrick, & Mooney, 2000). The author could find no studies that measured the effect of intensity of participation on recovery outcomes specifically for older adults. The role of age in such affiliation and attrition processes and the effects of intensity of self-help participation among adolescents and older adults deserve serious investigation.

QUALITY AND DURABILITY OF RECOVERY

Recovery and Global Health. The term recovery spans removal of drugs from an otherwise unchanged life to a complete and positive transformation of one's character, identity and lifestyle. This broader transformation has been referred to as *emotional sobriety* (Wilson, 1953) or *wellbriety* (Coyhis, 1999). While there is growing interest in measuring these broader changes in personal identity, physical and emotional health, personal relationships, and social and occupational functioning, research has yet to fully illuminate transformations in global health over time in recovery and the differences in the degree of such changes based on the age of recovery initiation.

The short time periods of treatment follow-up and the lack of longitudinal studies of untreated populations in long-term recovery have provided us with only anecdotal reports on these larger dimensions of health in the later stages of recovery. Such studies could be revealing. For example, it is quite possible that the risk factors that contribute to early onset AOD use, the failure to master major developmental tasks due to early onset AOD use, and the lack of resulting "recovery capital" might not only diminish one's prospects of recovery but also substantially compromise the quality of recovery for those who achieve this status. The resulting higher rates of relapse and failure to achieve personal, relational and occupational health might require considerably different post-treatment monitoring and support strategies compared to that needed for those with later onset of AOD use. Similarly, the successful treatment of late-onset AOD problems might require a much greater focus on achieving global health rather than a more restrictive focus on the elimination of AOD use.

Recovery Durability. When is recovery stable (point at which the probability of future lifetime relapse is very low)? The alcoholism literature suggests that persons who reach the 4-5 year window of sustained sobriety have a low (under 15%) risk for future relapse in their lifetime (De Soto, O'Donnel, & De Soto 1989; Dawson, 1996; Jin, Rourke, Patterson, Taylor, & Grant, 1998). Studies on such stability in recovery from addiction to drugs other than alcohol are less definitive and focus primarily on post-treatment follow-up of heroin addiction. In a twelve-year follow-up study of individuals treated for heroin addiction, Simpson, Joe, Lehman, and Sells (1986) found a low (19%) rate of future relapse after three years of cessation of daily heroin use. The fragileness of recovery from opiate addiction is indicated by other long-term follow-up studies reporting that 20-25% of those who achieve five or more years of abstinence from heroin later returned to opiate use (Simpson & Marsh, 1986; Hser et al., 2001). A recent study by Scott, Foss, and Dennis (2005) indicated that 83% of 1,326 clients followed up quarterly after discharge from addiction treatment experienced one or more recovery/relapse status transition over the three years of follow-up. Additional studies are required to determine if such recovery status volatility is greater or less for adolescents and older adults and whether these populations would benefit from more assertive models of post-treatment monitoring and support, active linkage to age-appropriate recovery support groups, and, when needed, early re-intervention.

CONCLUSION

This article has highlighted some of the literature on effects of age on the prospects and patterns of recovery from alcohol- and other drug-related problems. There appear to be significant differences in early- and late-onset substance use disorders, and available data suggests differences based on the age of recovery initiation. The emerging recovery research agenda should include focused attention on: (1) the influence of age of problem development upon the prospects for long-term recovery, (2) differences in pathways and styles of recovery across the developmental life cycle, and (3) the effects of age in interaction with other significant factors (e.g., gender, ethnicity, drug choice) on recovery processes. That knowledge base will lay the foundation for specialized approaches to treatment and recovery support for our youngest and oldest service consumers.

REFERENCES

Alcoholics Anonymous. (1999). *Alcoholics Anonymous 1998 membership survey.* New York: A.A. World Services.

Arria, A. M., Dohey, M. A., Mezzich, A. C., Bukstein, O. G., & Van Thiel, D. H. (1995). Self-reported health problems and physical symptomatology in adolescent alcohol abusers. *Journal of Adolescent Health, 16*(32), 226-231.

Atkinson, R. M., Tolson, R. L., & Turner, J. A. (1990). Late versus early onset problem drinking in older men. *Alcoholism: Clinical and Experimental Research, 14*, 574-579.

Brennan, P. L., & Moos, R. H. (1995). Life context, coping responses, and adaptive outcomes: A stress and coping perspective on late-life problem drinking. In T. Beresford & E. Gomberg (Eds.), *Alcohol and Aging* (pp. 230-248). New York: Oxford University Press.

Chappel, J. N. (1993). Long-term recovery from alcoholism. *Psychiatric Clinics of North America, 16*(1), 177-187.

Chen, J., & Millar, W. (1998). Age of smoking initiation: Implications for quitting. *Health Reports, 9*(4), 39-46.

Chen K., & Kandel, D. (1995). The natural history of drug use from adolescence to mid-thirties in a general population sample. *American Journal of Public Health, 85*(1), 41-47.

Chou, S. P., & Pickering, R. P. (1992). Early onset of drinking as a risk factor for lifetime alcohol-related problems. *British Journal of Addiction, 87*, 1199-1204.

Coyhis, D. (1999). *The wellbriety journey: Nine talks by Don Coyhis.* Colorado Springs, CO: White Bison, Inc.

Cunningham, J. A., Koski-Jannes, A., & Toneatto, T. (1999). Why do people stop their drug use? Results from a general population sample. *Contemporary Drug Problems, 26*, 695-710.

Cunningham, J., Sobell, L. Sobell, M., & Kapur, G. (1995). Resolution from alcohol problems with and without treatment: Reasons for change. *Journal of Substance Abuse, 7*, 365-372.

Dawson, D.A. (1996). Correlates of past-year status among treated and untreated persons with former alcohol dependence: United States, 1992. *Alcoholism: Clinical and Experimental Research, 20*, 771-779.

Dennis, M. L., Babor, T., Roebuck, M. C., & Donaldson, J. (2002). Changing the focus: The case for recognizing and treating marijuana use disorders. *Addiction, 97* (Suppl. 1), S4-S15.

Dennis, M. L., Titus, J. C., Diamond, G., Donaldson, J., Godley, S. H., Tims, F. et al. (2002). The Cannabis Youth Treatment (CYT) experiment: Rationale, study design, and analysis plans. *Addiction, 97*, S16-S34.

De Soto, C. B., O'Donnel, W. E., & De Soto, J. L. (1989). Long-term recovery in alcoholics. *Alcoholism: Clinical and Experimental Research, 13*, 693-697.

Emrick, D. C., Tonigan, J. S., Montgomery, H., & Little, L. (1993). Alcoholics Anonymous: What is currently known? In B. McCrady & W. R. Miller (Eds.), *Research on Alcoholics Anonymous: Opportunities and Alternatives* (pp. 41-78). New Brunswick, NJ: Rutgers Center on Alcohol Studies.

Fillmore, K. M., Hartka, E., Johnstone, B. M., Speiglman, R., & Temple, M. T. (1988). *Spontaneous remission of alcohol problems: A critical review.* Washington, DC: Institute of Medicine.

Fiorentine, R., & Hillhouse, M. (2000). Drug treatment and 12-step program participation: The additive effects of integrated recovery activities. *Journal of Substance Abuse Treatment, 18,* 65-74.

Frykholm, B. (1985). The drug career. *Journal of Drug Issues, 15,* 333-346.

Godley, M., Godley, S. H., Dennis, M., Funk, R., & Passetti, L. (2002). Preliminary outcomes from the assertive continuing care experiment for adolescents discharged from residential treatment. *Journal of Substance Abuse Treatment, 23,* 21-32.

Godley, M., & Payton, J. (2004). The urgent need for continuing care with adolescents: Recent research and recommendations. *Counselor, 5,* 49-54.

Goldman, M. S. (1983). Cognitive impairment in chronic alcoholics: Some causes for optimism. *American Psychologist, 38,*1045-1054.

Granfield, R., & Cloud, W. (1999). *Coming clean: Overcoming addiction without treatment.* New York: New York University Press.

Grant, B. F., & Dawson, D. A. (1997). Age at onset of alcohol use and its association with DSM-IV alcohol abuse and dependence. *Journal of Substance Abuse, 9,* 103-110.

Heather, N., & Robertson, I. (1983). *Controlled Drinking* (2nd ed.). New York: Methuen.

Hermos, J. A., Locastro, J. S., Glynn, R. J., Bouchard, G. R., & De Labry, L. O. (1988). Predictors of reduction and cessation of drinking in community-dwelling men: Results from the normative aging study. *Journal of Studies on Alcohol, 49,* 363-368.

Humphreys, K., Moos, R. J., & Cohen, C. (1997). Social and community resources and long-term recovery from treated and untreated alcoholism. *Journal of Studies on Alcohol, 58,* 231-238.

Humphreys, K., Wing, S., McCarty, D., Chappel, J., Galant, L., Haberle, B., et al., (2004). Self-help organizations for alcohol and drug problems: Toward evidence-based practice and policy. *Journal of Substance Abuse Treatment, 26,* 151-158.

Hser, Y., Anglin, M., Grella, C., Longshore, D., & Prendergast, M. (1997). Drug treatment careers: A conceptual framework and existing research findings. *Journal of Substance Abuse Treatment, 14*(3), 1-16.

Hser, Y., Hoffman, V., Grella, C., & Anglin, D. (2001). A 33-year follow-up of narcotics addicts. *Archives of General Psychiatry, 58,* 503-508.

James, W. (1985). *The Varieties of Religious Experience.* New York: Penguin. (Original work published in 1902.)

Jin, H., Rourke, S. B., Patterson, T. L., Taylor, M. J., & Grant, I. (1998). Predictors of relapse in long-term abstinent alcoholics. *Journal of Studies on Alcohol, 59,* 640-646.

Johnson, E., & Herringer, L. (1993). A note on the utilization of common support activities and relapse following substance abuse treatment. *Journal of Psychology, 127,* 73-78.

Keller, M., Lavori, P., Beardslee, W., Wunder, J., Drs., D., & Hasin, D. (1992). Clinical course and outcome of substance abuse disorders in adolescents. *Journal of Substance Abuse Treatment, 9,* 9-14.

Kelly, J. F., & Moos, R. (2003). Dropout from 12-step self-help groups: Prevalence, predictors, and counteracting treatment influences. *Journal of Substance Abuse Treatment, 24,* 241-250.

Kelly, J. F., Myers, M. G., & Brown, S. A. (2002). Do adolescents affiliate with 12-step groups? A multivariate process model of effects. *Journal of Studies on Alcohol, 63,* 293-304.

Kessler, R. C., Aguilar-Gaxiola, S., Berglund, P., Caraveo-Anduaga, J., DeWitt, D., Greenfield, S., et al. (2001). Patterns and predictors of treatment seeking after onset of a substance use disorder. *Archives of General Psychiatry, 58*(11), 1065-1071.

Kissin, W., McLeod, C., & McKay, J. (2003). The longitudinal relationship between self-help group attendance and course of recovery. *Evaluation and Program Planning, 26,* 311-323.

Kreichbaun, N., & Zering, G. (2000). Adolescent patients. In G. Zering (Ed.), *Handbook of Alcoholism* (pp. 129-136). Boca Raton, LA: CRC Press.

Labouvie, E. (1996). Maturing out of substance use: Selection and self-correction. *Journal of Drug Issues, 26*(2), 457-476.

Loder, J. E. (1989). *The Transforming Moment.* Colorado Springs, CO: Helmers and Howard.

Mäkelä, K., Arminen, I., Bloomfield, K., Eisenbach-Stangl, I., Bergmark, K., Kurube, N., et al. (1996). *Alcoholics Anonymous as a Mutual-Help Movement: A Study in Eight Societies.* Madison: University of Wisconsin.

Margolis, R., Kilpatrick, A., & Mooney, B. (2000). A retrospective look at long-term adolescent recovery: Clinicians talk to researchers. *Journal of Psychoactive Drugs, 32,* 117-125.

McIntyre, D. (2000). How well does A.A. work? An analysis of published A.A. surveys (1968-1996) and related analyses/comments. *Alcoholism Treatment Quarterly, 18*(4), 1-18.

Miller, W. R., & C'de Baca, J. (2001). *Quantum Change.* New York: Guilford.

Montgomery, H. A., Miller, W. R., & Tonigan, J. S. (1995). Does Alcoholics Anonymous involvement predict treatment outcome? *Journal of Substance Abuse Treatment, 12,* 241-246.

Moos, R. H. (1994). Why do some people recover from alcohol dependence, whereas others continue to drink and become worse over time? *Addiction, 89,* 31-34.

National Institute on Alcohol Abuse and Alcoholism. (2003). Underage drinking: A major public health challenge. *Alcohol Alert, 59,* 1-7.

Nordstrom, G., & Berglund, M. (1987). Ageing and recovery from alcoholism. *British Journal of Psychiatry, 151,* 382-388.

Presley, C. A., Meilman, P. W., & Lyerla, R. (1991). *Alcohol and Drugs on American College Campuses: Volume 1: 1989-91.* Carbondale, IL: Southern Illinois University Student Health Programs (The Core Institute).

Prochaska, J. O., Norcross, J. C., & DiClemente, C. C. (1994). *Changing for Good.* New York: Avon.

Rigler, S. K. (2000). Alcoholism in the elderly. *American Family Physician, 61*(5), 1710-1716.

Risberg, R., & White, W. (2003). Adolescent substance abuse treatment: Expectations versus outcomes. *Student Assistance Journal, 15*(2), 16-20.

Saunders, W. M., Phil, M., & Kershaw, P. W. (1979). Spontaneous remission from alcoholism: A community study. *British Journal of Addiction, 74,* 251-265.

Schutte, K. K., Brennan, P. L., & Moos, R. H. (1994). Remission of late-life drinking problems: A 4-year follow-up. *Alcoholism: Clinical and Experimental Research, 18*(4), 835-843.

Schutte, K. K., Byrne, F. E., Brannan, P. L., & Moos, R. H. (2001). Successful remission of late-life drinking problems: A 10-year follow-up. *Journal of Studies on Alcohol, 62*(3), 322-334.

Schutte, K. K., Nichols, K. A., Brennan, P. L., & Moos, R. H. (2003). A ten-year follow-up of older former problem drinkers: Risk of relapse and implications of successfully sustained remission. *Journal of Studies on Alcohol, 64*(3), 367-374.

Scott, C. K, Foss, M. A., & Dennis, M. L. (2005). Pathways in the relapse-treatment-recovery cycle over three years. *Journal of Substance Abuse Treatment, 28* (Supplement 1), S63-S72.

Simpson, D. D., Joe, G. W., Lehman, W. E., & Sells, S. B. (1986). Addiction careers: Etiology, treatment, and 12-year follow-up outcomes. *Journal of Drug Issues, 16*(1), 107-122.

Simpson, D. D., & Marsh, K. L. (1986). Relapse and recovery among opioid addicts 12 years after treatment. In F. Tims & C. Luekefeld (Eds.), *Relapse and Recovery in Drug Abuse* (NIDA Monograph 72, pp. 86-103). Rockville, MD: National Institute on Drug Abuse.

Simpson, D. D., & Sells, S. B. (1990). *Opioid addiction and treatment: A 12-year follow-up.* Malabar, FL: Krieger.

Snow, M. (1973). Maturing out of narcotic addiction in New York City. *International Journal of the Addictions, 8*(6), 921-938.

Sobell, L. C., Ellingstad, T., & Sobell, M. B. (2000). Natural recovery from alcohol and drug problems: Methodological review of the research with suggestions for future directions. *Addiction, 95,* 749-764.

Sobell, M. B., Sobell, L. C., Cunningham, J. C., & Agrawal, S. (1998). Natural recovery over the lifespan. In E. L. Gomberg, A. M. Hegedus, & R. A. Zucker (Eds.), *Alcohol problems and aging* (NIAAA Research Monograph No. 33, pp. 397-405). Bethesda, MD: National Institute on Alcohol Abuse and Alcoholism.

Starbuck, E. (1901). *The psychology of religion.* New York: Scribner's.

Stoltenberg, S. F., Hill, E. M., Mudd, S. A., Blow, F. C., & Zucker, R. A. (1999). Birth cohort differences in features of antisocial alcoholism among men and women. *Alcoholism: Clinical & Experimental Research, 23*(12), 1884-1891.

Substance Abuse and Mental Health Services Administration. (1999). *National Household Survey on Drug Abuse: Main Findings 1997.* Rockville, MD: Author.

U.S. Department of Justice, Bureau of Justice Statistics. (1994). *Drugs and Crime Facts, 1994.* Retrieved from http://www.ojp.usdoj.gov/bjs/dcf/contents.htm

Vaillant, G. (1966). A twelve-year follow-up of New York narcotic addicts: IV. Some characteristics and determinants of abstinence. *American Journal of Psychiatry, 123*(5), 573-584.

Vaillant, G. (2003). A 60-year follow-up of alcoholic men. *Addiction, 98,* 1043-1051.

Watson, A. L., & Sher, K. J. (1998). Resolution of alcohol problems without treatment: Methodological issues and future directions of natural recovery research. *Clinical Psychology: Science & Practice, 5*(1), 1-18.

White, W. (1996). *Pathways from the Culture of Addiction to the Culture of Recovery.* Center City, MN: Hazelden.

White, W. (1998). *Slaying the Dragon: The History of Addiction Treatment and Recovery in America.* Bloomington, IL: Chestnut Health Systems.

White, W. (2004). Recovery: The next frontier. *Counselor, 5*(1), 18-21.

White, W., Dennis, M., & Godley, M. (2002). Adolescent substance use disorders: From acute treatment to recovery management. *Reclaiming Children and Youth, 11*(3), 172-175.

White, W., Godley, M., & Dennis, M. (2003). Early age of substance experimentation: Implications for student assistance programs. *Student Assistance Journal, 16*(1), 22-25.

Wilson, W. (1953, January). Emotional Sobriety. *A.A. Grapevine,* 1-2.

Winick, C. (1962). Maturing out of narcotic addiction. *Bulletin on Narcotics, 14,* 1-7.

Index

Numbers followed by "f" indicate figure; "t" following a page number indicates tabular material.

Family(ies), alcohol abuse effects on,
171-184. *See also* Alcohol
abuse, marriage and family
contexts of
Family systems therapy, for alcohol
abuse, 177-178
Fetzer Institute, 39,93
Fetzer Study, 3,15
Fetzer/NIA Brief Multidimensional
Measure of
Religiousness/Spirituality,
103
Fillmore, K.M., 193
Finney, J., 61
Fitzgibbons, 148
Forgiveness
as altruistic gift, 137-138
aspects of, 134
decisional, defined, 136
described, 150
emotional, defined, 132-133,136
evidence-based intervention in
promoting of, 133-134
life-course theory of, 147-170. *See
also* Homeless veterans,
AOD problems among, study
of
model of alcohol and drug abuse
without, 152,152f
reconciliation and, 150
steps in reaching, 135-139
as altruistic gift, 137-138
commit to forgiveness you
experience, 138
declare decisional forgiveness,
136
define crucial terms, 135-136
empathize, 137
hold on to forgiveness in face of
doubts, 138
motivational interviewing, 135
recall hurts, 136-137
relapse prevention, 138-139
teach how to talk about
transgressions, 139

in treatment of persons with
alcohol-related problems,
125-145
interventions for, timing of, 140
Forgiveness and Reconciliation
through Experiencing
Empathy (FREE), 134
Foss, M.A., 196
FREE. *See* Forgiveness and
Reconciliation through
Experiencing Empathy
(FREE)

General Social Survey, 101
Global health, recovery across life
cycle from AOD problems
and, 195
Gorsuch, R.L., 15
Granfield, R., 37,59,190
Great Awakening, 23

Hargrave, T.D., 148
Hart, K.E., 133,138
HBQ. *See* Health Behavior
Questionnaire (HBQ)
Health, global, recovery across life
cycle from AOD problems
and, 195
Health Behavior Questionnaire (HBQ),
79
Hill, P.C., 15
Holy Scriptures, 148
Homeless veterans, AOD problems
among, 147-170
study of, 149-165,152f,153f
data analysis in, 157-158
discussion of, 161-165
findings in, 158-161,159t,160t
measures in, 154-157
method in, 153-158,155t,156t
procedures in, 154,156t
purpose of, 149-150

BOOK ORDER FORM!

Order a copy of this book with this form or online at:
http://www.HaworthPress.com/store/product.asp?sku= 5877

Spirituality and Religiousness and Alcohol/Other Drug Problems
Treatment and Recovery Perspectives

—— in softbound at $19.95 ISBN-13: 978-0-7890-3323-9 / ISBN-10: 0-7890-3323-2.
—— in hardbound at $39.95 ISBN-13: 978-0-7890-3299-7 / ISBN-10: 0-7890-3299-6.

COST OF BOOKS _____

POSTAGE & HANDLING _____
US: $4.00 for first book & $1.50
for each additional book
Outside US: $5.00 for first book
& $2.00 for each additional book.

SUBTOTAL _____
In Canada: add 7% GST. _____

STATE TAX _____
CA, IL, IN, MN, NJ, NY, OH, PA & SD residents
please add appropriate local sales tax.

FINAL TOTAL _____
If paying in Canadian funds, convert
using the current exchange rate,
UNESCO coupons welcome.

❑ BILL ME LATER:
Bill-me option is good on US/Canada/
Mexico orders only; not good to jobbers,
wholesalers, or subscription agencies.

❑ Signature _____

❑ Payment Enclosed: $_____

❑ PLEASE CHARGE TO MY CREDIT CARD:
❑ Visa ❑ MasterCard ❑ AmEx ❑ Discover
❑ Diner's Club ❑ Eurocard ❑ JCB

Account #_____

Exp Date_____

Signature_____
(Prices in US dollars and subject to change without notice.)

PLEASE PRINT ALL INFORMATION OR ATTACH YOUR BUSINESS CARD

Name

Address

City   State/Province   Zip/Postal Code

Country

Tel   Fax

E-Mail

May we use your e-mail address for confirmations and other types of information? ❑Yes ❑No We appreciate receiving
your e-mail address. Haworth would like to e-mail special discount offers to you, as a preferred customer.
We will never share, rent, or exchange your e-mail address. We regard such actions as an invasion of your privacy.

Order from your **local bookstore** or directly from
The Haworth Press, Inc. 10 Alice Street, Binghamton, New York 13904-1580 • USA
Call our toll-free number (1-800-429-6784) / Outside US/Canada: (607) 722-5857
Fax: 1-800-895-0582 / Outside US/Canada: (607) 771-0012
E-mail your order to us: orders@HaworthPress.com

For orders outside US and Canada, you may wish to order through your local
sales representative, distributor, or bookseller.
For information, see http://HaworthPress.com/distributors

(Discounts are available for individual orders in US and Canada only, not booksellers/distributors.)

Please photocopy this form for your personal use.
www.HaworthPress.com

 BOF06